savoring spices and herbs

ALSO BY JULIE SAHNI

Classic Indian Cooking (1980)

Classic Indian Vegetarian and Grain Cooking (1985)

Mogul Microwave (1990)

savoring spices and herbs

recipe secrets of flavor, aroma, and color

Julie Sahni

William Morrow and Company, Inc.

NEW YORK

Library of Congress Cataloging-in-Publication Data

Sahni, Julie.
    Savoring spices and herbs : recipe secrets of flavor, aroma, and color / Julie Sahni.— 1st ed.
      p. cm.
    Includes bibliographical references and index.
    ISBN 0-688-06976-2
    1. Spices. 2. Herbs. 3. Cookery (Herbs) I. Title.
TX406.S52 1996
641.6'383—dc20   96–1710
                                                          CIP

Printed in the United States of America

First Edition

1 2 3 4 5 6 7 8 9 10

BOOK DESIGN BY VERTIGO DESIGN

**To my parents for the gift of
sensual awakening**

acknowledgments

*S*avoring *Spices and Herbs* has been in the making for a very long time, as I traveled around the globe from South America to South Africa, from the Pacific Islands to the Spice Islands, and taught the techniques of using spices and herbs in cooking classes at my school in New York and at other cooking schools around the country. It was Maria Guarnaschelli, my longtime editor, however, who envisioned this book. She laid the foundation and the framework for it, and for that I owe her an immense debt of gratitude. I must also thank Ann Bramson for her enthusiastic support, wise guidance, and sound editorial judgment in giving the book its present form. Finally, I wish to thank Susan Derecskey, who entered into the spirit of the book with an energy and passion beyond words. For her valuable suggestions and superb editing I express my appreciation and affection forever. At this point I would also like to make special mention of Arthur Klebanoff, my agent, and Jennifer Kaye, assistant editor, for their constructive suggestions and moral support.

Over the years many people, both in the food world and outside, have provided encouragement and support. The list is endless. Those mentioned here are only a few, and naming them by no means reduces or takes away the importance of all the others.

I would especially like to thank Rebecca Alssid, Boston University Culinary Arts Program; Mary Risley, Tante Marie's Cooking School in San Francisco; Phyllis Vaccarelli, Let's Get Cookin' in Westlake Village, California; Bill Wallace, Draeger's Culinary Center in Menlo Park, California; Barbara Fairchild, *Bon Appetit;* Arthur Schwartz, host of WOR–Foodtalk in New York; Pat Brown, Food Write; and Greg Drescher, formerly of Oldways Preservation Trust in Boston, for giving me the opportunity to share experiences of my spice treks with the public. I would also like to thank the people at *The New York Times,* in particular, Nancy Newhouse, Trish Hall, Eric Asimov, and Ruth Reichl, for their support.

Special thanks are extended to the staff at the American Spice Trade Association; U.S. Food and Drug Administration and Department of Agriculture, Washington, D.C.; Spices Board India, Ministry of Commerce; Marshall Neale, Lewis & Neale Food Public Relations; and Niki Singer, Senior Vice President at M. Shanken Communications, publishers of *Wine Spectator* and *Food Arts,* for their help in research. I would also like to thank Charles Perry, of the *Los Angeles Times;* Dr. Joyce Toomre; Dr. Barbara Levine, Assistant Professor of Nutrition in Medicine, Cornell University Medical College; Charlie Sahadi, Sahadi Imports in New York; Arun Sinha, Sinha Trading Company in New York; Alan Wong; Mark Miller; Paul McIlhenny; Paula Wolfert; Dalia Carmel; Cara DeSilva; Grace Kirschenbaum; and Helen Witty, for our enlightening spice chats. Deepest thanks to Carol Shaw, Sue Perkins, Ambalika Misra, Doris Kaplan, Ann Nurse, and Jim Mellgrin.

No book would be a book without the meticulous behind-the-scenes work of many people. I would particularly like to thank food photographer Dana Gallagher and food and prop stylists Anne Disrude and Betty Alfenito for their clarity of vision in bringing life to the still photographs. Thank you also to Vertigo Design for a magnificent book design and stunning jacket design, and at Morrow, to Deborah Weiss Geline, for keeping the production on schedule, and Kim Yorio, for getting the word out in a most eloquent way. Finally my utmost gratitude to my son, Vishal, for making it all worthwhile.

preface

i gathered my belongings and headed for the harbor along Kivukani Front in Dar-es-Salaam, fringed with Arab dhows, dugout canoes, and rusty ocean freighters. Determined not to miss the first boat of the day, I walked briskly, weaving through the coconut palms and mangroves dotting the beach, and shut my senses to the irresistible aromas of chili-rubbed cassava fries and cumin-scented corn puffs rising from hawkers' baskets. I scrambled aboard the old battered ferry, found a niche near the helm, and settled in. Within minutes we were covering expanses of blue sea, cool breezes bringing relief to our sweat-soaked bodies scorching under the African sun. It did not matter that for the next five hours I was going to be confined to a boat jammed with Tanzanian men and their entourages of women in black veils, children, servants, goats, and chickens. What lay ahead was an experience I had waited a lifetime to savor—the exotic and mysterious island of Zanzibar.

A land of serene beauty, Zanzibar is a dreamer's paradise. But the real allure, I believe, is its unique history as the clove capital of the world. Strategically situated on the ancient sea route connecting West with East, Zanzibar since ancient times has served as a trading post. The Sumerians, Phoenicians, Persians, Aryan Hindus, Chinese, Malay, and in recent times, the Portuguese, Dutch, and English, have all left their mark on this remarkable land and its culture.

Interestingly, as recently as the eighteenth century there was not a single clove plant in Zanzibar. According to historical documents the Dutch, who monopolized the clove trade, had wiped out all the clove trees in the Moluccas except for one island, Amboina, to ensure their strict control and monopoly. But in 1770 a French botanist, Pierre Poivre, outwitted the Dutch by disguising himself as a mad sailor and smuggling live plants out of the Moluccas. He introduced them in the French colonies of Île de France (Mauritius), of which he was the administrator, and Bourbon (Réunion), and cultivated them successfully. Saleh ben Haramil al Abray, an Omani merchant from Zanzibar and a francophile, had his eyes set on cloves. In 1812, during one of several trips to Bourbon and Île de France, he charmed the French with his "perfect Frenchman manners" and got permission to take seedlings back to Zanzibar. With climatic conditions identical to the Moluccas, clove plants flourished in Zanzibar and within a couple of decades, during the reign of Seyyid Said, Sultan of Zanzibar, the island became the leading supplier in the world.

As I sat musing about the spice route and its impact on world history, a massive wave, generated by a passing ocean liner, suddenly crashed against the boat, jolting and spinning it—and me. Seasick, lightheaded, and queasy, I began to hallucinate. The whispers of Arabic and Swahili, the baaing of agitated goats, and the crashing waves carried me into the world of Ali Baba and the Forty Thieves. I woke to something warm and pungent startling my senses. I started to feel normal again, but the smell perplexed me. The captain, who was at my side, pointed into the air and said, *"Karafuu,"* clove in Swahili. So that's what clove-saturated air smells like, I thought. Now that made a lot of sense because clove, besides being used extensively in cooking, had since time immemorial been used medicinally, including as a remedy for motion sickness.

Zanzibar was now drawing closer and our boat, preparing to dock, turned course. Suddenly I noticed the pungent odor giving way to a sweet, more sensuously spicy aroma. This, the captain explained, was the true fragrance of Zanzibar. The odor we had first encountered en route came from the clove-processing plants. We had sailed right into the path of the wind currents that carried it out to sea.

Common sense suggested that immediately upon leaving the boat, I check into my hotel, where I planned to spend several nights, but with this hypnotic fragrance lingering in my mind, I was given to acting impulsively. I asked Maulidi, my driver and guide, to take my bags to the hotel, and, empowered with the phrases of Swahili, which I had picked up traveling through southern and central Africa in the past weeks, I hired a taxi and set out to see the spice market on Creek Road.

It was an open-air bazaar, bustling with a mesmerizing array of vegetables, fruits, spices, and herbs. It also had stalls selling meat, poultry, and local fish, some weighing several hundred pounds that needed to be portioned off by saw. I walked past mounds of okra, cassava, eggplant, coconut, green tamarind pods, breadfruit; tasted bitter oranges, tiny yellow limes, and red finger bananas; and inhaled the freshly packed spices in tiny bags. The fresh thyme had a unique smokiness, very distinct from the flowery thyme I had found in Greece or the strong and pungent Jamaican variety in the Caribbean. It was different even from the mellow one growing in my backyard in New York. I guess elements of nature bring this wonderful diversity.

What caught my attention most at the market was how the spices and fresh herbs were arranged in orderly fashion for sale. Chilies, garlic, cilantro, and thyme, for example, were in neat mounds or groups laid out in symmetrical rows, each containing just enough to flavor one dish or two. A stack of three semi-dry bay leaves, a bundle of three quills of cinnamon, a vine of green peppercorns, a bouquet of green clove buds, all arranged in neat lines. It brought to mind the fresh ginger knobs I had seen at similar stalls along the roadside in Canton, the saffron threads loosely wrapped in leaves in Kashmir, and bunches of annatto in Trinidad. How far apart these lands are and yet so similar in the practice of culinary art, I thought.

Later that evening, I was joined by a couple of Italians whom I had met earlier at the market, and we dined at a restaurant called Spice Inn. The meal—freshly caught sea bass braised in coconut milk with chilies and thyme, stewed spicy okra with cinnamon and cloves served over boiled rice, and roasted pepper-rubbed cassava—reflected the aromas of the spice market and a cuisine that had evolved out of an amalgam of cultures. Savoring this glorious food, we analyzed its flavors, tracing its Arab, Persian, African, French, Indian, and even Italian influences. Later we wandered out through the narrow cobblestone streets into the Chaga bazaar, exploring the tiny bakeries and food stalls and sampling nutmeg- and vanilla-scented puff-puff and chin-chin pastries. That night I slipped a few clove buds under my pillow and went to sleep dreaming of Arabian nights.

I rose early next morning to visit a clove plantation. The closest one was a good hour's ride by car. As in any tropical area, it was hot and humid with bright blue cloudless skies above. The road leading to the plantation wove through a countryside covered with coconut groves, banana plantations, cassava and breadfruit fields. Mud-plastered bamboo houses with thatched roofs appeared from time to time along the way. Before long, black clouds with thunder and lightning turned the bright day dark as night. Soon a blinding downpour flooded the land. We had no choice but to pull over to the side and wait for nature's fury to subside. Within minutes the pounding stopped, as though a two-hundred-piece orchestra had come to a sudden full stop, restoring the surroundings to an astonishing silence. The blue skies returned and the brilliant sun once again filled the world with light and heat. The significance of such downpours became clear to me. In a land of spices, this interplay of dark and light, cool and hot, moist and dry is fundamental. It is nature's way of curing ordinary barks, buds, and leaves, turning them into uniquely fragrant spices.

On the way to the plantation we made a brief stop at Maulidi's home. Thyme, parsley, chives, and chilies lined the walkway while a few tiny rose bushes graced the entrance. Like most country houses in spice lands, it had a cinnamon tree, a pepper vine wrapped around a tamarind tree, and a clove plant in the garden to supply flavorings for the household. We sat under the perfumed shade of a tamarind tree, and I was treated to cassava chips fried in clove-infused oil and Zanzibar-style vanilla tea. The captivating fragrance recalled the tranquillity of olive orchards in Lebanon and the grilled meats spiced with cardamom and cloves and cumin-scented fava bean purees with bread I had enjoyed with friends, sitting under the cool shade of olive trees in their garden in the old section of Beirut.

When we got to the plantation, I found myself surrounded by tall trees, about fifteen feet high, glistening with rainwater. The spices lent a magical aroma to the air. I held a bunch of tiny green buds, cool and moist from the rain, and inhaled their light, spicy bouquet. I considered the genius of man, who devised a way to transform a simple bud into a spice. Clove buds develop fragrance only when fully mature, at which point they must be harvested; once they open, they lose their fragrance. When dried, the buds turn dark brown and develop that pungency we are so familiar with and love. You don't have to visit the famous souks of Marrakech, their spice shops overflowing with cloves, coriander, cinnamon, turmeric, anise, cumin, pepper, oregano, and chilies, to experience the sensuous power of spices.

From the plantation, I could see the vast Indian Ocean. As I stood staring out, my senses saturated, I started thinking about the day I would return home, carrying memories from yet another land of spices and herbs and a newly felt awareness of their enriching influence on food and on my understanding of it. At that moment, I experienced the joy, the flavor, the aroma, the therapeutic calm, and the good health that spices and herbs bring to our lives.

contents

savoring spices and herbs

introduction

long before people learned to cook, or fish, or even hunt, when food was gathered from what grew around them, they knew of herbs and spices.

Archeological discoveries have shown that the precavemen who wandered the African land survived on a diet of vegetation. They lived close to nature and had more knowledge of things growing around them than most of us today and were familiar with groups of plants that possessed similar chemical properties. They knew what kind of reaction to expect when they ate a particular plant. Consequently, they learned to avoid certain plants that made them sick, and, in the event they did get sick, they knew which other plants to eat to feel better again. This was the earliest use of spices and herbs. As man raised livestock, cultivated crops, and formed organized societies, the pleasurable aspects of plants—fragrance, flavor, color, and bite—also became important. Thus began the use of spices and herbs as aromatics.

Spices and herbs can best be described as aromatic plants whose qualities are perceived through our sense of smell. Although often referred to collectively, they differ in botanical composition and in culinary use.

Spices are the dried aromatic parts of woody plants growing primarily in hot and dry climates (eastern Mediterranean) and hot and humid climates (Central America and

South Asia). Just about any part of the plant can be a spice as long as it is highly aromatic. Spices are usually low in moisture so that even after drying they retain almost all of their original fragrance and volume. Rhizomes (ginger), barks (cinnamon), leaves (bay leaf), fruits (chilies), kernels (nutmeg), arils (mace), seeds (anise), buds (cloves), berries (juniper), and flower stigmas (saffron) are all turned into spices. Because they are rough parts of plant matter, spices are not easy to digest, especially in large quantities. Spices should be used with discretion and moderation.

Herbs, on the other hand, are the highly fragrant leaves and tender stems of plants that never develop hard bark-covered trunks. They grow mostly in temperate climates (the Mediterranean basin) and cool climates (Europe). Oregano, thyme, basil, rosemary, parsley, dill, and cilantro, for example, are herbs. In order to bring out their true floral bouquet, herbs should be used fresh and added at the end of cooking. The contact with heat not only reduces their aroma but in most cases destroys their bright green color.

Spices can be purchased from any number of sources: supermarkets, specialty grocers, spice shops, and mail order outlets. Except for some spices, such as paprika and turmeric, which are sold only in ground form, all spices and herbs should be purchased whole. In the whole form they retain their fragrance longer, thus increasing their shelf life. According to your pattern of consumption, small quantities of spices should be freshly ground every few weeks. You also avoid adulteration, which is easy in the ground form, especially where expensive spices like saffron and cardamom are concerned.

There is no such thing as a clearance sale in spices. What you often find has most likely not moved for some time, maybe years. Make sure you can see the spices before buying—the quality can be confirmed only by looking at them. Spices packed in clear see-through containers are the best choice. When purchasing by mail order, where spices have to be purchased without inspection, deal only with reliable sources who specialize in spices and herbs.

There was a time when all kitchens had an adjoining room or area called a pantry. Spices and dried herbs were stored in that area in a cupboard, away from light and heat. The next best place is a cooler part of a kitchen cupboard. Certain spices, such as paprika and coriander, stay fresh longer if stored in the refrigerator. Store all spices in tightly covered containers to keep in the fragrance and to keep out moisture.

Fresh herbs should be purchased with roots attached if possible; they will keep longer that way. Herbs are available from supermarkets, greengrocers, and Asian and Latin markets. If very dirty, rinse the herbs briefly and shake off the excess water. Wrap them loosely in a paper or cloth towel and put them in a plastic bag. Do not tie up the bag, or the herbs will rot. Properly stored, herbs keep for as long as two weeks in the refrigerator.

All spices and herbs naturally contain certain essential oils and volatile oils. The chemical composition of these oils is what gives spices and herbs their characteristic aromas. These chemicals also define the fragrance from beyond spicy and aromatic to such specific scents as lemon, almond, lavender, rose, pine, and so on. When the chemical composition of any two spices or herbs differs, their characteristic aromas differ totally too, as can be seen in coriander versus clove. On the other hand, when two spices or herbs contain a common chemical in their composition, they have a similar aroma even though they are botanically very different, fennel and star anise for example.

Spices and herbs, though primarily aromatics, possess other qualities as well. Paprika, for instance, acts not only as a flavoring agent but as a coloring agent, adding a crimson color to food, and as an emulsifier. Sauces containing paprika often have body and a nice sheen. Turmeric adds a pleasant woodsy, piney fragrance and also changes the color of a dish. It does not turn everything yellow—it brings out the green in such vegetables as broccoli, artichokes, and asparagus and holds it for several days, and it turns even the palest tomatoes a glowing shade of red. Cardamom and nutmeg bring out the natural sweetness in food. These spices give satisfaction that eliminates the need or desire for salt and fat. Finally, a unique quality of spices and herbs is their ability to counter the effects of the hard-to-digest vegetable proteins in beans, peas, and root vegetables. A pinch of a spice like cumin, a piece of fresh ginger, or a few epazote leaves effectively render beans and chick peas harmless.

While some spices, cinnamon, cloves, and black pepper, for example, are fragrant whole, most need to be crushed, ground, chopped, or cooked, to release their fragrance. This is because their volatile oils are released only when the food cells are broken. Depending upon the end result, that is, how strongly or mildly you want the spice or herb to flavor the dish, the spice should be left whole, crushed, or ground or the herb should be left whole, chopped, or minced.

Whole spices are enhanced by being lightly toasted in an ungreased skillet. They develop a pleasant smokiness and their fragrance is concentrated. Ground spices, though, burn easily when brought into contact with direct heat. It's best to add them to moist ingredients during the cooking. Although whole spices may be milder than ground spices in a dish at the start, some spices, including cinnamon, clove, cardamom, and allspice, become unpleasantly strong when allowed to steep. Be sure to remove and discard whole spices at the end of cooking.

Working with spices and herbs can be challenging. Familiarity and experience are the keys to success. As long as you use spices and herbs judiciously, you can begin experimenting right from the start. As you become more familiar with the intricacies of their chemistry and the ways spices and herbs affect food, the more instinctive your style will become. In time you will develop a clear understanding of the full potential of spices and herbs and reach for them naturally as you cook.

everyday spices
and herbs

$\int$pices and herbs listed in this chapter are those you most likely have used in one form or another—black pepper ground freshly on eggs and salad, dried ground oregano sprinkled on pizza, cinnamon in apple pie, and jalapeño and fresh cilantro in salsas scooped up with tortilla chips.

These descriptive notes are intended to explain how they work in particular situations and to help you explore new avenues of use. If you like one spice or herb more than another, you will learn many different techniques for using it in cooking.

allspice

ALLSPICE, also known as pimenta, myrtle, and Jamaica pepper, is the fruit or berry of the evergreen tree *Pimenta officinalis,* which is indigenous to the West Indies and Latin America. The berries, ranging in size from a peppercorn to a pea, are picked green but fully mature. When dried, they shrivel and turn brownish-red.

Allspice is so named because it combines in one spice the fragrances of several spices, namely cloves, nutmeg, and cinnamon. The distinctive aroma of allspice is due to the abundant presence of eugenol, the spicy-smelling volatile oil that is mainly associated with cloves but is also present in nutmeg and cinnamon.

Allspice is grown mainly in Jamaica (hence the name Jamaica pepper) where it is called pimenta, not to be confused with pimiento (*Capsicum annuum*), a variety of red pepper (see page 13). The early Spanish explorers of the New World mistook the berry, which does possess some astringent bite, for the sought-after pungent black peppercorn of India. The spice was later brought to Europe and spread from there through Asia.

The flavor of fruits and such earthy winter vegetables as carrots, turnips, sweet potatoes, butternut squash, and pumpkin, are enhanced by the addition of allspice, as in Pumpkin with Allspice (page 216) and Dried Fruit Compote with Allspice (page 260). Allspice is particularly good with grains; in addition to lending them a rich flavor, it makes them digestible, as in Bulgur Salad with Allspice (page 173).

Allspice is one of the best natural food preservers available to man. For centuries the people of its lands of origins have known of the antibacterial and antifungal qualities of allspice and spiced their meat with the berries. The practice is still in wide use for cured meat and fish, as in Jerk Chicken (page 61) and Escabeche of Chicken in Allspice Sauce (page 105). Allspice is an extremely potent spice and must be used sparingly, in small pinches. An excess may overwhelm a dish and even lend it a bitter taste.

Allspice is used whole and ground in cooking. It is widely available in supermarkets. The berries should be purchased whole and ground as needed. Allspice has a husky skin that is not crushed or powdered easily with a mortar and pestle or with a rolling pin. To grind, use an electric spice/coffee grinder. (*Stored, tightly covered, in a cool dark place, allspice will keep indefinitely, though the color will dull with time.*)

If allspice is not available, a combination of cloves, nutmeg, and cinnamon is an acceptable substitute. For 1 teaspoon ground allspice, combine 1/2 teaspoon ground cloves, 1/4 teaspoon freshly grated or ground nutmeg, and 1/4 teaspoon cinnamon.

anise

ANISE belongs to the graceful *Umbelliferae* family of herbs, which also includes parsley and dill. Anise seeds, actually the dried ripe fruit of the plant, resemble cumin seeds. The plant, native to the eastern Mediterranean region, is widely cultivated in southern Europe, South America, and central Asia.

Anise (*Pimpinella anisum*) has a characteristic licorice flavor with a peppery bite and traces of vanilla. Although not directly related to fennel (*Foeniculum vulgare*), anise has the same flavor compound, anethole, which is responsible for the licoricelike aroma and flavor of both. Anise is, however, sweeter, smoother, and stronger than fennel.

From earliest times, anise has been used not only for its wonderful scent and flavor but for its carminative and antibacterial properties. The Romans flavored after-dinner confections and cordials with anise to act as a breath freshener, particularly after eating garlic meals, and as a digestive. Anisette, an anise-flavored liqueur; arak, distilled anise alcohol; aguardiente, distilled anise sugarcane alcohol; and Chilled Anise Tea (page 285) are a few examples of anise-flavored drinks.

Marinades for meat and poultry also benefit from anise, as in Grilled Chicken Kabobs with Anise (page 154). Anise's sweet flavor also lends itself naturally to seafood, as in Red Snapper with Anise-Tomato Sauce (page 140) and to baking, as in Anise Biscotti (page 276), Anise Cookies (page 277), and Anise-Pistachio Crêpes (page 256).

Anise is used whole and ground in cooking. It is widely available in supermarkets. Anise seeds should be purchased whole and ground as needed. When using seeds whole, gently bruise them to release the aroma. To bruise, run a rolling pin over the seeds. To grind, use a mortar and pestle or an electric spice/coffee ginder. (*Stored, tightly covered, in a cool dark place or in the refrigerator, anise will keep indefinitely.*) If anise is not available, fennel is an acceptable substitute.

basil

BASIL is so much a part of our summer salads, pizzas, and tomato sauces for pasta that it is hard to imagine that these peppery leaves are of Asian origin. Basil (*Ocimum basilicum*), an annual of the mint family, is indigenous to northwestern India. It is highly esteemed as a potherb and revered as a godhead, much the way the Christian world venerates the Holy Cross. Ancient Indian and Chinese medical treatises describe the warming properties of basil and recommend a basil infusion, as in Basil-Ginger Tea (page 285), as a remedy for coughs, sore throats, and head colds. Basil is also well known for its antispasmodic, carminative, and stomachic properties.

Due to differences in soil and climatic characteristics, the basil plant varies greatly from one country to another. The most popular variety, sweet basil, is cultivated in southern Europe. It is mildly saline to taste, with a distinct peppery bite; its scent and flavor are reminiscent of cloves with undertones of tarragon, French lavender, and rose. It is this complex bouquet that has captured the imagination of cooks around the world, making basil one of the most popular of all culinary herbs.

Basil has a natural affinity with tomatoes, as in Tomato Soup with Basil Cream (page 127). It is good with pasta, as in Angel Hair with Olives, Basil, and Chilies (page 188). Perhaps there is no better way to glorify basil than Pesto (page 232), a puree that captures the very essence of basil. Fish of any kind; shellfish, particularly lobster and crab; vegetables like eggplant, zucchini, and green peas; and grains all blend harmoniously with basil, as in Brown Rice Salad with Basil Dressing (page 174).

One variety of basil popular in Southeast Asian and Pacific Rim cooking is holy basil (*Ocimum sanctum*), also known as Thai basil or licorice basil. In addition to the flavors of sweet basil, this one has an added layer of anise and pepper. It is particularly good with pungent, more assertive seasonings, as in Chicken with Basil (page 148).

Basils with unique overtones also exist. These include lemon basil (*Ocimum basilicum citriodorum*), lemon tasting with a fruity aroma, which is particularly good with broiled white fish or steamed lobster, and purple basil (*Ocimum basilicum minimum*), with a peppery bite and hints of mint and cloves, which is good with orzo, couscous, or rice. Cinnamon basil (*Ocimum basilicum cinnamon*), slightly camphoric with overtones of cinnamon, is good with veal, tuna, and fruit, while Italian curly basil (*Ocimum basilicum crispum*) is essentially a sharper variety of sweet basil with a suppler texture.

Fresh basil is widely available during summer and occasionally in spring and autumn. It is used whole, shredded, chopped, and minced in cooking. Basil bruises easily and must be handled with care. It also turns black when cooked in an acid medium like tomato sauce; in addition, its volatile oil oxidizes and vanishes rapidly when exposed to heat. Basil should therefore be added at the very last minute to a dish. Dried basil is widely available in supermarkets. (*Loosely wrapped in a plastic bag, fresh basil keeps well in the refrigerator for 1 week, provided the leaves are not wet.*) Rinse basil thoroughly before use. Dried basil has a spicier, rougher edged flavor than the springlike bouquet of the fresh herb, but it may be substituted in an emergency. (*Stored, tightly covered, in a cool dark place, it will last for 3 months.*)

bay leaf

BAY is the fragrant leaf of a tree or shrub (*Laurus nobilis*) cultivated since antiquity in Mediterranean countries. The bright green leaves stay leathery and shiny on the top side even when dried. Bay leaves, also known as laurel or laurel leaves, are valued for their spicy aroma, which suggests cloves with layers of rose, lavender, and moss. Bay leaves also have a mild bitterness, considered by connoisseurs to be delightful on the palate.

Like olives, bay leaves are indispensable in Mediterranean dishes. Everything—from soups, stews, and stocks to marinades, pickles, and game dishes—is flavored with them. Packed with digestive and hallucinogenic properties, bay leaves are stimulants that make foods spiced with them highly sensuous.

Bay leaves are used whole and ground in cooking. Whole bay leaves are stubborn when it comes to releasing their fragrance. They must be simmered in liquid or steamed for the volatile oil, the flavor component, to be slowly released, as in Winter Bean Soup with Bay Leaf (page 117) and Red Lentil Soup with Bay Leaf and Pepper Cream (page 120). The longer the spice steeps in the liquid, the more pronounced its flavor becomes, as in Summer Peach Pilaf with Bay (page 197). Ground bay leaves, on the other hand, release aroma quickly but they lose it just as quickly. Ground bay is more suited to sautéed and grilled foods, as in Shrimp Sauté with Bay (page 141).

Bay leaves are widely available in supermarkets. They should be purchased whole and ground as needed. Bay leaves are not crushed or powdered easily with a mortar and pestle or a rolling pin. Tear the leaves into pieces and grind them using an electric spice/coffee grinder. Sift the ground bay leaf before use. (*Stored, tightly covered, in a cool dark place, bay leaves will keep for 1 year. They may become dull and slightly brittle with time, but the flavor will not be affected.*)

black pepper

BLACK PEPPER, the king of spices or black gold, is the most popular spice in the world, used in cooking primarily to lend hot taste and pungent aroma to food. Black pepper (*Piper nigrum*) is the pungent berry or fruit of a vine that is native to India but cultivated today in many hot and humid tropical countries. The whole spikes of fruit are picked when the berries are fully mature but still green to greenish yellow, before they turn red. The berries are removed from the spikes, spread on mats, and sun-dried. When fully dry, the outer skin wrinkles and turns dark brown to black. White pepper (page 41) and green peppercorn (page 41) are berries from the same plant; they are harvested and processed differently to produce different spices. Black pepper should not be confused with chili pepper (*Capsicum annuum*), a completely different species.

Black pepper has a distinctive bite and an aroma reminiscent of cloves with undertones of lemon and moss. The heat in black pepper is due to the abundant presence of the chemical irritants piperine and chavicine, which though insoluble in water are readily soluble in alcohol. In fact, the prolonged presence of pepper in water-based dishes turns them bitter. Black pepper should therefore be added to such dishes at the last minute, as in Black Pepper–rubbed Salmon (page 135), Lamb Shanks in Black Pepper Sauce (page 157), and Pepper Sticks (page 110). It is interesting to note that a water-based dish tastes hotter when prepared with alcohol. This is because of hydrolysis, which splits the hot bite-causing alkaloids, thus giving rise to even more pungent compounds. Pepper is always added together with other highly aromatic spices and/or herbs, which help temper and round off the flavor of pepper.

Black pepper's medicinal attributes have been known since antiquity. In ancient Indian, the word for black pepper means "poison killer." Pepper was one of the earliest food preservatives known. As an appetite stimulant, digestive, and carminative, black pepper is also vitalizing. In Chinese and Indian herbal medicine it is widely used in the treatment of coughs, asthma, heart ailments, and inflamed kidneys.

Black pepper is valued for its hot taste and sharp penetrating aroma. Several dozen varieties of pepper are produced around the world, with varying degrees of quality. Shape, color, and size, as well as taste, matter. Uniformly round and even-colored glossy peppercorns that give off a sharp peppery aroma and have a stinging hot taste are at the top of the list, the Tellicherry pepper in particular. Commercial names can be confusing, though. The Allepey pepper does not refer to any grade but simply the port of export. Peppercorns do not have to be large since they are almost always used cracked or ground.

Black pepper is used whole, cracked, ground, and powdered in cooking. Black peppercorns are widely available in supermarkets. Black pepper should be purchased whole and ground as needed. To crack peppercorns, use a mortar and pestle or a rolling pin; to grind them, use an electric spice mill/coffee grinder or peppermill. (*Stored, tightly covered, in a cool dark place, black peppercorns will keep indefinitely.*)

caraway

CARAWAY at first glance resembles cumin, but close examination reveals its crescent shape and sharp ridges. Cumin (*Cuminum cyminum*) is a completely different spice of central Asian origin. When crushed, caraway releases an aroma reminiscent of European bakeries and rye bread. Believed to be the oldest spice of Europe, caraway (*Carum carvi*) has been cultivated since antiquity.

It belongs to the highly aromatic *Umbelliferae* family, along with cumin, dill, coriander, and celery. The dark brown seeds have a sweetish-sharp flavor and a pleasant fragrance reminiscent of anise, oregano, and cedar with layers of lemon and vanilla.

Caraway is packed with medicinal benefits, particularly stomachic and carminative ones. A sprinkle of caraway is often added to hard-to-digest starches, as in Warm Potato Salad with Caraway Dressing (page 168) and Raisin and Caraway Rolls (page 245). In European cooking, caraway is also associated with cabbage because it both enhances the flavor and makes the cabbage more digestible, as in Chilled Borscht with Caraway (page 121) and Smothered Cabbage with Caraway (page 207). Caraway is also used as a digestive in cordials, like the famous Kümmel, and crackers, cakes, and cookies, as in Caraway Cookies (page 278). Ground caraway is used as a dough enhancer in yeast breads, rolls, and crackers.

Caraway is used whole and ground in cooking. It is widely available in supermarkets. The seeds should be purchased whole and ground as needed. When using whole, gently bruise the seeds to release the aroma by running the rolling pin over them. To grind, use a mortar and pestle or an electric spice/coffee grinder. (*Stored, tightly covered, in a cool dark place, caraway will keep for 1 year.*)

If caraway is not available, use a combination of equal portions of anise and cumin.

celery seed

CELERY also belongs to the highly aromatic *Umbelliferae* family. Celery (*Apium graveolens*) is native to southern Europe, and it is the seeds of the wild celery plant, not the cultivated vegetable, that are used as a spice. The tiny, brownish-gray seed is bitter to the taste with an intense but very pleasant citrusy bouquet. An excess of celery seed could very well lend a bitter taste to a dish. A pinch of this spice will give you a mountain of flavor, as in Tuna and Grape Salad in Celery Seed–Curry Dressing (page 134). Celery seed is an ideal flavoring in those sauces, soups, and stews where a green herb would normally turn dark, as in Fragrant Fish Chowder with Celery Seed (page 123), Fennel, Green Bean, and Cauliflower Soup with Celery Seed (page 122), and Celery Root Salad with Celery Seeds (page 167).

Celery seeds have many medicinal benefits. They are both a stimulant and a sedative that promotes inner calm and peace as well as a remedy for rheumatoid arthritis. The Romans considered celery seeds a carminative and an aphrodisiac. They used the seeds in herbal tonics.

Celery seeds are used whole and crushed in cooking. They are widely available in supermarkets. Celery seeds should be purchased whole and ground as needed. When using them whole, gently bruise the seeds to release the aroma by running a rolling pin over them. To crush, use a mortar and pestle or an electric spice/coffee grinder. (*Stored, tightly covered, in a cool dark place or the refrigerator, celery seeds will keep indefinitely.*)

If celery seeds are not available, twice the amount of finely minced celery tops will make a reasonable substitute.

chili

CHILI, the spice that gives food a hot taste, was a rarity not so long ago. Except for some adventurous people who made it to the Asian or Latin neighborhoods, few knew of chilies. Today it seems that no amount of heat is too formidable. Supermarkets are now stocked year round with several varieties of fresh chilies. The growth in popularity of hot foods in America in recent years has been phenomenal.

Chili pepper, also known as capsicum (*Capsicum annuum*), is native to tropical America. For centuries before Christopher Columbus and the Spanish conquistadors, the Mayan Indians of Central America were using chilies to flavor and preserve their meats. The Spaniards thought the chili to be a new, more colorful variety of black pepper, the spice they had set out to find, and called it pepper, an error that has continued to cause great confusion. Chilies were introduced in Europe in the early sixteenth century and very shortly thereafter spread to Africa and Asia.

Although many chilies are picked green, they also come colored red, yellow, and orange; they range in heat from mildly sweet to fiery hot. They can be as tiny as a pea or as large as an eggplant. In Mexico alone, the world of chilies is baffling, a proliferation of shapes, colors, aromas, flavors, and heat. Many of the two hundred or so varieties possess unique flavor and textural characteristics. Two of them, the smoky, licorice-flavored ancho and the chocolaty pasilla, both dried chilies, form the core of the spice blend Chili Powder (page 54).

Chilies are rich in Vitamin C, even more so than orange juice, and in palate stimulants and digestives; they are said to be an aphrodisiac. Capsaicin, a chemical irritant, is what gives chilies their bite. The higher the concentration of capsaicin, the hotter the chili. Eating a chili causes a sensation like a rush or high. The body responds with warning signals and releases endorphin, a morphine-like chemical that is the body's own painkiller. As one eats more chilies, the secretion of endorphin builds to a point where the chilies are neutralized and the pain is transformed into an almost euphoric feeling. The secret of cooking with chilies lies in knowing exactly when and how to add them to a dish to temper and round off their heat, as in Chili-stuffed Prawns (page 104), Green Chili Vinegar (page 76), Angel Hair with Olives, Basil, and Chilies (page 188), and Chili Tortilla Bread (page 241).

How to extinguish the fire? Everything from eating a bowl of rice to drinking iced beer to chanting a mantra has been suggested. Many find a chilled yogurt or milk shake, with or without fruit, effective, probably because of the presence of certain natural enzymes. However, what works for others may not work for you. Experiment with a few antidotes and stick with the one that is best for you.

Fresh chilies fall into two categories, hot and mild. Jalapeño, serrano, Thai, and Scotch bonnet chilies, are commonly available hot varieties while anaheim, arbol, and yellow wax peppers are mild varieties. Chilies are easy to grow.

Chilies are used fresh and dried, whole, shredded, sliced, chopped, minced, and pureed, in cooking. They are widely available in supermarkets. Because of the presence of capsaicin, hot chilies can burn the skin. Wear surgical gloves while handling chilies and don't touch your eyes. Chilies bruise easily and should be handled with care. (*Loosely wrapped in a plastic bag, fresh chilies will keep in the refrigerator for several weeks provided they are not wet. Stored, tightly covered, in a cool dark place, dried chilies will keep for up to 6 months.*)

If chilies are not available, use the same amount of green bell pepper mixed with ground red pepper.

crushed red pepper

Crushed red pepper flakes came into vogue with the pizza generation. Together with oregano, black pepper, and salt, crushed red pepper is on the condiment tray at all pizza parlors. Very pungent varieties of chili (*Capsicum annuum*) are used to make this product. Dried ripe chilies are carefully crushed into even-size flakes. The commonly available crushed red pepper has a very pleasant, tolerable level of pungency.

Although it is a common practice to sprinkle pepper flakes on pizza, that is not the best way to use them. Dried hot pepper in all forms—whole, crushed, or ground—tastes best when smoked, with or without oil, as in Smoked Chili Pepper Oil (page 88), and Grilled Leg of Lamb with Smoked Chili Pepper Oil (page 88). The idea is to bring out the rich earthy flavors and create a gentle glow in the mouth, as in Penne with Mushrooms and Crushed Red Pepper (page 189).

Crushed red pepper is widely available in supermarkets. It is processed and treated, hence does not deteriorate easily when exposed to heat, light, and air. (*Stored on a kitchen shelf, it will keep indefinitely.*)

If crushed red pepper is not available, use half the amount of ground red pepper or an equal amount of minced fresh hot chilies.

ground red pepper

Ground red pepper is powdered dried red chili (*Capsicum annuum*). The chilies are allowed to ripen on the plant, then they are picked, sun-dried, and ground. Different chilies with varying degrees of strength are combined to produce the desired level of heat. For example, what is labeled ground cayenne pepper is not any particular variety of chili but a combination with an extremely high level of heat. Ground red pepper ranges in color from brilliant red to dull red, depending on the color of the chilies. The commonly available ground red pepper has a very pleasant, tolerable level of pungency. Since ground red pepper is a fine powder, it blends easily into a dish, as in Roast Duck with Hot Pepper and Plums (page 155).

Ground red pepper is widely available in supermarkets. It has a high content of volatile oils and should be stored in a cool dark place or the refrigerator, or it will turn rancid. (*Stored, tightly covered, in the refrigerator, it will stay fresh for 1 year.*)

If ground red pepper is not available, use an equal amount of crushed red pepper or double the amount of minced fresh hot chilies.

paprika

Paprika, a kind of ground red pepper, is highly esteemed for its mild flavor and brilliant red color. Although there is hot paprika, what is on the market is mostly mild or sweet. The paprika pepper (*Capsicum annuum*) grows in several countries around the world, notably Hungary, and in California. When the Spaniards introduced the chili to Europe, it took on new characteristics due to differing soil and climatic conditions. Thus the paprika pepper was born. Paprika is a rich source of beta-carotene and vitamin C; it is a stimulant, carminative, and digestive.

In order to preserve the color of paprika and its delicate flavor, the spice should never be added directly to hot oil. For best results, paprika should be added to the liquid or with other moist ingredients. Paprika is a natural emulsifier, well suited to sauces and soups as in Green Beans and Potatoes in Paprika Broth (page 114), Warm Tomato Butter with Paprika (page 236), and Mild Indian Chile with Paprika (page 163).

Paprika is widely available in supermarkets, usually found in red tins. It is light, air, and heat sensitive. (*Stored, tightly covered, in a cool dark place or the refrigerator, paprika will keep for 1 year.*)

In the event paprika is not available, use Annatto Oil (page 90) or tomato paste if appropriate in the recipe.

cilantro

CILANTRO, also known as fresh coriander and Chinese parsley, has become a household word thanks to the popularity of Asian and Mexican foods, in America in recent years. The coriander plant (*Coriandrum sativum*), native to southern Europe and the Mediterranean region, produces both the herb cilantro—the leaves—and the spice coriander—the seeds (see page 34). Cilantro, the Spanish name for the herb, is used to avoid confusion between the two.

Cilantro has a piquant taste and a strong scent reminiscent of lemon, parsley, and seaweed with undertones of pepper, mint, and moss. Although cilantro is one of the most widely used herbs in cooking, it is an acquired taste. This is because cilantro contains a chemical compound with a penetrating odor. Although most people find it sensuous and a necessary component of flavor, some find it objectionable. Coriander seeds do not have this unique aroma.

Cilantro is indispensable in Mexican salsas, Chinese dim sum, and Indian curries. A rich source of vitamins C and A, it is ideally suited to salads, dips, and sauces, as in Pesto (page 232), Linguine with Cilantro Sauce (page 186), and Cilantro-Walnut Dip (page 229).

Cilantro bruises easily and must be handled with care. It is used whole, shredded, chopped, and minced in cooking. Cilantro turns black when cooked in an acid medium like a tomato-based sauce; in addition, its volatile oil, the prime flavor compound, oxidizes and vanishes rapidly when exposed to heat. Cilantro should therefore be cooked briefly, added to the dish at the very last minute.

Cilantro, fresh as well as dried, is widely available year round at greengrocers and in supermarkets. (*Loosely wrapped in a plastic bag, cilantro will keep well in the refrigerator for 1 week, provided the leaves are not wet. Stored, tightly covered, in a cool dark place, dried cilantro will keep for 3 months*.) Cilantro usually comes with soil and grit clinging to the leaves and stems. Rinse the cilantro before use.

Although dried cilantro is less floral, it is an acceptable substitute for fresh cilantro in an emergency.

cinnamon

CINNAMON is one of the oldest spices known to man. The Babylonians traded with the Indians for cinnamon forty-five hundred years ago. King Solomon (about 960 B.C.) declared the scented quills, a gift of the Queen of Sheba, the prized possession of his royal treasury. There is frequent reference to cinnamon in the Bible, as in Exodus 30:23–25. Greek and Roman kitchens used cinnamon, known for its medical attributes, as a stimulant, carminative, and fungicide.

Cinnamon is the scented bark of the evergreen tree *Cinnamomum zeylanicum,* native to India and Sri Lanka. The inner bark of the tree branches is stripped by scraping off the corky outer layer and dried. As it dries, the bark curls up into quills. These are cut into manageable three-inch sticks before being shipped. The market-ready cinnamon is sweet tasting and mahogany colored. Cinnamon's camphoric aroma and sensuous flavor come from the essential oil of cinnamon.

The cinnamon commonly available in the American market is a teak brown thick bark that is rolled up like a scroll, very aromatic but slightly astringent. This is cassia cinnamon, the bark of the Asian evergreen *Cinnamomum cassia,* native to eastern India and Vietnam. Cassia cinnamon is not true cinnamon but is widely used because it is much cheaper. Mexicans, however, insist on getting true cinnamon for their hot chocolates and moles. To cooks in the rest of the world, the difference does not seem to matter.

Cinnamon's natural sweetness and high flavor match well with tart fruits, mildly flavored berries, and simple cakes, as in Blueberry-Cinnamon Sauce (page 257) and Cranberry Relish with Apricots, Walnuts, and Cinnamon (page 237). A pinch of cinnamon adds a delightful twist to savory dishes, as in Orange-Cinnamon Pilaf (page 196). And it is hard to imagine holiday baking without cinnamon, which fills the air with its warm sensuous fragrance, as in Warm Spice Blend (page 64).

Cinnamon is also refreshing in ices and beverages, as in Chocolate-Cinnamon Ice (page 270) and Great Chocolate Milk with Cinnamon (page 287). Just drop a small piece into a brewed cup of tea or coffee, or for a more intense flavor, add half a teaspoon ground cinnamon to the ground coffee or tea leaves before brewing, as in Cinnamon Coffee (page 288).

Cinnamon is used whole and ground in cooking. It is widely available in supermarkets. It should be purchased whole and ground as needed. True cinnamon, which has a flaky, paper thin bark, is easy to crush or powder with a mortar and pestle or with a rolling pin, but cassia cinnamon is not. Crush the cinnamon sticks first into small bits and then grind them using an electric spice/coffee grinder. Sift ground cinnamon before use. (*Stored, tightly covered, in a cool dark place, cinnamon keeps for 1 year.*)

clove

CLOVE is the highly aromatic bud of the tree *Eugenia aromatica,* native to the Moluccas or Spice Islands, which are today part of Indonesia. It is now widely cultivated in Zanzibar, Madagascar, and Granada. The pale green buds are harvested while still unopened, spread on mats, and sun-dried. When fully dry, they shrivel and turn dark brown to black.

The use of cloves in Asia dates back to the Han dynasty (206 B.C.–A.D. 220) when courtiers were obliged to keep a clove in their mouth when addressing the emperor, apparently to sweeten their breath. *De Materia Medica,* authored by Dioscorides, the outstanding Greek botanist and physician of the first century A.D., describes in detail many virtues of cloves in cooking, medicine, and perfumery.

The essential oil of clove has a penetrating peppery aroma and sweet taste reminiscent of bitter almond, rue, and vanilla. Clove goes well with saline flavors, such as ham, pork, and sausage, and with game. In stocks and stews, clove has the ability to fuse and bind flavors. Famous for its antibacterial properties, clove is added to such preserved condiments as ketchup, cured meats, jams, and conserves, as in Sweet Tomato Conserve with Cloves (page 272).

An inherent quality of cloves is to add a caramelized scent to vegetables and fruits without adding a sweet taste, as in Glazed Carrots with Cloves (page 208), Seared Pears with Cloves (page 219), and Roasted Sweet Potatoes with Cloves (page 218). It is one of the three most important spices in baking (cinnamon and dried ginger being the other two). Clove is an extremely strong spice and must be used sparingly, in small pinches. An excess of clove may overwhelm a dish and will lend it a bitter-hot taste.

Clove is used whole and ground in cooking. It is widely available in supermarkets. Cloves should be purchased whole and ground as needed. To grind, use a mortar and pestle or an electric spice/coffee grinder. (*Stored, tightly covered, in a cool dark place, clove keeps indefinitely, although the color may dull with time.*)

No other spice has the characteristic aroma of clove; there is no substitute for the real thing. Allspice, which has some clove fragrance, may be substituted in an emergency.

cumin

CUMIN, a light brown seed, resembles the caraway seed but is smaller and plumper. Cumin (*Cuminum cyminum*) belongs to the same highly aromatic *Umbelliferae* family as caraway, dill, coriander, fennel, and celery.

This ancient spice, cultivated in the valley of the Nile since antiquity, was in popular use during the building of the pyramids. Eber's Papyrus (about 1550 B.C.) details many medical virtues of cumin. It has been in use in Asia since the Han dynasty (206 B.C.–A.D. 220). There is constant reference to cumin in the Bible by Isaiah and in the two-thousand-year-old Indian medical treatise, *Susruta Mushkakadigana*. From earliest times, cumin has been used both for its wonderful scent and flavor and as a stimulant, a carminative, and a cure for colic.

Today cumin is indispensable to Mediterranean, Indian, Middle Eastern, Mexican, and Latin American cooking. It has a piercing spicy-lemony aroma and a stinging bite, which is due to the presence of certain chemical irritants similar to capsaicin. This is why a dish containing cumin but no chili tastes spicy or hot. Beans and peas and meats flavored with cumin are rendered more digestible, as in Chick Pea Salad with Cumin (page 172) and Chile con Carne (page 55). A pinch of cumin adds a spicy twist to marinades, vinegars, and spice blends, as in Cumin Vinaigrette (page 82) and Barbecue Spice Blend (page 70). It can turn a simple starch into something extraordinary, as in Cumin Potatoes (page 215) and Tomato-Cumin Rice (page 193).

Cumin is used whole and ground in cooking. Cumin is widely available in supermarkets. You can bring out more aroma and add a slight smokiness by lightly toasting the seeds. The seeds should be purchased whole and ground as needed. To grind, use a mortar and pestle or an electric spice/coffee grinder. (*Stored, tightly covered, in a cool dark place, cumin will keep for 1 year.*)

In the event cumin is unavailable, substitute half the amount of caraway seeds.

toasted cumin seeds

Place about 2 tablespoons cumin seeds in an ungreased skillet. Toast over medium-high heat until the seeds turn a few shades darker. Remove from the heat and cool completely. If not using right away, transfer to a container. (*Stored, tightly covered, in a cool dark place, the toasted seeds will keep for 3 months.*)

They can be sprinkled, whole or ground, over soups and vegetables, or used in marinades and rubs for fish, as in Cool Yogurt Soup with Toasted Cumin Seeds (page 128), Cucumber with Toasted Cumin Seeds (page 211), and Barbecue Spice Blend (page 70).

dill

DILL, also known as dillweed, is native to the Mediterranean and northwestern Asia. The plant (*Anethum graveolens*) produces both an herb—the feathery leaves—and a spice—the yellowish-brown dillseeds, actually the dried fruit of the plant.

Dill has many medicinal benefits, which were known to the peoples of ancient Egypt, India, and Rome. A very effective stomachic and carminative, a dill infusion was a common remedy for colic during the Middle Ages. Dill has a somewhat bitter flavor and exudes a pleasant fragrance reminiscent of anise, oregano, and cedar with hints of lemon and vanilla. Mellow sauces, delicate fish, and simple breads all perk up with a touch of dill, as in Cool Yogurt Dill Sauce with Dried Cranberries and Almonds (page 230), Steamed Sea Bass with Dill (page 138), and Dill Tortilla Bread (page 240).

Dill is used whole, chopped, and minced in cooking. It is widely available in both fresh and dried form in supermarkets. (*Loosely wrapped in a plastic bag, dill will keep in the refrigerator for 1 week, provided the leaves are not wet. Rinse before using. Stored, tightly covered, in a cool dark place, dried dillweed will keep for 3 months.*)

fennel

FENNEL seeds, tiny and yellowish-green, resemble cumin seeds except that when bruised they explode with a licorice fragrance reminiscent of anise. Although not directly related to anise, fennel (*Foeniculum vulgare*) contains anethole, the same essential oil and flavor component that is present in anise. Fennel, however, is milder, and less sweet and fragrant than anise.

The spice, native to southern Europe and the Mediterranean, was used in ancient India and Egypt for its sweet pleasant flavor and its medicinal attributes. Fennel is effective as a carminative and stimulant and helps sharpen the senses, particularly sight and smell. In some parts of the world, it is used in candies. During the Middle Ages, fennel reached heights of popularity in cure-all tea infusions. Fennel is the primary flavoring spice in the Italian liqueur sambuca.

Fennel brings out the sweetness in foods it is paired with, as in Apple Compote with Fennel (page 221). Brussels sprouts are hard to digest, but not when a little fennel is added, as in Brussels Sprouts with Fennel (page 206). Fennel goes particularly well with poultry, fish, and tomatoes, as in Spaghetti with Fennel-Tomato Sauce (page 185).

Fennel seeds are used whole and ground in cooking. They are widely available in supermarkets. Fennel seeds should be purchased whole and ground as needed. When using whole, bruise the seeds to release the aroma by lightly crushing them with a mortar and pestle or with a rolling pin. To grind, use an electric spice/coffee grinder. (*Stored, tightly covered, in a cool dark place or the refrigerator, fennel seeds will keep indefinitely.*)

If fennel is not available, anise seeds make an acceptable substitute.

mace

MACE is the membrane covering the shell of nutmeg from the tree *Myristica fragrans,* native to the Moluccas or Spice Islands, now widely cultivated, particularly in Grenada. The apricotlike nutmeg fruit is harvested when ripe and slit open to expose the seed shell. The brilliant red membrane covering the shell, the aril, is carefully removed and spread on mats. Under the hot tropical sun the aril dries into yellowish-brown flakes called blades. This is the spice mace.

Mace has a pungent flavor and sweet, peppery fragrance reminiscent of cloves and mint with undertones of rose, French lavender, and pine. Mace is a baking spice. Like nutmeg, it is used in everything from cookies and pies to puddings and custards to elaborate cakes. Mace is more aromatic than nutmeg and slightly astringent, qualities that make it suitable for saline dishes as well, notably luncheon meat (it is a flavoring of frankfurters), ham, and poultry. Its natural orange color recommends it for light-colored cakes, cream pies, and cream soups, as in Chilled Carrot Soup with Mace (page 119), Currant and Mace Puffs (page 242), and Raspberry Yogurt Bavarian with Mace and Pistachio (page 265). Both nutmeg and mace bring out the sweetness in vegetables, add buttery flavor even when there is no butter, and fuse flavors.

Mace is used whole as blades and ground in cooking. Mace blades are available at specialty spice stores and outlets. Ground mace is widely available in supermarkets. To grind blades, use a mortar and pestle or an electric spice/coffee grinder. (*Stored, tightly covered, in a cool dark place, mace blades will keep indefinitely. Stored, tightly covered, in a cool dark place, ground mace will keep indefinitely.*)

If mace is not available, nutmeg makes a good substitute.

marjoram

MARJORAM, an aromatic herb of the mint family, is very similar to oregano (see page 23), but more delicate, more refined in flavor. Grown since antiquity in western Asia and the eastern Mediterranean regions, marjoram (*Origanum majorana*) is widely cultivated and used in many temperate regions of the world, including England, northern Europe, India, and the United States. The small oval light-green satiny leaves are mildly pungent and pleasantly bitter, with an aroma reminiscent of basil and thyme with undertones of French lavender, lemon, and pepper.

Marjoram has been highly valued since ancient times for cooking, medicine, and perfumery. The delicate springlike bouquet of fresh marjoram is unmatched, particularly for ices, salads, uncooked tomato sauces, and herb butters, as in Peach Ice Cream with Marjoram (page 267) and Marjoram Risotto with Water Chestnuts (page 200).

Fresh marjoram is available at greengrocers and supermarkets from late spring until late fall. Dried marjoram is widely available in supermarkets. (*Tightly sealed in a plastic bag, marjoram will keep in the refrigerator for 2 weeks, provided the leaves are not wet. Rinse before using. Stored, tightly covered, in a cool dark place, dried marjoram will keep for 1 year.*)

If marjoram is not available, oregano makes an acceptable substitute.

mint

MINT, or more specifically spearmint (*Mentha spicata*), is a common weedlike herb. Grown since antiquity in many temperate regions of the world, mint is native to southern Europe and the Mediterranean region. The Romans and Greeks relished its refreshing scent and penetrating flavor in cordials, condiments, and fruit compotes and scented their baths and bedchambers with it. Hippocrates (460–377 B.C.), known as "the father of medicine," frequently prescribed mint, a well known carminative, stomachic, and restorative, for digestive ailments. Mint made its way from the Mediterranean to China, India, and central Asia as early as the first century.

Mint has a sweetish-sharp flavor and a pleasant fragrance reminiscent of caraway with undertones of lemon, peppermint, and vanilla. This complex flavor is loved by Middle Eastern and central Asian cooks because it blends gracefully with their pungent spices. As a result, a whole spectrum of dishes—from yogurt dips, soups, and grilled meat to soothing beverages—is given a mint treatment, as in Iced Pear Soup with Mint (page 126) and Mint Tea (page 284), the ever-present beverage of North Africa.

In America, mention of mint brings up visions of mint jelly, mint julep, and mint–chocolate chip ice cream. It is the ubiquitous garnish on fruit compotes, ices, ice creams, and tarts. But in reality, mint has not been a popular culinary herb. Considered too strong, mint was said to be unable to blend harmoniously with other more subtle herbs, thus limiting its use in European cooking.

With the arrival in our markets of new seasonings from many parts of the world and our changing palate, though, mint is being given a fresh look. A touch of mint is refreshing, as in Basil-Pineapple Ice (page 269), while in Mango-Mint Salsa (page 231), it retains the integrity and tropical allure of the mango.

Fresh mint is used whole, chopped, and minced in cooking. It is widely available at greengrocers and in supermarkets. It bruises easily and must be handled with care. It also turns black when cooked in an acid medium like tomato sauce. Its volatile oil, the prime flavor compound, oxidizes and vanishes rapidly when exposed to heat. Mint should therefore be added to a dish at the very last minute. Dried mint is widely available in supermarkets. (*Loosely wrapped in a plastic bag, mint will keep in the refrigerator for 1 week, provided the leaves are not wet. Stored, tightly covered, in a cool dark place, dried mint will keep for 3 months.*)

nutmeg

NUTMEG is the magical fragrance of the holidays, imbuing everything from eggnog, mulled wine, and cakes to goose. Nutmeg is the dried seedlike kernel of the fruit of the evergreen tree *Myristica fragrans,* native to the Moluccas or Spice Islands, which are today part of Indonesia. It is now widely cultivated in many tropical regions of the world, particularly in Grenada. The fruit is harvested when ripe and slit open. The lacy membrane covering the seed or shell is removed and the seed is dried. The shell is cut open to release the oily dark-brown kernel, the spice nutmeg.

The use of nutmeg in Asia dates back to pre-Christian days when courtiers carried little boxes of the ground spice, well known for its euphoric and hallucinogenic properties, to sprinkle on wine. Ancient Indian medical treatises describe in detail the many virtues of nutmeg as a stimulant, carminative, and aphrodisiac. Nutmeg has a pungent flavor and sweet, camphoric, mildly peppery fragrance reminiscent of cloves and mint with undertones of rose, French lavender, and pine.

Nutmeg is slightly sweeter and more delicate than mace, hence better suited to desserts and delicate sauces, vegetables, and fruits, as in Mango Sauce with Nutmeg (page 259). Both nutmeg and mace have the quality of bringing out the sweetness in vegetables, adding buttery flavor even when there is no butter, and fusing flavors, as in Potato and Cheese Croquettes with Nutmeg (page 175).

Nutmeg is used grated in cooking. Nutmeg and little graters are widely available in supermarkets. Nutmeg should be purchased whole and freshly grated as needed. (*Stored, tightly covered, in a cool dark place, it will keep indefinitely.*)

If nutmeg is not available, mace makes a good substitute.

oregano

OREGANO, familiarly known as the pizza herb, is technically wild marjoram. This hardy perennial (*Origanum vulgare*) is native to the Mediterranean region. The dark-green fuzzy leaves, larger than marjoram's, are astringent and have a bold aroma reminiscent of thyme with undertones of lemon and pepper.

Oregano has been in wide use, both for its culinary flavor and medicinal properties, since before recorded history. A well-known carminative and stomachic, oregano was widely used in ancient Egypt to flavor fish, meat, and wine. Oregano's ability to stimulate hair growth and a clear complexion was known to the Romans, who used it in special tea infusions and lotions. Today, oregano is indispensable to Italian, Greek, and Mexican cooking. It is the main herb flavoring in Chili Powder (page 54). Oregano pairs well with robust vegetables such as eggplant, zucchini, peppers, and tomatoes.

Many different varieties of oregano are grown around the world; they can be grouped into two broad categories: strong and mild. Those grown in hot and dry regions, like Italy, Spain, Greece, and Mexico, are highly perfumed and assertive, particularly those grown in Mediterranean soil; oregano grown in cool climates, like North America and northern Europe, are mild and subtle. The oregano grown in your garden or from the market is more like sweet marjoram (see page 21) and should be used in such recipes as Risotto of Cauliflower with Oregano (page 198).

Imported dried oregano is widely used in Italian cooking in soups, simmered tomato sauces, and casseroles because oregano dries well, holding its highly fragrant and pungent volatile oils. Use it in Bean and Pasta Soup with Oregano (page 116) and Cajun Spice Blend (page 58). Although all imported dried oreganos are highly aromatic, rigani, the intensely floral Greek oregano, is preferred.

Dried Greek oregano is available in some supermarkets, at specialty foodstores, and by mail order (see page 289). (*Stored, tightly covered, in a cool dark place, it will keep for 1 year, though the color may dull with time.*) If Greek oregano is not available, Italian, Spanish, or Mexican, in that order, may be substituted.

Fresh oregano is available at greengrocers and supermarkets from late spring until late fall. (*Tightly sealed in a plastic bag, fresh oregano will keep in the refrigerator for 2 weeks, provided the leaves are not wet.*)

parsley

PARSLEY, the best known of all garnishing herbs, is a native of Sardinia; it is widely cultivated in the Mediterranean region, Europe, central Asia, and the United States. Parsley (*Petroselinium crispum*) has a mildly piquant, almost bitter taste with a delicate camphoric aroma reminiscent of French lavender and lemon. Parsley is a rich source of vitamins C and A. It is an effective stimulant, carminative, and digestive. Parsley has been used since Roman times as a breath freshener in tea infusions. Today parsley capsules are in great demand among people of garlic-eating cultures.

Parsley comes in two varieties: curly leaf, which is mild and more suited for garnish, and flat leaf, also known as Italian parsley, which has a strong pronounced aroma. Parsley's mild floral bouquet blends well with seafood, chicken, rice, and pasta and lends a streak of balminess to marinades, sauces, and vinaigrette, as in Parsley Sauce (page 226) and Parsley-Garlic Noodles (page 184). One of the greatest and simplest ways to enjoy it is as a parsley zest.

Parsley is used whole, chopped, and minced in cooking. Fresh parsley, both curly and flat, and dried parsley are widely available year round in supermarkets. (*Loosely wrapped in a plastic bag, fresh parsley keeps well in the refrigerator, provided the leaves are not wet. Stored, tightly covered, in a cool dark place, dried parsley keeps for 3 months.*)

Although dried parsley is less floral than the fresh, it makes an acceptable substitute in an emergency.

parsley zest

Combine 1 tablespoon minced parsley with 1 teaspoon minced garlic and 1 teaspoon grated lemon zest.

Sprinkle over soups, seafood, and vegetables, or beat it into butter.

rosemary

ROSEMARY, a bushy evergreen shrub of the mint family, is native to the Mediterranean coasts. Its Latin name, *Rosmarinus officinalis,* means "dew of the sea." The herb now thrives all over Europe and the United States. Closely connected with Europe culture, rosemary marks many traditions and rituals, with sprigs of it always present at baptisms, weddings, and funerals.

Since the Middle Ages, the silver-tipped dark green pine-needlelike leaves of rosemary have been valued as a culinary and medicinal herb. It is a stimulant and, due to the presence of certain antioxidants, one of the most potent food preservatives known. Rosemary has a bittersweet taste and a powerful piney aroma with undertones of pepper, mint, camphor, and sea moss. Robust foods, like lamb, pork, veal, chicken, and grains, taste wonderful enveloped in rosemary essence, as in Rosemary-crusted Veal Chops (page 160), Pot Roast of Chicken with Rosemary, Figs, and Pine Nuts (page 146), and Savory Millet Cake with Rosemary (page 181). Like other Mediterranean herbs, it is good in marinades, vinegars, and stocks. Because of rosemary's sweet camphoric quality, ices, teas, chilled beverages, and fruit tarts all benefit from rosemary.

Rosemary is used both whole and ground, both fresh and dried, in cooking. Fresh rosemary is available at greengrocers and supermarkets from late spring until late fall. A sprig or a pinch is all you need as anything more will overwhelm the dish and, possibly, make it acrid. Buy only whole rosemary and chop or grind it as needed with a mortar and pestle or an electric spice/coffee grinder. Dried rosemary is widely available in supermarkets. (*Tightly sealed in a plastic bag, rosemary keeps in the refrigerator for 2 weeks, provided the leaves are not wet. Rinse before using. Stored, tightly covered, in a cool dark place, dried rosemary will keep for 1 year, though the color may dull with time.*) The herb also grows easily in a pot on a sunny windowsill. The leaves dry quickly and well, retaining most of their fragrance.

sage

SAGE, the leaf of a woody evergreen shrub, is native to southeastern Europe. Since Roman times sage (*Salvia officinalis*) has been valued in Europe as a medicinal herb that revitalizes the mind and body, a cure-all. Its wide culinary use is relatively recent, beginning with the arrival of the herb in American gardens in the nineteenth century. Breakfast sausage and turkey stuffing, two American classics, get their distinctive flavor from sage. In these preparations, the herb not only lends flavor but acts as a digestive—and as a preservative since sage has antioxidant properties. The grayish-green leaves of sage are astringent and spicy-bitter. Their camphoric aroma suggests layers of thyme, lemon, pine, and moss. In some varieties one can even detect a floral undertone.

Sage is a powerful flavoring. A leaf is all you need; anything more will overwhelm the dish and, possibly, make it acrid. Sage pairs well with rich meat, game, fatty fish, poultry, and grain preparations, as in Roasted Chicken Legs with Sage (page 149) and Stuffed Sage Roti Bread with Olives (page 251). Sage is calming and soothing in tea infusions and in fruity aromatic beverages in summer, as in Peach Cooler with Sage (page 282) and Raspberry Tea with Sage (page 283).

Fresh sage is used whole and minced in cooking. It is available at greengrocers and supermarkets from late spring until late fall. Dried sage is available whole, crushed (known as rubbed), and ground. It is widely available at supermarkets. Buy whole dried sage and grind the amount needed with a mortar and pestle or an electric spice/coffee grinder. (*Loosely packed in a plastic bag, sage will keep in the refrigerator for 2 weeks, provided the leaves are not wet. Stored, tightly covered, in a cool dark place, dried sage will keep for 1 year.*) The herb also grows easily in a pot close to a sunny window. Sage dries well, retaining much of its fragrance.

tarragon

TARRAGON can easily be mistaken for an overgrown weed—until you crush the long thin leaves, and they start giving off a licorice fragrance. Tarragon (*Artemisia dracunculus*) is native to western and northwestern Asia.

Tarragon is a delicate herb with a distinct sweet fragrance and licorice flavor. It pairs beautifully with chicken, seafood, particularly lobster and scallops, and salmon, as in Barbecued Tarragon Game Hens with Quick Cherry Coulis (page 152), Tarragon Scallops Kedgeree (page 201), and Lentil Soup with Smoked Turkey and Tarragon (page 118). It is good with sautéed okra, mushrooms, cauliflower, and roasted onions, as in Stuffed Tarragon Roti Bread with Ham and Mushrooms (page 252). Sauces, particularly cream-based and reduction sauces, benefit from tarragon: Its sweetness tempers polarizing flavors, thus giving the sauce a more rounded, balanced taste. Tarragon can easily be infused in vinegar by pouring warm vinegar over the herb and letting it stand, covered, for a week. Tarragon-infused vinegar is delicious over such tropical fruits as papaya, mango, and pineapple and in salads of steamed and broiled fish and chicken. Because of its unusual mildness and sweet licorice flavor, tarragon does not blend harmoniously with other popular Mediterranean herbs.

Tarragon is used whole, chopped, and minced in cooking. Fresh tarragon is available at greengrocers and supermarkets from late spring until late fall. (*Tightly sealed in a plastic bag, tarragon will keep in the refrigerator for 2 weeks, provided the leaves are not wet.*) The volatile oil that gives tarragon its characteristic flavor evaporates during drying, leaving the dried herb practically tasteless. Use only the fresh herb.

In the event tarragon is not available, substitute a pinch of ground star anise.

thyme

THYME, a small shrub of the mint family, is native to the Mediterranean region, where it grows wild between the cracks in the rocks. Thyme (*Thymus vulgaris*) has many medicinal attributes, including digestive, antibacterial, and aphrodisiac qualities. Thyme smoke was used to scent ancient Greek temples during rituals; it was supposed to have a hypnotizing effect.

There are hundreds of varieties of thyme, each a little different in flavor and fragrance. The most interesting ones for culinary purposes are lemon thyme, anise thyme, orange thyme, and lavender thyme. The characteristic fragrance of thyme is due to the presence of thymol, which is also present in ajowan (see page 32).

Common garden thyme has a pleasant peppery taste and a very floral piney aroma that suggests mint, French lavender, and moss with underpinnings of clove and lemon. This complex flavor makes thyme very versatile and adaptable to a whole spectrum of dishes. The aroma of thyme is highly appetizing in stocks, soups, and stews, in marinades, and with chicken and lentils, as in Island Vegetable Stew with Thyme (page 177), Thyme Pita Bread (page 248), Kale Soup with Crabmeat and Thyme (page 124), and Thyme Roasted Chicken (page 151).

Fresh thyme sprigs and leaves, whole or minced, are used in cooking. Fresh thyme is available at greengrocers and supermarkets from early spring until late fall. It turns black when cooked in an acid medium like tomato sauce; in addition, its volatile oil, the prime flavor compound, oxidizes and vanishes rapidly when exposed to heat. For a full-flavored effect, thyme should be added to a dish at the very last minute. Dried thyme is widely available in supermarkets. (*Loosely wrapped in a plastic bag, it will keep in the refrigerator for 2 weeks, provided the leaves are not wet. Stored, tightly covered, in a cool dark place, dried thyme will keep for 6 months.*)

If thyme is not available, marjoram may be substituted.

vanilla

VANILLA, the world's most beloved spice, was unknown to the world outside the tropical rain forests of southeastern Mexico and Central and South America until 1521. The Spanish invader Hernán Cortés was the first European to taste this divine flavoring, which was offered to him by Montezuma when he welcomed him to the Aztec capital of Tenochtitlan. Later vanilla was introduced to Europe by the Spanish, and it quickly spread around the world.

Vanilla is the cured and dried fruit of a creeping perennial plant of the orchid family, *Vanilla planifolia.* The word vanilla is derived from the Spanish *vainilla,* diminutive of *vaina,* or pod. The distinct flavoring and aroma in vanilla is due to the chemical vanillin. Surprisingly, the green vanilla pods, which resemble green beans, have no vanillin or vanilla flavor when harvested. This is because the vanillin is bound to a sugar molecule and is released only when the pods are subjected to a unique curing process, which brings about enzymatic changes.

Although there are many curing processes in practice around the world, they share one common factor: They are all tedious and time consuming, often lasting several weeks. In Madagascar, the largest producer of vanilla, the pods are first boiled in water for several minutes to stop the growth process. Then the curing begins as they are piled into wooden boxes and steamed at intervals for several days. During the sweating and fermentation, the vanillin separates as a white crystalline compound that settles on the surface of the pod. The cured pods, deep brown, shriveled but pliable, and highly fragrant, are sun-dried for three to six months. The pods are then graded for quality— length, aroma, pliability, and sheen all being factors—tied into bundles and packed in tightly covered containers to conserve their fragrance.

Vanilla's sweet flavor and aroma naturally lend themselves to everything imaginable associated with sweets, particularly cakes, cookies, puddings, and ice creams, of which vanilla is the all-time favorite flavor, as in Old-fashioned Vanilla Ice Cream (page 266). Vanilla is also used in soft drinks, liqueurs, and perfumes. The use of vanilla in savory dishes is still shrouded in history, but there are indications that the Aztecs used vanilla and chilies in conjunction, and in Africa vanilla is seen flavoring such beverages as tea and coffee and fish preparations, as in Fish Fillet Braised in Vanilla Sauce (page 139).

Pure vanilla extract is made by steeping crushed vanilla beans in alcohol for several weeks, until the desired concentration of fragrance is achieved. Often the extract is allowed to mature for a few months, to clarify the flavor. Artificial or synthetic vanilla essence used to be extracted from eugenol, which is found in clove oil; although it was not as delicate and mellow as the vanilla, it was reasonably aromatic and acceptable. Artificial vanilla today, however, is extracted from coal-tar products and paper mill wastes! It is often harsh smelling and bitter tasting. Buy only pure vanilla—it's well worth the extra cost.

Pure vanilla is commercially available in two forms: as a bean or as an extract. Though expensive, a vanilla bean can be used over and over again until it is no longer fragrant and flavorful. After each use, simply rinse the bean and dry it thoroughly before storing. Store vanilla beans in a tightly covered container away from light. A practical way to store vanilla, particularly when using it for sweet dishes, is to bury it in a container of sugar. After a few weeks, the vanilla scent and flavor will permeate the sugar. Use this vanilla sugar in recipes calling for vanilla and sugar.

Pure vanilla extract is also widely available. It is a high-quality product and expensive, but there is no substitute. You can also make your own extract by breaking a vanilla bean into small pieces and putting it in a small bottle of vodka or brandy. Close the bottle tightly and set it aside in a cool dark place for at least a month. Use your homemade extract in place of the commercial kind. (*Stored, tightly covered, in a cool dark place, vanilla beans, vanilla sugar, and pure vanilla extract will keep indefinitely.*)

uncommon
spices and herbs

this section covers spices and herbs that may be less familiar to you than those in the previous chapter. Some are widely known but only when associated with certain products—mustard seed with prepared mustard, coriander with pickling spices, and fresh ginger with Chinese food. Others, though associated with ethnic cooking, have gained wide acceptance in recent years. These include wasabi, the Japanese green horseradish paste; annatto, used in Mexico, Puerto Rico, and South India to give food an orange color; and sumac, the eastern Mediterranean berries used as a souring agent. Then there are lesser known spices that possess special attributes worth serious consideration. These include epazote, ajowan, and turmeric. While most of these spices and herbs are available in supermarkets, some need to be purchased from specialty food stores or by mail order (page 289). I have given specific information for each spice and herb.

ajowan

AJOWAN, also known as carum, bishop's weed, omam, and ajwain, resembles celery seeds except that these seeds are light brown as compared to green celery seeds and that when bruised they explode with the fragrance of thyme. Although not directly related to thyme (*Thymus vulgaris*), ajowan (*Carum copticum*) contains thymol, the same essential oil that is present in thyme. This ancient spice, cultivated in Egypt and central Asia since antiquity, belongs to the *Umbelliferae* family along with caraway, cumin, dill, coriander, fennel, and celery.

Ajowan has many medicinal attributes, digestive and antibacterial ones, in particular. An infusion of ajowan called "omam water" or "gripe water" has long been a common cure for stomach ailments. Ajowan makes starch, such as beans, and meat easy to digest, preventing flatulence. A sprinkle of it enhances the flavor of crackers and of grilled food, as in Ajowan Crackers (page 112) and Milk-marinated Grilled Pork Chops with Ajowan (page 161). Since ajowan retards food spoilage, it is ideal in marinades for delicate fish and seafood, as in Flash-grilled Flounder with Ajowan (page 132). Ajowan is an extremely powerful spice and should be used judiciously. An excess may overwhelm a dish and lend it a bitter taste.

Ajowan is used whole and ground in cooking. Ajowan is available at specialty food stores and by mail order (page 289). Buy it whole and grind it as needed. When using whole, gently bruise the seeds with your fingertips to release the aroma. To grind, use a mortar and pestle, a rolling pin, or an electric spice/coffee grinder. (*Stored, tightly covered, in a cool dark place, it will keep indefinitely.*)

If ajowan is not available, dried thyme makes an acceptable substitute.

annatto

ANNATTO or achiote is to Puerto Rican cooking as chilies are to Mexican cooking. The Portuguese introduced annatto in India; it is used in limited quantities in South Indian cooking. Without annatto's color, flavor, and fragrance, dishes do not quite have the proper authenticity. Annatto comes from the evergreen tree *Bixa orellana,* native to Mexico, Latin America, and the Caribbean. Each fruit has about 50 seeds, the pulpy arils of which contain a red pigment. The pulp and seeds are scraped off and dried. Annatto was the basis of the dye that the Indians painted on their faces and bodies. This practice confused the discoverers of the New World, who labeled the Indians red Indians. Annatto, a safe and natural dye, is used today to color butter, margarine, cheese, ice cream, and sausage.

The brownish-red annatto seeds themselves are inedible. For cooking, color is leached into oil, as in Annatto Oil (page 90). In addition to turning a dish brilliant orange, annatto lends a sweet balmy aroma reminiscent of a rain forest. Annatto oil makes an excellent cooking base, particularly when added to marinades, sauces, and vinegars, as in Seared Red Chicken (page 91). A little annatto oil turns plain white rice saffron gold, an inexpensive alternative to the pricey spice. And it is a prerequisite for the classic Puerto Rican version of Sofrito (page 92), and the base for Arroz con Pollo (page 93).

Annatto seeds are available in markets selling Latin American products, at specialty food stores, and by mail order (page 289). (*Stored, tightly covered, in a cool dark place, annatto keeps indefinitely.*)

cardamom

CARDAMOM, the queen of spices (black pepper being the king), is a dried seed pod native to India that has been cultivated since antiquity. Eber's Papyrus (about 1550 B.C.), the medical treatise of the Egyptians, describes several uses of cardamom (*Elettaria car-*

damomum) in the royal court. When crushed, the tiny seeds contained in the pod give off a sweet aroma so seductive that Cleopatra is said to have filled her chambers with cardamom smoke during Mark Antony's visit to Egypt.

Cardamom is highly aromatic. Its sweet-spicy aroma is reminiscent of lemon and pine, with hints of pepper and mint. Cardamom is also a well-known digestive, stimulant, and breath freshener. It is ideal for candies, cakes, and cookies, as in Cardamom Cookies (page 279). A pinch of cardamom adds a delightful twist to pie crusts, crêpes, flans, puddings, and ice cream as in Cardamom Ice Cream (page 268) and Rice Pudding with Cardamom (page 264). Because of its volatile oil, cardamom is extremely strong and must be used sparingly, in small pinches, so as not to overwhelm the dish.

Cardamom is also refreshing in beverages. Just float a pod or two in a brewed cup of tea or coffee. For a more intense flavor, add ground cardamom to ground coffee or to tea leaves before brewing, as in Cardamom Coffee (page 288) and Cardamom-Citrus Tea (page 286). Cardamom's complex flavor melds equally well with savory dishes, as in Chicken Braised in Cardamom Sauce (page 147).

Cardamom is used whole and ground in cooking. It is widely available in supermarkets. Whole pods, hulled seeds, and ground cardamom are sold. For maximum flavor, purchase only pods or seeds. The pods come in two colors, green (natural) and white (bleached). The difference is due to the difference in the color at the time of harvesting. Cardamom with an even deep green color fetches a higher price than unevenly colored pods, even though it is only a cosmetic factor. The evenly colored pods are separated out and packed as they are while the rest are bleached. Although visually appealing, the ivory white cardamom is a dud because the bleaching wipes out much of the fragrance as well as the pigment. Buy green pods when buying whole cardamom.

To hull, lightly crush the pods with a mallet or the flat side of the blade of a kitchen knife. Peel away the skin and discard. Separate the bunched-up seeds clinging to the membrane and discard the membrane. To crush or grind, use a mortar and pestle, a rolling pin, or an electric spice/coffee grinder. (*Stored, tightly covered, in a cool dark place, cardamom will keep for 1 year, although the color may dull with time.*)

coriander

CORIANDER is native to southern Europe and the Mediterranean but has been in use in Asia since the Han dynasty (206 B.C.– A.D. 220). Constant reference is made to coriander (*Coriandrum sativum*) in a three-thousand-year-old Indian medical treatise.

Coriander seeds come from the same plant that produces the herb cilantro (see page 15). When the fruit is ripe, the plant is pulled out by the roots and laid out to dry.

The seeds are threshed and winnowed. The yellowish-brown coriander seed, slightly smaller than a peppercorn, has a mildly piquant taste and a distinct scent reminiscent of French lavender and cedar with undertones of peppery mint, orange, and rose. Fresh coriander fruit contains certain unusual odor compounds (also present in the leaves), which evaporate during drying. Coriander's mild taste and floral aroma make it one of the most widely used spices in cooking, medicine, and perfumery.

Coriander works well in many dishes—from soups to candies—but it displays particular flair when combined with chick peas, tomatoes, eggplant, zucchini, cauliflower, and onion, a combination the Mediterranean peoples have worked out in more variations than imaginable, as in Bluefish with Tomato-Coriander Sauce (page 130) and Carrot Salad with Coriander Vinegar (page 166). Since powdered or ground coriander acts as an emulsifier, it is ideally suited to any soup, stew, or any gravy-based dish that needs natural thickening. It is this spice that gives Curry Powder (page 56) its characteristic flavor.

Coriander is used whole and ground in cooking. You can bring out more aroma in coriander by lightly toasting the seeds. It is widely available in supermarkets. It should be purchased whole and ground as needed. Except when added as a flavoring not to be eaten, as in dill pickle, coriander is used ground or crushed because the skin is hard and stays that way even after cooking. It is particularly important to grind coriander for spice mixtures intended to be used as rubs for grilled meats. The skin is difficult to crush with a mortar and pestle or rolling pin, so grind the seeds in an electric spice/coffee grinder. (*Stored, tightly covered, in a cool dark place, coriander keeps for 1 year.*)

If coriander is unavailable, substitute twice the amount of cilantro or a combination of oregano and minced lemon zest.

toasted coriander seeds

MAKES 1 ½ TABLESPOONS

Place about 2 tablespoons coriander seeds in an ungreased skillet over medium-high heat. Toast the seeds until they turn a few shades darker, about 4 minutes. Remove and cool completely before grinding to a powder, transfer to an airtight container. (*Store, tightly covered, in a cool dark place for up to 3 months.*) Ground toasted coriander seed is lovely sprinkled over salads, lentils, soups, sandwich spreads, yogurt, cheese, and fruits.

epazote

EPAZOTE, also known as wormseed, goosefoot, Mexican tea, and Jerusalem oak, is the highly aromatic leaf of a wild herb plant that is native to Mexico. Long naturalized in North America, epazote (*Chenopodium ambrosioides*) grows everywhere, both as a culinary herb and as a garden weed. (Although you might very well have epazote growing in your backyard, it is strongly advised not to experiment: Many varieties are poisonous.) In Europe, where it was introduced in the late eighteenth century, epazote is very popular in herbal tea infusions.

Epazote comes from the Nahuatl expression, *epatl tozil,* meaning "animal of strong smell." As the name suggests, it is a powerful herb with a highly camphoric piney-balmy odor reminiscent of a tropical rain forest; it has a pleasantly bitter taste. For centuries before Christopher Columbus's voyage of discovery and the arrival of the Spanish conquistadors, the Mayan Indians of Central America had been using epazote to flavor their beans. It is one of the most effective neutralizers of the stomach gas often produced by beans. It is used medicinally as an anthelmintic.

To be effective, both as a flavoring and medicinally, epazote needs to be incorporated into the dish and not served as a garnish. Use it in flavoring meats and beans and peas, as in Black Bean Soup with Epazote (page 115) and Grilled Pork with Epazote (page 162). It is also used with heavy starches such as taro root and plantain, and to flavor rye, barley, and corn doughs.

Epazote is used shredded, chopped, and minced in cooking. Fresh epazote is sometimes available at Mexican groceries and specialty food shops. It has a wild, very pronounced fragrance. Epazote dries quickly and retains much of its pungency. Dried epazote is widely available at Mexican groceries and by mail order (page 289). (*Stored, tightly covered, in a cool dark place, dried epazote will keep for 3 months.*)

If epazote is unavailable, substitute a combination of equal portions of oregano and powdered dried Polish mushrooms.

ginger

GINGER is an aromatic rhizome that grows out like fingers from the ginger plant (*Zinziber officinale*), which is indigenous to the Pacific islands and southern Asia but is now cultivated in most tropical countries. It is used both fresh and dried.

fresh ginger

Fresh ginger is widely consumed in China and India. The botanical name *Zinziber* comes from *ingivere* in Dravidian, the ancient language of southern India, where ginger grows. Early Hindu medical treatises dating back to 500 B.C. give 35 specific uses of ginger for invigorating life. The Greek physician Dioscorides describes in detail many digestive properties of ginger in his *De Materia Medica* (A.D. 90).

Ginger contains strong antioxidants. A small amount added to *ghee* (clarified butter) or oil infusions keeps them from turning rancid. Marinades, rubs, and vinaigrettes made with ginger are similarly effective on meats. Recent experiments have also discovered that ginger has a noticeable effect on lowering cholesterol. The Indians and Chinese have known for centuries of the meat tenderizing properties of ginger, which have only recently been proven by the modern scientific community. Protease, the protein-digesting enzyme in ginger, works the same way as papain, which is present in papaya. Thus, the ginger in Ginger Ragout of Lamb (page 158) first tenderizes the meat and later retards spoilage.

Ginger has a camphoric spicy flavor and peppery scent reminiscent of cloves and lemon with undertones of cedar and mint. Ginger is a hot-tasting spice. Its stinging bite is due to the presence of zingerone, a chemical irritant similar to the piperine in black pepper. That is why a dish containing fresh ginger but no chilis tastes spicy hot. Ginger, however, mellows with cooking and lends a dish a nice warm glow, as in Tomato-Ginger Jam (page 271), Pan-grilled Pineapple with Young Ginger (page 222), and Steamed Fish with Ginger Essence (page 131). A little grated ginger enhances sautéed or roasted vegetables, and makes squash dishes taste more intense and flavorful. A slice of ginger added to chamomile tea, sweetened with a little honey, is very soothing, particularly for a head cold.

Fresh ginger is used sliced, julienned, chopped, grated, and crushed in cooking. Ginger is widely available in supermarkets. Except for very tender pink ginger from Hawaii, which has hardly any skin, ginger must be peeled before use. To julienne, thinly slice the ginger, stack a few slices at a time, and cut into fine julienne. To chop, gather julienned ginger and cut crosswise into very fine dice. To grate, use a ginger grater, the fine hole of a grater, or a mini processor. To crush, use a food chopper or food processor. To make ginger juice, place grated or crushed ginger in a double layer of dampened cheesecloth and extract the juice by squeezing. (*Loosely wrapped in plastic, fresh ginger will keep in the refrigerator for 3 weeks.*)

If fresh ginger is not available, substitute half the amount of ground ginger.

young ginger

Ginger comes to market in late spring and early summer. This is immature ginger, with skinless translucent flesh and pink shoots. It has a delicate aroma and a crisp, juicy, pearlike texture. Young ginger is lovely raw in salad dressings and sauces, as in Sweet-and-Hot Wasabi Sauce (page 86); with fruits and fish, as in Pan-grilled Pineapple with Young Ginger (page 222) and Steamed Fish with Ginger Essence (page 131); and in Thai curries, notably Green Curry Paste (page 94).

Young ginger is usually minced, chopped, or shredded in cooking. It is available in Asian markets and specialty food stores. (*Loosely wrapped in plastic, young ginger will keep in the refrigerator for 3 weeks.*)

If young ginger is not available, substitute the same amount of juicy fresh ginger.

ground ginger

Ground ginger is used in baked goods, in sweet confections, and in beverages. The rhizomes of ginger are dug up, washed, scraped clean, boiled, and spread out on mats. When thoroughly dry, they are ground. Ground ginger is buff colored. It has a warm sweet aroma and hot taste, spicy and pungent with clove undertones. It is worlds apart from fresh ginger in aroma.

Ground ginger was popular in the West as early as the fourth century B.C. By the Middle Ages, Europe had made painstaking attempts to transport living rhizomes, and ginger was a favorite spice in Elizabethan England. The use of fresh ginger in America, on the other hand, did not come about until the eighteenth century, when the mass movement of Asians to the New World took place. Even so, fresh ginger is still considered an exotic spice.

With cinnamon and clove, ground ginger is one of the three most important baking spices. It is used in cookies, pies, cakes, and puddings, as in Banana-Ginger Cream (page 258) and Ginger Crisps (page 274). Ground ginger also makes refreshing drinks and beverages. (Ginger beer and ginger ale are well-known soft drinks.) It brings out the natural flavor and sweetness in squashes and starchy fruits, as in Pan-grilled Plantains with Ginger (page 223).

Ground ginger is widely available in supermarkets. (*Stored, tightly covered, in a cool dark place or in the refrigerator, it will stay aromatic for 1 year.*)

juniper

JUNIPER is native to the British Isles. The bluish-black, allspice-size berry is astringent and has a highly camphoric aroma reminiscent of pine with undertones of lemon and cloves. Gin gets its characteristic flavor from juniper.

Juniper (*Juniperus communis*) was known to the Romans who used it in many meat and wine preparations for its carminative and stimulant effects. For centuries juniper has been used in northern Europe and England to flavor game, pâtés, and vegetables of the cabbage family. Juniper berries are wonderful in sauerkraut, for example. They go particularly well with venison, pork, squab, quail, wild duck, and goose, especially when cooked with apples and cider. Juniper's powerful aroma lends itself well to the richness of cheese, as in Goat Cheese Spread with Dried Tomatoes and Juniper Berries (page 100). The clean woodsy scent also enhances foods as different as lobster and lentils in the most delicate way, as in Steamed Lobster in Juniper Berry Vapor (page 142) and Lentil and Endive Salad with Juniper Berries (page 171). A little crushed juniper sprinkled over carrots or rice pilaf lends a delicate sweetness.

You can also add finely crushed juniper to give plain vanilla or fruit ice cream an interesting twist. Juniper is extremely refreshing in chilled beverages and tea. Juniper is a very strong spice and must be used sparingly, in small pinches, as an excess may overwhelm a dish and lend it a bitter taste.

Juniper berries are used whole, crushed, and coarsely ground in cooking. They are available in some supermarkets, at specialty food stores, and by mail order (page 289). The berries should be purchased whole and crushed or ground as needed. To crush, use a mortar and pestle or a rolling pin. To grind, use an electric spice/coffee grinder. (*Stored, tightly covered, in a cool dark place, juniper berries will keep indefinitely.*)

If juniper berries are not available, substitute a shot of gin.

mustard

MUSTARD, indigenous to southern Europe and the Mediterranean region, has been known since before the Greco-Roman period. It was appreciated for its pungent spicy flavor as well as its countless medicinal properties. It is a well-known tonic for the hair and skin and for rheumatism. Of all the spices and herbs, mustard is the most effective food preservative.

There are some 150 varieties of cabbage and mustard plants (species: *Brassica*) that produce edible greens, but only three yield the spice mustard: black mustard seeds (*Brassica nigra*), white or yellow mustard seeds (*Brassica alba*), and brown mustard seeds

(*Brassica juncea*). Brown mustard seeds are also known as Oriental or Indian mustard seeds. Brown and white mustard seeds are the only ones popularly used today.

Mustard is used in cuisines around the world in two forms: ground seeds (powdered dry mustard), which is popular in Asian cooking, and ground seeds combined with vinegar, salt, and spices (prepared mustard). Sinigrin, a chemical irritant present in mustard seeds, is responsible for its penetrating odor. Sinigrin, however, is dormant in ground dry mustard; that is why the spice has no aroma or taste in its natural state. But when it is steeped in water for ten minutes, certain enzymatic reactions are triggered by hydrolysis, and the sinigrin breaks down into new pungent compounds with a characteristic tear-producing odor and pungent taste. Since the aroma disappears with the end of the enzymatic activity, the mustard paste needs to be consumed within a very short period. For the aroma to last, mustard must be combined with vinegar or lemon juice as in prepared mustard; the acid base stops the enzymatic action and holds the pungency. This is why citric-based mustard sauces are more pungent than those made with cream. See Grilled Mustard Tuna (page 133) versus Green Beans in Mustard Sauce (page 204).

In Indian cooking, brown mustard seeds are used either toasted or infused in oil to release their volatile oil and turn them sweet and mellow and distinctly perfumed, as in Pasta with Mustard Shrimps (page 190) and Apple-Mustard Salsa (page 233).

Mustard seeds are used whole, crushed, and ground in cooking. Prepared mustard, powdered dry mustard, and mustard seeds are all widely available in supermarkets. Brown mustard seeds, which often look red, are available at specialty food stores and by mail order (page 289). Mustard seeds should be purchased whole and crushed or ground as needed. To crush, use a mortar and pestle or a rolling pin. To grind, use an electric spice/coffee grinder. (*Stored, tightly covered, in a cool dark place, mustard seeds and powdered dry mustard will keep for 1 year. Once opened, prepared mustard must be refrigerated.*)

If mustard seeds are not available, substitute an equal amount of powdered dry mustard. If prepared mustard is not available, substitute 1 tablespoon powdered dry mustard mixed with 1 tablespoon white wine.

pepper

PEPPER berries from the pepper vine (*Piper nigrum*) are harvested at different times and processed in different ways to produce black pepper (see page 10), white pepper (see page 41), and green peppercorns.

green peppercorn

Green peppercorns are removed from the spikes of berries that are picked when fully mature but green. The berries are then cleaned and either packed in brine or blanched and dried. In countries where green peppercorns are grown, they are used fresh, in sauces, salads, pastas and pilafs, and sandwiches, as in Rolled Vegetable-Cheese Sandwich with Green Peppercorns (page 176), Yellow Tomato and Green Peppercorn Salsa (page 235), and Polenta with Green Peppercorns (page 191). Freshly picked berries, are crisp, fragrant, and floral with a peppery bite. Reconstituted dried green peppercorns have a clear herbal flavor and a hotter bite than brined green peppercorns. Rinsed brined green peppercorns have a mild, cured, olivelike flavor. According to the herbal medical treatises, green peppercorns are an antiseptic and a digestive; they are valued particularly for the care of the skin and eyes.

Green peppercorns are available at specialty food stores and by mail order (page 289). They are available dried or packed in brine. Dried green peppercorns are extremely flavorful. They can be reconstituted in warm water in a matter of minutes; the berries soak up the water, plumping up to look like fresh green peppercorns. Brined peppercorns are available in jars and cans; once a can is opened, the contents should be transferred to a jar with a lid. Brined green peppercorns should be drained and thoroughly rinsed before use. Once opened, the jar must be refrigerated. (*Stored, unopened, on the kitchen shelf, green peppercorns in brine will keep for 1 year; once opened, they will keep in the refrigerator indefinitely. Dried peppercorns will keep for 9 months.*)

If green peppercorns are not available, white or black pepper or green chilies may be substituted.

white pepper

White pepper, a favorite of French and Chinese chefs, results when the berries are harvested when fully ripe, yellowish-red to red. They are soaked in water for several days. The skin comes off the fruit, which is then bleached, rinsed, and sun-dried to yield grayish-white peppercorns.

The heat in pepper is due to the presence of the alkaloids piperine and chavicine. Since most of these chemicals are in the skin, which is soaked away, white pepper is less pungent than black pepper and has a rather delicate piney aroma. It is ideal in delicate white sauces, cream soups, seafood, and fruit dishes, as in Stewed Apples with White Pepper and Fennel (page 220).

White pepper is not water soluble, but it is instantly soluble in alcohol. In fact, a prolonged presence in water-based dishes turns pepper bitter. White pepper should therefore always be added to such dishes at the very last minute, as in White Pepper Cashew Nuts (page 109). A dish with white pepper tastes hotter when prepared with an alcohol base compared to a water base. This is because of chemical reactions that split the alkaloids and give rise to more pungent compounds. In Chinese and Japanese cooking, where rice wine is added to many dishes, white pepper is preferred over black to ensure abundant flavor and heat. This is true also when white wine is used, as in Peppery Squid Puffs (page 107). White pepper is always added in conjunction with other highly aromatic spices and/or herbs, which help temper and round off the peppery flavor.

White pepper is used whole and ground in cooking. It is widely available in supermarkets. White pepper should be purchased whole and ground as needed. To grind, use a mortar and pestle, rolling pin, electric spice mill/coffee grinder, or peppermill. (*Stored, tightly covered, in a cool dark place, white pepper will keep indefinitely.*)

If white pepper is not available, substitute black pepper.

pomegranate

POMEGRANATE, literally many-seeded apple, has symbolized abundance, prosperity, fertility, and hope from time immemorial. Native to southwest Asia, it was grown in the hanging gardens of Babylon and was known to the ancient Egyptians. Highly esteemed for its flavor, beauty, and medicinal properties, the pomegranate (*Punica granatum*) is indispensable to eastern Mediterranean cooking. It is well known as being good for the heart and stomach; it is one of the easiest fruits to digest. It is also known to help build the body's immune system.

The scarlet red fruit, about the size of an apple, is filled with a juicy red pulp enclosing angular seeds. Pomegranate is sweetish-sour to the taste with a distinct astringent nip; it has a scent and flavor reminiscent of oregano, bay, and pine. The juice makes an excellent punch and sorbet. Pomegranate juice is used in cooking to lend piquancy, as in Pomegranate Braised Chicken (page 150) and Chicken and Papaya Salad with Pomegranate Dressing (page 153).

The fresh pomegranates available in the United States often lack the acidity naturally present in Middle Eastern pomegranates. Taste the pomegranate before using it and add a tablespoon or so of lemon juice to adjust the tartness. Pomegranate molasses does not pose this problem since it is all made from tart varieties. Pomegranate molasses is made by cooking down pomegranate juice to a syrup. It has a long shelf life.

For fresh pomegranate juice, quarter the fruit lengthwise and remove the seeds from the membranes. Extract the juice using a juicer or potato ricer. Be careful of staining. If fresh pomegranate juice is not available use pomegranate molasses or syrup, or dehydrated seeds, or balsamic vinegar. To reconstitute the molasses, mix 2 teaspoons in $1/2$ cup water. To make pomegranate juice from dried seeds, grind 2 teaspoons seeds into a fine powder and put it into a measuring cup. Add $1/2$ cup boiling water, stir well, and let soak for 10 minutes. Strain through a double thickness of dampened cheesecloth.

Grenadine, the well-known pomegranate-flavored syrup, is lovely in salad dressings, fruit compotes, and ice cream sauces, but it cannot be used in savory dishes.

Although technically a fall fruit, fresh pomegranate is available almost year round from greengrocers and supermarkets. Pomegranate molasses and dried seeds are available in Middle Eastern and Indian groceries and specialty food shops and by mail order (page 289). The dried seeds should still be somewhat moist and brightly colored. (*Loosely wrapped in a brown paper bag, fresh pomegranate will keep for 6 weeks in the refrigerator. Pomegranate molasses keeps indefinitely on the kitchen shelf; once opened, it must be refrigerated. Stored, tightly covered, in a cool dark place or the refrigerator, the seeds will keep for 1 year.*)

If pomegranate is not available, light balsamic vinegar, sour prune, and tamarind all make acceptable substitutes.

saffron

SAFFRON, the dried, brilliant red stigmas of a crocus indigenous to Persia (present-day Iran), is a spice of antiquity. The English name saffron comes from the Arabic *za'-faran* meaning thread or yellow.

Saffron (*Crocus sativus*) was introduced in India four thousand years ago by the invading Aryans, who reserved its use exclusively to the privileged caste. Saffron is mentioned in the Old Testament. The Hebrew word *carcom* for saffron is derived from *cumcum,* the ancient Indian word for saffron, which is still in use today in India. The Greeks, Romans, and Egyptians all knew of saffron and used it in food, medicine, and perfumery.

Although the Arabs introduced saffron in Spain as early as 960, it was only later in the tenth century, with the return of the Crusaders from the Holy Land, that the spice gained immense popularity and spread through Europe. Saffron, brought back by a pilgrim, was cultivated in medieval England and widely used in savory dishes and cakes. It was brought to China by the invading Mongol, the great Genghis Khan, in the thirteenth century.

Saffron has a bitter taste, a spicy flavor, and a sweet floral bouquet. Saffron also contains several red and yellow color pigments. Depending on the concentration of the spice, the color of a dish can vary from lemon yellow to deep orange. Saffron added beyond the saturation point, however, will be wasted both in color and aroma and will lend bitterness to a dish. Only a small amount, often just a pinch, is enough. Saffron's appeal is unparalleled. Its magical fragrance, subtle color, and delicate sensuous flavor are so captivating that many cuisines have developed classic dishes using the spice, including paella, bouillabaisse, risotto alla milanese, and zafran pilao.

Saffron blends equally well with savory and sweet flavors. In addition, it draws out the sweetness of food. Saffron flavor goes as well with ice cream and milk shakes, flans, puddings, and custards; cakes and cookies; as with seafood, or with rice and polenta, as in Saffron Pilaf with Peas and Almonds (page 199), Baked Saffron Custard (page 263), Saffron Cream (page 261), Saffron Scones (page 275), and Blueberry Tart with Saffron Cream (page 262). It can be brewed with tea.

Saffron is the most expensive spice in the world because its production is tedious and time-consuming. The lilac-colored flowers of the crocus bloom only for fifteen days in autumn, revealing the brilliant orange-red stigmas, which are hand-picked, one stigma at a time. During drying the stigmas lose most of their moisture, and thus weight. It takes 225,000 stigmas from about 75,000 flowers to produce a mere pound of saffron. Being so precious and popular a commodity, saffron is often adulterated with such ingredients as corn silk and safflower (called bastard saffron) and, in ground saffron, turmeric. In the Middle Ages in Germany, merchants were burned at the stake or buried alive for such practices.

Saffron is available at some supermarkets, specialty food stores, and by mail order (page 289). Pure high-grade saffron commands a high price, and today such quality comes from Spain. Deep burgundy saffron threads are packaged in small amounts—one to two grams—in sealed and dated containers to prevent adulteration. To release the fragrance, either powder the saffron threads with your fingertips or soak them in tepid water or milk and crush them with the back of a spoon before adding them to a dish. Toasting saffron makes the threads more brittle and easier to powder, a step recommended for Indian saffron, which being sun-dried is soft and limp. Mechanically dried and toasted Spanish saffron does not require this step. (*Stored, tightly sealed, in a cool dark place, saffron will keep indefinitely.*)

If saffron is not available, change the menu—there is no substitute.

sesame

SESAME, also called benne, til, and gingili, is one of the oldest edible seeds known to man. The Babylonians and the Sumerians flavored their wine with sesame and baked bread with ground seeds; bread is still baked the same way today in Iraq. The Egyptians and Indians pressed oil from it; this practice is also still in use today.

The subtropical sesame plant (*Sesamum indicum*) is indigenous to India but grows in most temperate zones, including China, the Middle East, and Mexico. The small shiny oval seeds are used in countless ways in China, the Middle East, and the eastern Mediterranean, but in most of Europe and the United States they are mainly a pretty nutty garnish sprinkled on breads, rolls, and pastries, as in Sesame Pita Bread (page 249).

There are two kinds of sesame seeds, white and black. Black seeds are cultivated mainly for oil, white seeds for cooking. Sesame has a sweet sugary aroma and rich buttery taste. Sesame seeds can be ground to a smooth creamy sauce, which is protein rich (26 percent) and contains several essential minerals. These milklike properties have made sesame very popular in Chinese and Middle Eastern cuisines that lack cow's milk or coconut milk. Tahini Dip (page 80) is one such sesame seed sauce.

Sesame seeds are extremely versatile. Whole, they make an attractive garnish for salads, vegetables, and meats, lending a nice textural touch, as in Fresh Fig Salsa with Sesame (page 234). A smoky fragrance, an added dimension, can be achieved by lightly toasting the seeds in an ungreased skillet beforehand, as in Zaatar Dip (page 228). In a sauce, sesame seeds interchange flavors, making the sauce taste creamy while they become soft and chewy as in Sweet Sesame Dipping Sauce (page 227). Sesame seeds lend a rich flavor to any dish to which they are added.

Sesame seeds are widely available packaged in supermarkets; they are sold in bulk at Middle Eastern markets and health food stores. Since sesame seeds are oil rich, they easily turn rancid if left out in a warm kitchen. (*Stored, tightly covered, in the refrigerator or freezer, they last indefinitely.*)

sichuan peppercorn

SICHUAN PEPPERCORN, also called fagara, has become more familiar thanks to the popularity of Chinese food, particularly the hot and spicy Sichuan style of cooking. Sichuan peppercorn is the dried maroon-brown berry of a prickly ash tree (*Zanthoxylum piperitum*) indigenous to China. The berry, although called a peppercorn, is in fact not a peppercorn, which grows on a vine. Sichuan peppercorns resemble true peppercorns in appearance and texture and have a mild bite, hence the confusion. This prickly ash tree grows throughout south and east Asia, from Pakistan to Japan. For thousands of years, before the spread of the black peppercorn from India or chilies from the New World, the people of east Asia used these berries to flavor food. They have a distinct anise aroma with traces of ginger, clove, and pepper and a mild peppery bite. The Chinese value it highly, both for medicinal and culinary applications. Sichuan peppercorn is also a well known stomachic and cold remedy. Its antifungal and antibacterial properties were known to the ancient Chinese, and the spice was often used with meat, not only to add flavor but to ensure safe consumption.

In processing, the bitter black seeds of the peppercorns are removed and discarded. Hollow, split-open Sichuan peppercorns, sometimes with a small stalk attached, are what is sold commercially. Sichuan peppercorn is a strong spice, and should be used judiciously, as an excess of it may overwhelm a dish.

Sichuan peppercorn is used ground (both coarse and fine) in pepper mixes and spice rubs, as in Five Pepper Mix (page 68) and crushed to accent vegetables, as in Green Beans with Sichuan Peppercorns (page 205), and in sauces. Sichuan peppercorns are available in some supermarkets, Asian markets, specialty food stores, and by mail order (page 289). You can bring out more aroma and add a smoky flavor by lightly toasting Sichuan peppercorns. The spice should be purchased whole and crushed or ground as needed. To crush, use a mortar and pestle or a rolling pin. To grind, use an electric spice/coffee grinder. (*Stored, tightly covered, in a cool dark place, Sichuan peppercorns will keep indefinitely.*)

toasted sichuan peppercorn

MAKES 2 TABLESPOONS

To toast, place about 2 tablespoons Sichuan peppercorns in an ungreased skillet over medium-high heat. Toast the peppercorns until they turn a few shades darker, about 3 minutes. Remove and cool completely. Transfer to an airtight container. (*Store in a cool dark place for up to 4 months.*)

Sprinkle toasted peppercorns, crushed or ground, on salads, vegetables, dips, and sauces.

star anise

STAR ANISE, shaped like a starfish, is stunning. Friends have told me that they use it because "it's so pretty." Although most people associate star anise exclusively with Chinese cooking, as in marinades for red simmered beef and soy chicken, it has been a popular spice in Europe since the eighteenth century for flavoring conserves, syrups, and cordials. The flavoring in the anise-flavored French liqueurs Pernod and Pastis is not anise but star anise.

Star anise is the dried reddish brown fruit of a small evergreen tree (*Illicium verum*) of the magnolia family, which is native to southwestern China. In Chinese the spice is called *jiao hui xiang,* which means "eight-horned fennel" because the ripe fruit opens out into eight points around a central core. In addition, star anise has a fennel-like sweet flavor and fragrance. Star anise is similar to both fennel (see page 19) and anise (see page 7), except that it is sweeter, more licorice-caramel smelling. Star anise is a stomachic, carminative, and preservative. The Chinese have used star anise as an herbal medicine for centuries.

Star anise is lovely used whole—the fragrance is less pronounced and the beauty of the spice is left intact. It is good with simmered and steamed poultry, as in Steamed Duck with Star Anise (page 156), and in fruit punches and syrups for poaching fruits such as figs, pear, and litchis. Fresh dates are wonderful baked with a sprinkling of star anise and grated lemon zest.

Star anise, though sweet smelling, should be used judiciously so as not to overwhelm the dish, particularly since star anise can lend a bitter aftertaste. Star anise gets stronger as it steeps in a sauce, so remove the whole spice as soon as the cooking is finished if a mild flavor is desired.

Star anise is used whole and ground in cooking. It is available at Asian markets and by mail order (page 289). Purchase it whole and grind it according to need. To grind, use an electric spice/coffee grinder. (*Stored, tightly covered, in a cool dark place, star anise will keep indefinitely.*)

If star anise is not available, substitute anise or fennel.

sumac

SUMAC, called *sim'meh* in the Middle East, is the dark red berry of the shrub *Rhus corioria,* native to temperate regions of the eastern Mediterranean. Today, it grows anywhere from the Mediterranean to the northwestern regions of India. Sumac is highly esteemed for its distinct sour taste, which is fruitier and more floral than lemon or vinegar and less sweet than pomegranate (see page 42), and for the sheer beauty of the burgundy powder. Before the introduction of the lemon, sumac was used as a souring agent in food by the Egyptians and Romans.

There is no limit to the way sumac can be used. In Lebanon, where every dining table has a bottle of sumac on it, I sprinkled it on just about every savory dish that needed a little lift. Salads, pilafs, and vegetables, as in Cauliflower with Sumac (page 210), grilled food, yogurt sauces, and creamy soups—all embrace sumac. Sumac is combined with toasted sesame seeds, thyme, and marjoram or oregano in zaatar, a blend that is used as a garnish for vegetables and a flavoring for pita bread. Combined with olive oil and garlic, it makes an unusual dipping sauce, as in Zaatar Dip (page 228).

Sumac is used ground in cooking. It is available whole or ground from Middle Eastern markets, specialty food stores, and by mail order (page 289). I prefer to purchase this spice ground. I have found the quality is not compromised, and grinding one's own requires removing the seeds first, a tedious and time-consuming process. (*Stored, tightly covered, in a cool dark place, sumac will keep indefinitely.*)

turmeric

TURMERIC is the yellow spice that gives Curry Powder (page 56) its characteristic color. Turmeric (*Curcuma longa*) is a rhizome native to India. The rhizomes are dug up, cleaned, boiled, dried, and powdered to produce this very aromatic yellow powder.

Turmeric has a mildly bitter-spicy taste and a very floral bouquet with mint, clove, and lemon undertones. It is one the most important and ancient spices in use today. In India, where the use of turmeric in religious rituals, cooking, and remedies dates back to pre-Aryan times (2500 B.C.), it is still widely and frequently used in cooking and as a stomachic, carminative, antiseptic, and antiparasitic agent. Recent studies have further proven that turmeric possesses anticancer and antioxidant properties.

Turmeric contains a color pigment, which dyes yellow anything it touches. Although the stain is usually not permanent—it comes off with a strong cleanser—the experience can be annoying. When cooking with turmeric, use pots and pans that are stain resistant.

Turmeric is a good spice to use with vegetables, lentils, and rice, to which it gives a lovely woodsy fragrance and yellow color. With green vegetables, it arrests the leaching of color, so that broccoli, for example, cooked with a pinch of turmeric turns even greener and stays that way for several days without any loss in flavor or aroma, as in Penne with Broccoli and Turmeric (page 187). It also adds color to Turmeric

Escabeche of Vegetables (page 106) and Turmeric Cauliflower (page 209). With tomatoes, it deepens the red color and makes the dish glow, as in Forever Red Tomatoes (page 217).

Turmeric is a very strong spice; you need only a pinch to color a dish brilliant golden yellow. It is widely available in supermarkets. (*Stored, tightly covered, in a cool dark place, turmeric will keep for 2 years.*)

wasabi

WASABI is the tear-provoking, parrot green pastelike condiment that accompanies sushi. With the new craze for hot-and-spicy condiments, America is in love with wasabi. Anything—from marinades and dipping sauces to salad dressings and butter for soup—gets a lift and a nip from wasabi, as in Sweet-and-Hot Wasabi Sauce (page 86) and Clear Mushroom and Shrimp Soup with Wasabi (page 125). What makes wasabi's pungency, though extreme, so desirable is that it is floral and produces a cool heat, which is short and instantaneous, unlike that of chili, which is warm and lingering. Because of that, wasabi naturally lends itself to fish, summer salads, chilled soups, and the like.

Although not related to the horseradish plant, wasabi (*Wasabia japonica*) is often referred to as Japanese horseradish because it contains the same pungent compound sinigrin that is present in horseradish and, incidentally, mustard seeds. Wasabi is native to Japan, where it grows near mountain streams.

The wasabi rhizomes are dug up, scraped clean, and kept immersed in water. Just before serving, they are rubbed on a fine grater to a paste. Grating or slicing tears the cells of the rhizome, releasing the pungent tear-producing volatile oils and causing enzymatic reactions that break down the sinigrin into new compounds with a characteristic penetrating odor.

Fresh wasabi is seldom available outside Japan, but dried powdered wasabi and wasabi paste are. Wasabi is available at some supermarkets, Japanese markets, and by mail order (page 289). Powdered wasabi comes in small round tins, containing as little as one ounce of the green powder. Wasabi paste comes packaged in tubes like toothpaste. Although these are less fragrant and more pungent than fresh wasabi, they are an acceptable substitute. To reconstitute wasabi powder, combine some with a little tepid water and let stand for ten minutes for the aroma to build. If you are using wasabi paste, squeeze it out at the very last minute to retain maximum flavor and pungency. (*Once exposed to air all wasabi products must be refrigerated.*)

spice and herb blends and seasonings

two diverse trends—an increased interest in the flavors of food and an emphasis on its nutritional value—have overlapped in recent years. It was a predictable merger since natural and fresh ingredients are the basis for those dishes that are both the *best* tasting and the *best* for you. The innovative methods of cooking today follow none of the set rules and hard-and-fast standards set centuries ago. They borrow freely from all over the world and adapt ingredients and techniques to suit the increasingly sophisticated American palate.

The inventive use of spices and herbs is one way to create truly imaginative recipes that are also nutritionally sound. Becoming familiar with each spice's and each herb's special contribution enables the creative and health-conscious cook to improvise with seasonings instead of being completely bound by tradition or, worse, randomly adding handfuls of this and that in hopes of coming up with a flavorful dish. When correctly utilized, spices and herbs can take the place of salt, sugar, and fats and eliminate much unhealthy cholesterol and sodium and many calories, while enhancing food's natural flavors. In Asian, Mediterranean, and Latin American cooking, the skillful use of aromatics is highly developed and as such is a strong influence on the recipes that follow. The results are adventurous, creative combinations and exciting flavors.

ten great spice
and herb blends

Spice and herb blends are one of the cook's great flavoring tools. The ones in this chapter are carefully thought out to combine intricate flavors in natural harmony. All these blends are practical yet authentic adaptations of great spice blends from cuisines around the world. They have been tried and tested over and over again and in my mind represent truly universal flavors. For example, Chili Powder, a traditional seasoning for Chile con Carne, makes a great marinade for fish and scallops (I particularly like the color), a rub for grilled meat, and a garnish to sprinkle over eggs or potatoes. Similarly, the Cajun Spice Blend can be used as a rub or to season boiled shrimp or lobster.

Spice blends are extremely simple to make. All you do, in most cases, is assemble the ingredients and mix them together. The recipes are purposely worked out in small quantities, usually a quarter of a cup, or just enough to season one recipe, so that your kitchen cabinet is not cluttered with little jars. All recipes can be doubled, tripled, or increased to any amount by increasing the ingredients proportionally. Most of the blends will keep well for a couple of months. Packed attractively, they make excellent holiday gifts.

chili powder

Chili powder blend should not be confused with the chili powder sold at ethnic markets or Latin American, Middle Eastern, and Indian groceries. That is not a blend, it is pure ground red pepper (see page 14). This Chili Powder is a blend of mild and hot dried chilies, oregano, cumin, and other spices. It is used as flavoring for the famous Southwest beef stew, Chile con Carne. The generous presence of chilies is what gives this blend an authentic character. Thanks to spice mail order companies and the popularity of Southwestern and Mexican foods, you can now get many varieties of chilies in ground form and make your own Chili Powder.

In this combination, I have used four varieties of chilies: The smoky ancho and the chocolatey pasilla give the blend richness and depth; the red pepper adds pure heat; and the paprika, in addition to adding color, sweetens and lightens the other chilies. The blend is aromatic and mildly spicy, so as not to mask the aromas of the various chilies. You can make it hotter if you like by adding more ground red pepper. Chili Powder can be used as rub for pork and for flank or skirt steak. Sprinkle a little on hash-brown potatoes (see page 214) or scrambled eggs to really liven up your morning.

chili powder

MAKES ¼ CUP

2 teaspoons ancho chili powder

2 teaspoons pasilla chili powder

1 tablespoon Hungarian paprika

1 tablespoon ground red pepper

1 teaspoon dried oregano

1 teaspoon ground cumin

spoon celery seeds

teaspoon ground bay leaf

Combine all the ingredients and transfer to an airtight container. (*May be stored in a cool dry place for up to 3 months; the pungent aroma begins to diminish after 3 weeks.*)

chile con carne

While you can make chile[...] nothing is more pleasing than this one made [...] and finely diced. Both its flavor and texture a[...]ense flavors of the chilies. Whether or not to a[...] are a purist, substitute an equal amount of beef [...]laden dishes; they soak up and smooth out the [...] a few hours, preferably a day, ahead. For som[...] Eggplant, and Lima Bean Chile (page 180).

ERRATA
Page 54

The missing measures for the celery seeds and ground bay leaf are $1/2$ teaspoon of each.

2 pounds lean beef, preferably sirloin, finely diced

2 tablespoons minced garlic

2 cups chopped onions

3 tablespoons Chili Powder

2½ cups pureed peeled tomatoes, fresh or canned

1½ cups beer, beef or chicken stock, or water

4 cups cooked red or pink beans, homemade or canned

Freshly ground black pepper and kosher salt

Relish Topping

1 cup chopped Spanish onion

1 cup chopped tomatoes

½ cup chopped cilantro

[...]S 8 SERVINGS

1. Place t[...] high heat. Cook, stirring, u[...]ng until the moisture evaporates and the bee[...] minutes. Add the garlic and onions and cook until the vegetables look soft, about 5 minutes. Stir in the Chili Powder, tomatoes, and beer and bring to a boil.

2. Reduce the heat and simmer, covered, until the meat is tender, about 45 minutes. Add the beans and cook for another 45 minutes, or until the sauce is very thick and flavorful. For even richer flavor, simmer the chile on the gentlest of heat for 1 hour more. Add a generous grinding of pepper and season to taste with salt. (*The chile can be refrigerated for 4 days or frozen. The high aromas of pasilla chilies and oregano, however, dull with chilling.*)

3. When ready to serve, ladle the chile into bowls. Combine the relish ingredients and spoon over the top.

Serving Suggestions: For great chilly winter evenings and entertaining, serve Chile con Carne with Chili Tortilla Bread (page 241), Parmesan-Chive Puffs (page 243), or Cumin Rolls (page 246).

curry powder

Curry powder is an old spice blend of Indian origin, introduced and made famous by early English traders. It is a blend of coriander seeds, which give it the curry flavor we are accustomed to, turmeric, which provides the yellow color, red pepper for a little bite, and other spices and herbs. I like my blends to be light and herbal, not too yellow, and definitely not very hot. A good Curry Powder, properly used, is a valuable seasoning to add to the flavor possibilities of a dish. Used creatively, it can flavor anything from mayonnaise and salad dressings, ragouts and roasts, to soup, vegetables, and rice, as in Curried Rice (page 194).

curry powder

MAKES ¼ CUP

2 teaspoons cumin seeds

2 teaspoons coriander seeds

2 teaspoons mustard seeds

1 teaspoon fennel seeds

1 teaspoon whole cloves

½ teaspoon dill seeds or 1 teaspoon dried dillweed

½ stick (1½ inches) cinnamon, crushed into bits

1 teaspoon black peppercorns

1 teaspoon ground red pepper

2 teaspoons ground turmeric

Combine all the spices, except the red pepper and turmeric, in the container of an electric spice/coffee grinder and grind until finely powdered. Add the red pepper and turmeric and continue to process until thoroughly blended. Transfer to an airtight container. (*May be stored in a cool dry place for up to 3 months; the pungent aroma begins to diminish after 3 weeks.*)

curry-grilled scallops

Here is a basic recipe using Curry Powder as a rub. The curry rub is perfect for seafood, fish, chicken breasts, and such vegetables as eggplant, potatoes, zucchini, and Belgian endive. For a stronger curry flavor, increase the amount of Curry Powder by one teaspoon, but remember too that it becomes disagreeable if used in excess. If extra heat is what you want, add a little more ground red pepper to the blend.

1½ teaspoons Curry Powder

1 teaspoon minced garlic

1 teaspoon minced fresh thyme or ½ teaspoon dried thyme

1½ tablespoons olive oil

1½ pounds large sea scallops

Freshly ground black pepper and kosher salt

2 lemons, cut into wedges

MAKES 4 MAIN COURSE SERVINGS, 8 FIRST COURSE SERVINGS

1. Combine the Curry Powder, garlic, thyme, and oil and rub over the scallops in a bowl.

2. Heat a frying pan over high heat until very hot. Add the scallops and reduce the heat to medium-high. Cook the scallops, shaking and tossing, until they turn ivory white inside (they will be yellowish-brown outside) and feel firm to the touch, about 4 minutes. Season to taste with pepper and salt. Transfer to a serving plate, garnish with lemon wedges, and serve.

Serving Suggestions: Serve for lunch or dinner, accompanied with Mango-Mint Salsa (page 231). Parsley Rice (page 192), Parsley-Garlic Noodles (page 184), or Smothered Cabbage with Caraway (page 207) are nice additions.

cajun spice blend

Cajun spice blend brings a wonderful blend of paprika and red pepper, cumin, mustard, thyme, oregano, basil, and other herbs alive with the essence of bayou country. It is used in Louisiana specialties like gumbo and jambalaya and as a rub for fish and meat. The large quantity of herbs makes the blend extremely aromatic. Traditionally, it contains garlic and onion, but I prefer to add these separately for more control and freshness. Cajun Spice Blend without onion and garlic is also easier to store since it's a dry blend. The clean, spicier flavor is more suitable for boiling vegetables, particularly starchy ones, and seafood, as in Cajun Shrimp Boil (page 143).

cajun spice blend

MAKES ¾ CUP

1 tablespoon black peppercorns

1 tablespoon cumin seeds

1 tablespoon celery seeds

2 tablespoons dried thyme

1 tablespoon dried sage

2 tablespoons dried basil

2 tablespoons dried oregano

2 tablespoons dried parsley

1 tablespoon powdered dry mustard

2 tablespoons ground red pepper

2 tablespoons Hungarian paprika or a combination of paprika and ancho chili powder

1 teaspoon freshly grated nutmeg

Combine the black peppercorns and cumin seeds and grind in an electric spice/coffee grinder until the spices are coarsely ground. Add all the other spices and herbs. Working in batches, continue to process with an on-off motion until fully blended. Be careful not to overgrind and turn the mix into a powder. Transfer the mix to an airtight container. (*May be stored in a cool dry place for up to 3 months; the pungent aroma begins to diminish after 3 weeks.*)

pan-grilled flounder with cajun spices

Delicate sweet flounder is a perfect contrast to the spicy coating. For this dish, I prefer thick, meaty fillets so that the moistness that is held within has a mellowing effect. Be sure to watch and regulate the heat so as not to let the coating burn. This dish can also be prepared with Jerk Spice Blend (page 60).

2 skinless and boneless fillets of flounder or sole (about 6 ounces each)

¼ cup grated onion

1 teaspoon minced garlic

¼ teaspoon sugar

Kosher salt

2 teaspoons all-purpose flour

4 teaspoons Cajun Spice Blend

2 tablespoons olive oil

MAKES 2 SERVINGS

1. Place the fish fillets flat in a shallow dish. Add the onion, garlic, sugar, and salt to taste and rub to coat the fish.

2. Put the flour and Cajun Spice Blend on a plate, mix them together, and spread the mixture out on the plate. Place it near the stove. Heat the oil in a large nonstick frying pan over high heat until hot. Dip the fish in the flour, coating it thickly, and add to the hot oil. Reduce the heat and cook, turning once with a spatula, until cooked and lightly browned, about 2 minutes per side. Remove and serve immediately.

Serving Suggestions: Serve with Orange-Cinnamon Pilaf (page 196) or Summer Peach Pilaf with Bay (page 197); Five Pepper Rolls (page 247) or Dill Tortilla Bread (page 240); and Cucumber with Toasted Cumin Seeds (page 211). A tall glass of sweet Peach Cooler with Sage (page 282) is lovely to wash it all down.

jerk spice blend

Jerk refers to barbecuing Jamaican style. There the meat is rubbed with special spices and pit roasted. Jerk Spice Blend, a highly aromatic and pungent blend, is a combination of allspice, cinnamon, black and red peppers, thyme, and other spices and herbs. Combined with a little garlic and lemon juice, jerk spices make a fabulous rub for chicken, chops, beef, fish, and even vegetables like eggplant, corn on the cob, and sweet potatoes. You can use Jerk Spice Blend in place of Curry Powder in Curry-grilled Scallops (page 57), in place of Cajun Spice Blend in Pan-grilled Flounder with Cajun Spices (page 59), or in place of Herb Citrus Blend in Herb Citrus–rubbed Filet Mignon (page 67).

jerk spice blend

MAKES ABOUT ¼ CUP

1 tablespoon allspice berries

1 teaspoon black peppercorns

1 teaspoon ground cinnamon

2 teaspoons ground red pepper

1 tablespoon Hungarian paprika

1½ teaspoons dried thyme

¾ teaspoon freshly grated nutmeg

Place the allspice berries in a small frying pan and toast over medium heat for 5 minutes, or until the spice gives off a delicate aroma. Remove and let cool. Transfer to an electric spice/coffee grinder, add the black peppercorns, and grind until the spices are finely ground. Remove to a bowl, add all other ingredients, and mix well. Transfer to an airtight container. (*May be stored in a cool dry place for up to 3 months; the pungent aroma begins to diminish after 3 weeks.*)

jerk chicken

One of the most delicious, yet simple, ways to use the Jerk Spice Blend is with chicken. The spice blend is combined with shallots, scallions, lemon juice, vinegar, sugar, and rum to turn it into a paste. Chicken, whole or cut-up, is rubbed with the paste and marinated before roasting, whether in a pit or, as in this recipe, a home oven. Often fresh minced chilies (the sky's the limit) are added to the paste to give the chicken plenty of bite. The end result is absolutely delicious but hot. I have tried to keep as much heat in the recipe as possible without having the tongue fall out of the mouth. While authenticity would demand accompanying Jerk Chicken with an equally hot or even hotter chili sauce, I prefer light fruity salsas, herbal pilafs, sweet vegetables, and fragrant bread rolls, so that you can savor the magic of allspice.

2 small chickens, each halved into serving portions

Olive oil spray

Jerk Marinade

3 tablespoons fresh lemon juice

3 tablespoons wine vinegar

3 tablespoons dark rum or grapefruit juice

3 tablespoons minced shallots or 1 teaspoon minced garlic

⅓ cup minced scallions, green and white parts

¼ cup Jerk Spice Blend

2 teaspoons brown or granulated sugar

Kosher salt

Fresh chilies, minced (optional)

MAKES 4 SERVINGS

1. Trim the chicken of all visible fat, slash randomly into the flesh, and place in a shallow dish. Combine the ingredients of the marinade, adding as much or as little salt and minced chilies as desired. Rub the marinade over the chicken. Turn and toss to coat thoroughly. Cover and marinate for 1 hour at room temperature or from 4 hours to overnight in the refrigerator. Remove the chicken from the refrigerator at least 30 minutes before cooking.

2. Preheat the oven to 350° to 375°F.

3. Remove the chicken from the marinade, scraping off and reserving the excess. Place a rack over a baking dish and spray with oil. Place the chicken on top. Bake in the middle level of the oven, basting with the reserved marinade, for 1 hour, or until the juices run clear when the flesh is pierced and the skin is nicely browned. Remove from the oven and let the chicken rest for 5 minutes, to let juices settle, before serving. Serve hot, at room temperature, or cold.

Serving Suggestions: Serve Jerk Chicken with Mango-Mint Salsa (page 231) or Cool Yogurt Dill Sauce with Dried Cranberries and Almonds (page 230), Parsley Rice (page 192), Pan-grilled Plantains with Ginger (page 223), and Raisin and Caraway Rolls (page 245) or Thyme Pita Bread (page 248). An icy concoction, like Basil-Pineapple Ice (page 269), will make a nice finale.

fragrant spice rub

Fragrant spice rub is neither hot nor sweet, just plain fragrant with fennel, cumin, mustard, rosemary, and thyme. It is particularly good on butterflied leg of lamb, squab, duck, quail, and fish. The spices form a crust, sealing in moisture. Although called a rub, this spice blend can also be used for flavoring sauces, as in Scrod Ragout with Fragrant Spices (page 137). You can vary the texture of the blend by using spices whole or lightly crushed for large pieces of meat or finely ground for fish and sauces.

fragrant spice rub

MAKES ABOUT ¾ CUP

1 tablespoon mustard seeds

1 tablespoon cumin seeds

1 teaspoon fennel seeds

½ teaspoon black peppercorns

½ teaspoon whole cloves

1½ teaspoons dried thyme

1 teaspoon dried rosemary

Combine the mustard, cumin, and fennel seeds, the peppercorns, and cloves in the container of an electric spice/coffee grinder. Grind to a coarse powder. Add the thyme and rosemary and process with an on-off motion until thoroughly blended. Transfer the mixture to an airtight container. (*May be stored in a cool dry place for up to 3 months; the pungent aroma begins to diminish after 3 weeks.*)

grilled squab with fragrant spice rub

Squab takes naturally to the Fragrant Spice Blend which enhances its flavor. In this recipe, I have given detailed instructions for preparing squab so as to ensure an attractive looking bird.

4 squabs

Fragrant Marinade

1 tablespoon Fragrant
   Spice Rub

1 tablespoon fresh
   lemon juice

1 tablespoon maple syrup

2 teaspoons minced garlic

2 teaspoons grated or crushed
   fresh ginger

Freshly ground black pepper
   and kosher salt

Olive oil spray

Radishes and 8 lemon
   wedges, for garnish

MAKES 4 SERVINGS

1. Using poultry shears, cut out the backbones of the squabs and place them, breast side up, on the work surface. Press down with the heel of your hand to break the breastbone and flatten the bird. Prick the squabs all over with a fork and make diagonal slashes, $1/2$ inch deep and 1 inch apart, on the meat, along the grain. Make a slit in the skin between the thigh and the breast and secure the end of the leg through the slit. Repeat on the other side. Place the squabs in a shallow dish.

2. Combine Fragrant Spice Rub, lemon juice, maple syrup, garlic, ginger, and pepper and salt to taste. Rub over the squabs. Turn and toss to coat thoroughly. Cover and marinate for 15 minutes at room temperature or for 4 hours to overnight in the refrigerator. Take the squabs out of the refrigerator at least 30 minutes before cooking.

3. Light and preheat a covered charcoal grill until white ash covers the coals and the heat subsides to a moderately hot level. Lightly spray the rack with oil.

4. Spray the squabs with oil and place them, breast side down, on the rack. Barbecue, covered, with the vents open, turning 3 times, for 18 minutes, or until the meat is cooked medium rare (the meat will be pink near the joints). Transfer the squabs to a heated platter and surround with radishes and lemon wedges. Serve immediately.

Serving Suggestions: Serve with Polenta with Green Peppercorns (page 191) or Tomato-Cumin Rice (page 193), Brussels Sprouts with Fennel (page 206), and Cranberry Relish with Apricots, Walnuts, and Cinnamon (page 237).

warm spice blend

Warm spice blend conjures up images of winter and the holiday season, of the buttery-fruity aromas of cookies and fruitcakes baking, of the air scented with sweet cinnamon, clove, nutmeg, allspice, and ginger. The holidays are unthinkable without this extremely aromatic blend. Use it in fruitcakes, spice cakes, spice cookies, and, if you fancy, spice tea. Although predominantly associated with sweet baking, Warm Spice Blend is equally good in savory dishes, particularly winter vegetable stews, as in Split Pea and Winter Vegetable Stew with Warm Spices (page 178).

warm spice blend

MAKES ¼ CUP

4 teaspoons ground cinnamon

2 teaspoons ground allspice

2 teaspoons ground ginger

2 teaspoons ground cloves

2 teaspoons freshly grated nutmeg

1 teaspoon ground star anise or ground anise (optional)

Combine all the spices and transfer to an airtight container. (*May be stored in a cool dry place for up to 3 months; the pungent aroma begins to diminish after 3 weeks.*)

steamed spice cakes

This is really a spiced custard, but the Cream of Wheat lends it an unusual cakelike texture. The addition of cereal to custards is quite common in the eastern Mediterranean, where I first tasted it. The blending of wheat cereal with warm spices comes naturally.

4 cups milk

3 tablespoons regular Cream of Wheat cereal

1/2 cup (packed) light brown sugar

1 teaspoon Warm Spice Blend

3/4 teaspoon pure vanilla extract

3 large eggs, lightly beaten

1/4 cup dark raisins

1/4 cup sliced almonds, toasted

1. Preheat the oven to 375°F.

2. Combine the milk, cereal, brown sugar, and Warm Spice Blend in a 3-quart saucepan and bring to a boil over high heat. Reduce the heat and simmer, stirring constantly, until the cereal is cooked and the milk thickened. Turn off the heat and stir in the vanilla. Add the eggs in a slow stream, while whisking or stirring the milk mixture rapidly.

3. Pour into 6 greased 6-ounce custard cups. Place the custard cups in a baking pan. Add boiling water to the pan to a depth of 1 inch. Bake in the middle level of the oven for 50 minutes, or until a toothpick inserted in the center comes out clean. Remove from the oven, cool, and refrigerate. Unmold and serve chilled or at room temperature, garnished with raisins and almonds.

Serving Suggestions: Serve after Pomegranate Braised Chicken (page 150) and Mint Pilaf (page195) or Pasta with Mustard Shrimps (page 190) and Sesame Pita Bread (page 249).

herb citrus blend

Herb citrus blend, like all spice blends and seasonings, has the inherent ability to replace or reduce the need for strong salt and fat flavors while providing satisfaction to the palate. This blend, a very floral bouquet indeed, goes to new heights. It combines thyme, oregano, rosemary, basil, and sage with dried citrus peel. A little fennel is added to fuse the flavors and lend sweet undertones. Keep this blend on the dining table alongside pepper and sprinkle it on steamed vegetables, fruit salads, and grilled fish. It works well with starchy lentil and grain dishes, which generally demand more salt for flavor, as in Black Bean and Mango Salad with Herb Citrus Dressing (page 170). The blend also serves as a rub for lean meats.

herb citrus blend

MAKES ⅓ CUP

1 tablespoon dried thyme

1 tablespoon dried oregano

2 teaspoons dried basil

1 teaspoon ground dried rosemary

1 teaspoon ground dried sage

1½ teaspoons coarsely ground dried orange zest

1½ teaspoons coarsely ground dried lemon zest

1 teaspoon coarsely ground fennel seeds

Combine all the ingredients and mix until thoroughly blended. Transfer to an airtight container. (*May be stored in a cool dry place for up to 3 months; the pungent aroma begins to diminish after 3 weeks.*)

herb citrus–rubbed filet mignon

This herb coating lends flavor and also prevents the outer layer of the meat from getting tough when cooked in a greaseless pan. The filet steaks are cooked medium-rare and then topped with a fine sauce made from their juices and a reduction of wine and stock. The steaks are equally good without any sauce.

2 filet mignon steaks, about ¾ inch thick (8 ounces each)

1 teaspoon olive oil

1 tablespoon Herb Citrus Blend

Freshly ground black pepper

¼ cup red wine

¼ cup beef stock or low-sodium canned broth

MAKES 2 SERVINGS

1. Place the steaks on a plate and coat evenly with olive oil. Combine the Herb Citrus Blend and pepper to taste in a small bowl and sprinkle over the steaks, pressing to make the mixture adhere to the meat. Set aside for 15 minutes.

2. Heat a medium-size heavy skillet until very hot. Add the steaks and pan-broil over medium to medium-high heat, turning, until browned outside and medium-rare inside, about 7 minutes. For medium and well done, cook the steaks longer. Remove the steaks to a plate and loosely cover with aluminum foil to keep warm.

3. Add the wine and stock to the skillet and bring to a boil, scraping up the browned bits. Boil rapidly to reduce the liquid by half. Turn off the heat. Slice the steaks into neat strips and arrange, slightly fanning them, on a dinner plate. Pour the sauce over and serve.

Serving Suggestions: Serve with Glazed Carrots with Cloves (page 208) and a green salad or Cumin Potatoes (page 215) and Green Beans in Mustard Sauce (page 204) or Penne with Broccoli and Turmeric (page 187). Accompany with a basket of breads, including Raisin and Caraway Rolls (page 245), Thyme Pita Bread (page 248), and Parmesan-Chive Puffs (page 243).

five pepper mix

Five pepper mix is a careful combination of five different peppers that brings out the finer points of peppers and their pungency. Use it on grilled seafood, as a rub for meat, as in Pepper-rubbed Rack of Lamb (page 159), in marinades and vinegar, in bread or rolls, as in Five Pepper Rolls (page 247), or sprinkle it over salads and soups, as in the recipe that follows.

five pepper mix

MAKES ¼ CUP

2 teaspoons black peppercorns

2 teaspoons white peppercorns

1 tablespoon dried green peppercorns

1 tablespoon Sichuan peppercorns or a combination of 1½ teaspoons anise seeds and 1½ teaspoons allspice berries

2 teaspoons crushed red pepper

Combine the black, white, green, and Sichuan peppercorns in a small ungreased frying pan over medium heat. Toast, shaking and tossing, until the peppercorns give off an aroma and are lightly toasted, about 3 minutes. Add the red pepper and continue toasting for another 2 minutes. Remove from the heat. Transfer the pepper to a bowl.

When completely cool, place in the container of an electric spice/coffee grinder and grind until the peppercorns are coarsely ground. Do not powder the mixture; a little texture adds to its appeal. Transfer the peppercorn mix to an airtight container. (*May be stored in a cool dry place for up to 3 months; the pugent aroma begins to diminish after 3 weeks.*)

five pepper–laced creamy cauliflower soup

The almond-colored cream of cauliflower soup has a mild, almost bland flavor; with just a dusting of pepper mix, it becomes vibrant.

2 cups chopped cauliflower

1/2 cup chopped peeled potatoes

1/2 cup finely chopped onions

1/2 teaspoon ground dried sage

2 cups rich chicken stock or low-sodium canned broth

1 1/2 cups lowfat (2%) milk

Kosher salt

1 to 2 teaspoons Five Pepper Mix

MAKES 4 SERVINGS

1. Combine the cauliflower, potatoes, onion, sage, and stock in a medium-size saucepan and bring to a boil. Lower the heat and cook, covered, until the vegetables are very soft, about 25 minutes.

2. Transfer the mixture to a food processor and process until smoothly pureed. If necessary, do this in batches. Return the soup to the pot. Pour 1/2 cup milk into the food processor and process briefly to wash down the pureed vegetables clinging to the sides of the workbowl. Add to the soup. Add the remaining milk to the soup and season to taste with salt.

3. Just before serving, heat the soup until piping hot and ladle into soup plates. Sprinkle with Five Pepper Mix and serve.

Note: You can make this soup with pumpkin, zucchini, sweet potatoes, turnip, green peas, or fava beans. Simply substitute two cups of the other vegetable for the cauliflower.

Serving Suggestion: Follow the soup with Rosemary-crusted Veal Chops (page 160), Polenta with Green Peppercorns (page 191), Mushrooms with Nutmeg (page 213), and Mini Pita with Basil and Dried Tomatoes (page 250). Anise Cookies (page 277) with Cardamom Coffee (page 288) make a fine ending to this elegant meal. For pure indulgence you may also squeeze in a dessert like Blueberry Tart with Saffron Cream (page 262).

barbecue spice blend

Barbecue spice blend, one of the great pleasures of summer, heightens barbecuing. No American barbecue would be considered real or complete without the use of a sauce or marinade. So here it is: a blend of spices that will turn ordinary ketchup into great Barbecue Sauce (page 72). Don't forget, though, that it is a basting sauce and not a marinade. Any prolonged exposure to heat will char the sauce and the skin. The barbecue blend is also great as a rub for grilled fish or butterflied leg of lamb and as a seasoning in batter-fried seafood, as in Fried Clams with Barbecue Spices (page 108). You can also use the blend in marinades made with white wine and onion or vinegar and soy sauce or the citrus one that follows.

barbecue spice blend

MAKES ¼ CUP

1 tablespoon Hungarian paprika

2 teaspoons ground cumin

2 teaspoons powdered dry mustard

2 teaspoons ground red pepper

1 teaspoon ground ginger

1 teaspoon ground dried sage

½ teaspoon ground cloves

½ teaspoon ground cinnamon

Combine all the ingredients and transfer to an airtight container. (*May be stored in a cool dry place for up to 3 months; the pungent aroma begins to diminish after 3 weeks.*)

barbecued chicken wings

The barbecue spice blend is excellent in citrus-based marinades like this one. The chicken picks up the fragrance of herbs and citrus while it gets tenderized. In recent years chicken wings have become very popular, partly because they are great for entertaining but mainly because they really take to being barbecued. The recipe works just as well with chicken drumsticks or a cut-up whole chicken.

4 pounds chicken wings

Freshly ground black pepper
  and kosher salt

Barbecue Marinade

¼ cup Barbecue Spice Blend

3 tablespoons wine vinegar

3 tablespoons olive oil

1 tablespoon minced garlic

½ cup fresh grapefruit juice

½ cup apple juice or fresh
  orange juice

MAKES 8 APPETIZER SERVINGS

1. Put the chicken wings in a large bowl. Sprinkle generously with pepper and salt. Combine all the ingredients of the marinade and pour over the chicken. Turn and toss to coat thoroughly. Cover and marinate for 30 minutes at room temperature or for 4 hours to overnight in the refrigerator. Take the chicken wings out of the refrigerator at least 30 minutes before cooking.

2. Light and preheat a charcoal grill until white ash covers the coals and the heat subsides to a moderately hot level. Or preheat an oven broiler.

3. Remove the chicken from the marinade, scraping off and reserving the excess marinade. If grilling, lightly brush the rack with oil. Place the chicken wings on the rack. Grill, turning and basting with the barbecue sauce, for 12 minutes, or until the juices run clear when the flesh is pierced. If broiling, put the chicken wings on the pan and place it under broiler, 4 to 5 inches from the heat. Broil, turning and basting with the sauce, for 12 minutes, or until cooked. Transfer the wings to a heated platter.

continued

Serving Suggestions: For a buffet, serve with Brown Rice Salad with Basil Dressing (page 174), Warm Potato Salad with Caraway Dressing (page 168), Turmeric Escabeche of Vegetables (page 106), and Five Pepper Rolls (page 247).

barbecue sauce

MAKES 1 ½ CUPS

Combine ¼ cup Barbecue Spice Blend (page 70) with 1¼ cups ketchup, ¼ cup olive oil, and 1 tablespoon minced garlic. Baste with the sauce during the last 10 minutes of cooking.

mogul potpourri

Mogul potpourri was a favorite of the Moguls, who ruled India for three hundred years and left the magnificent legacy, the Taj Mahal. What could be more simple a gift to put together than this potpourri of highly fragrant spices, herbs, and dried flower petals? The spices can be displayed whole, arranged attractively in a basket, or they can be tied in a sachet. Lightly crush the spices with a mallet or rolling pin to release more aroma if you are packing the potpourri in sachets. Placed in a warm place, the potpourri will last for a month. Although created as a decorative item, Mogul Potpourri can be used for tea, as in Mogul Spice Tea (page 284).

mogul potpourri

MAKES 1 ½ CUPS

- 3 tablespoons green cardamom pods
- 6 cinnamon sticks (3 inches each)
- 2 tablespoons whole cloves
- 1 star anise, separated
- 1 tablespoon mace blades or 1 teaspoon ground mace
- 1 tablespoon juniper berries
- 8 bay leaves

- ¼ cup coriander seeds
- 2 sprigs of dried sage or 1 teaspoon ground dried sage
- 3 sprigs of dried marjoram or 1 teaspoon dried marjoram
- Dried zest of 1 orange, broken into small bits
- Dried petals of 4 red roses (optional)

Combine the cardamom, cinnamon, cloves, star anise, mace juniper, bay, and coriander in a small ungreased frying pan over medium-low heat. Toast the spices, stirring, until they give off an aroma, about 5 minutes. Turn off the heat. Transfer the spices to a bowl and let cool. Add the sage, marjoram, orange zest, and rose petals, if using.

ten great spice and herb seasonings

Cuisines around the world have unique ways of seasoning a dish, ways of cooking a dish with a seasoning, and ways of serving a dish with a seasoning. These traditions have been handed down from one generation to the next until they have become classic.

With the popularity of ethnic foods in the United States, many such ways of seasoning are becoming familiar and are being incorporated into mainstream cooking. Some seasonings in this chapter—Harissa from North Africa, Sofrito from Latin America, Tahini Dip from the Middle East, Green Curry Paste from Thailand, and Sweet-and-Hot Wasabi Sauce from Japan—are classics. They are appealing and highly versatile even outside their own realms.

All herb seasonings are perishable, some more so than others, and must be kept refrigerated at all times. Harissa, for example, will keep for three months while Green Chili Paste will keep only for two days. Although some require a few steps in cooking, all are extremely simple to make. All you do, in most cases, is assemble the ingredients and mix or cook them.

All the recipes for seasoning blends are worked out in small quantities, just enough to flavor a batch or two of a dish. All recipes, if necessary, can be doubled or tripled with no problem. Packed attractively, many of these seasonings make excellent gifts. The labels should clearly indicate their perishability.

green chili vinegar

Green chili vinegar is one of the most popular seasonings in Asia. It came into vogue around the turn of the sixteenth century, shortly after the chili was introduced in Asia. Cooks, not yet familiar with this novel spice and its natural place in their traditional foods, presented it separately, as a condiment, to be enjoyed according to taste. Today every home, from Afghanistan to China, has its version of Green Chili Vinegar, but I believe the Chinese one, in its original simplest form, is the most eloquent.

Green Chili Vinegar is a true condiment that can grace any table. It is the Asian equivalent of putting black pepper on the table with every meal. Green Chili Vinegar is generally not used in cooking but rather with cooked dishes, particularly fried, roasted, and grilled foods. You can use it on anything from hamburger and hot dogs to salads and grilled fish. You can even stir a few shreds into a Bloody Mary. You can also use this vinegar to flavor fried food, as in Green Chili Vinegar Shrimp Fritters.

green chili vinegar

MAKES ⅓ CUP

4 small fresh chilies, stemmed, seeded, and very thinly sliced

¼ cup rice wine vinegar or white wine vinegar

½ teaspoon finely shredded lime zest

½ teaspoon sugar

¼ teaspoon kosher salt

Combine all the ingredients and transfer to a jar, tightly cover, and refrigerate. Let the vinegar ripen for 1 hour before use. (*May be stored in the refrigerator for up to 1 week.*)

green chili vinegar shrimp fritters

Choose small to medium shrimps for this recipe. They will be the most succulent. The batter-coated shrimps look like golden nuggets. You can also make this dish with bay scallops or quick-cooking vegetables like scallions, zucchini, asparagus, and artichoke hearts.

1¼ pounds small to medium shrimps, shelled and deveined

1 teaspoon minced garlic

⅓ cup Green Chili Vinegar

2 cups all-purpose flour

¼ teaspoon baking powder

½ teaspoon kosher salt

Canola, olive, or vegetable oil, for deep-frying

2 large eggs, separated

½ cup dry white wine or water

¼ cup minced cilantro

MAKES 4 FIRST–COURSE SERVINGS

1. Put the shrimps in a small bowl. Add the garlic and 1 tablespoon of the Green Chili Vinegar, both chilies and vinegar. Toss well. Marinate the shrimps for 15 minutes.

2. Combine 1½ cups of the flour, the baking powder, and salt in a large bowl. Mix 1 tablespoon oil, the egg yolks, and wine in a measuring cup and pour over the flour. Add the cilantro and mix only until blended. Do not overmix. Beat the egg whites in a clean medium bowl until stiff and fold into the batter. Have the bowl near the deep-fryer.

3. Heat the oil in a deep-fryer until hot (365°F.). Put the remaining ½ cup flour in a shallow soup plate and keep close by. Dip the shrimps, one at a time, first in the flour, then in the batter and drop into the hot oil. Fry a few at a time so as not to crowd them in the oil, turning once, for 3 minutes, or until golden. Remove with a slotted spoon and drain on paper towels. Make all the same way, bringing the oil up to 365°F. before frying a new batch. Serve immediately with the remaining Green Chili Vinegar.

Serving Suggestions: These fritters are rather filling, so serve a light main course like Spaghetti with Fennel-Tomato Sauce (page 185) or Steamed Duck with Star Anise (page 156), or a soup like Chilled Borscht with Caraway (page 121) or Green Beans and Potatoes in Paprika Broth (page 114). A nice addition to this meal, served as a separate course, would be Summer Peach Pilaf with Bay (page 197) or Risotto of Cauliflower with Oregano (page 198).

harissa

Harissa, one of many ever-present chili seasonings in kitchens throughout Africa, is associated mainly with Moroccan food. It is a garlic-flavored puree of chilies, mellowed with a little salt. Often a spice or two enters into the mix to add subtle flavor and, more important, help preserve it. The paste is thinned into a sauce with olive oil.

Some cooks like to heat the sauce briefly to remove the raw garlic taste, but I leave that to your personal discretion. Although not traditional, some cooks also stir in a little lemon juice and herbs to lend a lighter feel on the palate and waistline. Here is my recipe, one that I have treasured for over three decades. It is very hot but pleasantly so because for some of the hot pepper I substitute paprika, which, incidentally, lends a lovely red color. Use Harissa as a condiment, the way you use mustard, with sandwiches, grilled chicken, salads, cooked vegetables, rice pilafs, and, of course, couscous. It makes a piquant sauce for bland ingredients such as marinated mozzarella.

harissa

MAKES ABOUT 1 CUP

$1^1/_2$ **tablespoons ground red pepper**

$1^1/_2$ **tablespoons crushed red pepper**

1 **teaspoon minced garlic**

2 **tablespoons ground cumin**

$1/_4$ **teaspoon ground anise**

$1/_2$ **teaspoon kosher salt**

$1/_2$ **cup olive oil**

$1^1/_2$ **tablespoons Hungarian paprika**

$1/_4$ **cup fresh lemon juice**

Combine all the ingredients in a bowl.

If you wish to cook the sauce, combine all the ingredients, except the paprika and lemon juice, in a small saucepan. Cook over low heat until the ingredients are heated through and tiny bubbles appear around the garlic. Remove from the heat. Do not fully cook the garlic as the hot oil will continue to cook the mixture long after the heat is turned off. When completely cool, stir in the paprika and lemon juice.

Transfer the sauce to a jar. Cover tightly and refrigerate. Let the Harissa rest in the refrigerator for 1 day before serving. (*May be stored in the refrigerator for up to 3 months.*)

marinated mozzarella and carrots in harissa sauce

In the summer when my friends drop in, I often make this appetizer using fresh mozzarella, which is available at my local market. It is a simple and very quick preparation, particularly welcome for warm weather outdoor entertaining.

1 pound whole milk or part skim milk mozzarella, cut into ³/₄-inch cubes

¹/₂ pound tiny carrots, or 1 medium carrot, peeled and cut into ¹/₄ x ¹/₄ x 2-inch pieces, cooked (about 1 cup)

3 tablespoons plain nonfat yogurt or buttermilk

1 tablespoon Harissa

¹/₂ teaspoon tomato paste

2 tablespoons chopped fresh chives or 1 tablespoon dried chives, lightly crushed

Lettuce leaves, for serving

Freshly ground black pepper

MAKES 3 CUPS

Combine the mozzarella, carrots, yogurt, Harissa, tomato paste, and chives in a bowl. Toss well to distribute the seasonings evenly. Cover and marinate for 30 minutes or refrigerate for 1 hour. (*May be stored tightly covered in the refrigerator for up to 3 days.*) When ready to serve, arrange lettuce leaves on a platter. Season the mozzarella and carrots generously with black pepper. Mound over the lettuce and serve.

Serving Suggestions: Follow this appetizer with Tomato Soup with Basil Cream (page 127). For the main course, Thyme Roasted Chicken (page 151) accompanied with Turmeric Cauliflower (page 209) and Parsley Rice (page 192) would be a nice choice.

tahini dip

Tahini is the famous toasted–sesame seed butter of Middle Eastern origin. Widely available in jars, it looks like smooth peanut butter, except thinner and creamier in color. Tahini, with its mild delicate flavor, can be used in countless ways, as an enrichment for sauces and spreads—once thinned with yogurt or fruit juice—to a dressing for grilled foods and vegetables. Two very popular spreads using tahini are hummus, made with chick peas, and baba ghanoush, with smoked eggplant, which are scooped up with pita bread. Tahini, or sesame paste as it is commonly called, is combined with lemon juice, garlic, salt, and sometimes parsley to make an all-purpose dip for vegetables and breads.

tahini dip

MAKES 1 CUP

$1/2$ cup toasted white sesame seeds or tahini

$1/4$ cup fresh lemon juice

1 small clove garlic, peeled

$1/4$ cup fresh parsley leaves

$1/4$ teaspoon kosher salt

3 tablespoons water, or more as needed

Mix all the ingredients in a food processor or blender until finely blended, adding enough water to achieve a consistency like thick whipped cream or mayonnaise. Cover and refrigerate. (*May be stored for up to 1 week in the refrigerator.*)

avocado spread with tahini

This avocado spread has the appearance of plain guacamole, but it is made with tahini, scallions, and lots of lemon juice. Since no chilies are added, the spread has no bite, but a touch of Curry Powder makes it mysteriously spicy. My friends Galli and Danny Meyer of Hebron, Israel, shared this recipe of theirs with me a very long time ago. I have enjoyed it with them and with other friends many, many times. It is important that the avocado be very ripe because large chunks of unripe avocado will not blend together into a creamy cohesive spread.

2 small ripe Haas avocados, peeled and pitted

¼ cup fresh lemon juice

1 teaspoon minced garlic

1½ tablespoons Tahini Dip

½ teaspoon Curry Powder (page 56)

Freshly ground black pepper and kosher salt

3 scallions, trimmed and chopped or shredded

Rye or pita bread, for serving

MAKES 1 CUP

Roughly mash or crush the avocado in a medium bowl. Add the lemon juice, garlic, Tahini Dip, and Curry Powder. Mix well. Season to taste with pepper and salt and fold in the scallions. Serve immediately with rye or pita bread.

Serving Suggestions: Follow the appetizer with Mild Indian Chile with Paprika (page 163), Mint Pilaf (page 195), Cucumber with Toasted Cumin Seeds (page 211), and Apple-Mustard Salsa (page 233). Conclude with soothing Old-fashioned Vanilla Ice Cream (page 266) topped with Blueberry-Cinnamon Sauce (page 257).

cumin vinaigrette

Cumin vinaigrette is one of the most popular of all Middle Eastern salad dressings. It is good on a basic green salad, but it is great with beans, peas, and lentils, where cumin adds a spicy touch to otherwise mellow flavors. Cumin Vinaigrette is also suitable for chicken salad and potato salad and as a marinade for seafood and lamb.

cumin vinaigrette

MAKES 1 CUP

1/4 cup wine vinegar

1/4 cup olive oil

1/4 cup vegetable broth, white wine, or water

1/2 teaspoon kosher salt

1/8 teaspoon ground allspice

1/2 teaspoon Hungarian paprika

1/2 teaspoon ground cumin

4 arbol chilies (2 to 3 inches long), stemmed, seeded, and minced

1/4 cup finely chopped basil, cilantro, parsley, and mint

Whisk all the ingredients in a mixing bowl. Transfer to a jar, cover tightly, and refrigerate. (*May be stored for up to 3 days in the refrigerator. Shake well before using.*)

lima bean spread with cumin vinaigrette

My friend Dalia Carmel is hard to describe. She is not in the food business and yet makes it her business to know food. Everyone who cares about food either knows her or knows of her and of her encyclopedic knowledge of culinary facts and lore. Those who have tasted her food know that hers is a unique gift. Dalia is a treasure.

One summer afternoon, Dalia introduced me to her new lima bean spread. It was unusually light and refreshing. I had to have more. Nothing was in writing, but in a very clear descriptive way, Dalia told me how to make the spread. Going on the memory of the flavor and aroma, I recreated the spread as best I could. It turned out to be wonderful. So here I share with you those delicious memories.

1 cup fresh or frozen lima beans

1 tablespoon Tahini Dip (page 80)

3 tablespoons Cumin Vinaigrette

1 cup parsley, leaves and tender stems only

1 cup peeled, seeded, and diced tomatoes

Warm pita bread, for serving

MAKES 2 CUPS

Cook the lima beans in boiling water for 30 minutes, or until very soft. Drain, cool, and put in the work bowl of a food processor. Process until the beans are coarsely chopped. Add the Tahini Dip, Cumin Vinaigrette, and parsley. Process until the mixture is pureed, but do not overprocess to a paste. The puree should have a little texture. Arrange the bean spread on a platter, surround with diced tomatoes, and serve accompanied with warm pita.

Serving Suggestions: Follow the appetizer with Iced Pear Soup with Mint (page 126). For the main course, a good choice is Salmon Steamed in Bay Leaf Vapor (page 136) accompanied with Curried Rice (page 194) and Pan-grilled Pineapple with Young Ginger (page 222). Chocolate-Cinnamon Ice (page 270) makes a fine ending to this cool summer meal.

curry mayonnaise

Curry mayonnaise is nothing new, but this one is prepared in a different way. Curry Powder is toasted first in a little oil along with a clove of garlic, for a rich mellow flavor with no bitterness or floury taste. If you prefer a milder curry flavor, reduce the amount of Curry Powder to one tablespoon. For mayonnaise to emulsify properly, you need to have the ingredients at room temperature.

curry mayonnaise

MAKES 1 ½ CUPS

½ cup canola oil

½ cup olive oil

1 large clove of garlic, thinly sliced

2 tablespoons Curry Powder (page 56)

2 large egg yolks, at room temperature

1 teaspoon Dijon mustard

1 tablespoon fresh lemon juice

1 tablespoon hot water

Freshly ground white pepper and kosher salt

Combine the 2 oils in a measuring cup. In a small heavy skillet, combine the garlic with 3 tablespoons of the oil. Cook over medium-high heat until the garlic is fragrant but not browned, about 30 seconds. Reduce the heat to low and add the Curry Powder. Cook, stirring, until it begins to sizzle and darken, 1 to 1½ minutes. Immediately remove from the heat. Remove and discard the garlic. Scrape the curry-oil mixture into the remaining oil in the cup.

Combine the egg yolks, mustard, and lemon juice in a food processor or blender. Process until mixed. With the machine on, very gradually add the oil, drop by drop at first until the mayonnaise begins to thicken, and then in a slow stream. Add the water and process until mixed. Add pepper and salt to taste and process until blended. Transfer to a jar, cover, and refrigerate. (*May be stored in the refrigerator for up to 1 week.*)

lobster sandwich with curry mayonnaise

One of the nicest features of this elegant sandwich is that it takes very little time at all to put it together if you have lobster meat on hand. I usually prepare this for Sunday lunch when I serve lobsters for dinner on Saturday. With these sandwiches in mind, I cook up two extra lobsters. No, I do not feel overwhelmed having lobsters a couple of days in a row, particularly not when they taste and look so totally different.

³⁄₄ cup cooked lobster meat, from 2 cooked medium-size lobsters

¹⁄₄ cup Curry Mayonnaise

2 tablespoons chopped walnuts, toasted

1 tablespoon chopped basil leaves

2 large round or oval sandwich rolls

8 arugula leaves

MAKES 2 SERVINGS

Place the lobster meat in a bowl. Add the mayonnaise, walnuts, pepper, and basil. Fold carefully. Cut the rolls in half horizontally. Divide the lobster mixture between the bottom halves of the rolls. Top with arugula leaves and the other half of the roll.

Serving Suggestions: For a light summer luncheon, serve the sandwich with Chilled Carrot Soup with Mace (page 119) or Tomato Soup with Basil Cream (page 127) and conclude with Blueberry Tart with Saffron Cream (page 262).

sweet-and-hot wasabi sauce

Sweet-and-hot wasabi sauce is a popular all-purpose Japanese dipping sauce. Wasabi, the aromatic Japanese horseradish (see page 49), here lends its pungent bite to an otherwise sweet sauce. As is, the sauce can be served with meat, poultry, and fish dishes and fritters, for example, Steamed Duck with Star Anise (page 156), Thyme Roasted Chicken (page 151), Fried Clams with Barbecue Spices (page 108), and Peppery Squid Puffs (page 107). You can also use it to marinate tofu, seafood, and chicken, as in the recipe that follows, to dress steamed vegetables, or, thinned slightly, to dress salad greens.

sweet-and-hot wasabi sauce

MAKES 1 CUP

$1/2$ cup white wine

2 tablespoons light (low-sodium) soy sauce

1 tablespoon dark sesame oil

2 tablespoons red wine vinegar

1 tablespoon light brown sugar

1 teaspoon minced garlic

1 tablespoon finely diced young ginger (see page 38) or very fresh juicy ginger

$1/4$ cup chopped cilantro

1 to 2 tablespoons wasabi paste or 1 teaspoon wasabi powder

Combine the wine, soy sauce, sesame oil, vinegar, and brown sugar in a bowl and mix until the sugar dissolves. Stir in the garlic, ginger, and cilantro. Cover and refrigerate. Just before serving, stir in the wasabi.

pan-grilled chicken with sweet-and-hot wasabi sauce

This is a very simple, quick way to fix chicken breast. The chicken is tender and aromatic. The trick to getting the chicken really tender is to pound it very thin. The chicken can then be flash-grilled in the pan with a minimum loss of moisture. You can substitute flattened turkey breast cutlets for the chicken.

2 whole boneless and skinless chicken breasts (about 1½ pounds each)

¾ cup Sweet-and-Hot Wasabi Sauce

Olive oil spray

MAKES 4 SERVINGS

1. Cut the chicken breasts in half and trim all visible fat. Pound with a mallet to make them as thin as possible. Place the chicken in a shallow dish and add half the wasabi sauce. Turn and toss to coat thoroughly. Set aside for 15 minutes.

2. Heat a heavy well-seasoned or nonstick skillet over medium-high heat until hot. Remove the chicken from the marinade, scraping off the excess. Spray lightly with oil and add to the skillet. Pan-grill until nicely seared on both sides, turning once, about 2 minutes, or until the meat feels firm to the touch. Serve accompanied with the remaining wasabi sauce.

Serving Suggestions: Serve with Broiled Vegetables with Oregano (page 103), Stewed Apples with White Pepper and Fennel (page 220), and Tomato-Cumin Rice (page 193). Ginger Crisps (page 274) and Basil-Pineapple Ice (page 269) are a good way to end the meal.

smoked chili pepper oil

Smoked chili pepper oil is made by cooking dried chilies—either whole, crushed, or ground—in oil. As the chilies turn dark, they lend the oil hot taste, smoky aroma, and caramel color. The oil, with or without the peppers, is an integral part of Chinese, Indian, and African cooking and that of the Persian Gulf states. The seasoned oil can be used in anything from boiled eggs to cocktails. The possibilities are limitless—as long as you like it hot, very hot.

smoked chili pepper oil

MAKES 1 CUP

1 cup light vegetable oil

1/2 cup small whole dried red chilies or crushed red pepper

Heat the oil in a small pan over medium-low heat until hot. Add the chilies and fry until they turn almost black, stirring often to ensure that they do not burn, about 4 minutes for whole chilies, 3 minutes for crushed red pepper. Turn off the heat. Transfer the oil, with the peppers, to a jar. When completely cool, cover tightly with a lid. (*May be stored in a cool dry place for up to 1 year.*)

grilled leg of lamb with smoked chili pepper oil

To give the lamb a fiery taste, stir into the marinade some coarsely crumbled smoked whole chilies or crushed red pepper from the Smoked Chili Pepper Oil. For a milder taste, omit the chilies and dilute the chili pepper oil with olive oil. This treatment is just as good with beef flank steak as with lamb. Both lamb and beef, imbued with a smoky chili flavor, are excellent in fajitas.

1 leg of lamb, boned and butterflied, trimmed of all fat (5 to 6 pounds)

Spiced Marinade

4 tablespoons fresh lemon juice

2 tablespoons minced garlic

1 tablespoon ground cumin

1 teaspoon ground cinnamon

1/2 teaspoon ground cloves

Kosher salt

4 tablespoons Smoked Chili Pepper Oil, with chilies, or 2 tablespoons Smoked Chili Pepper Oil and 2 tablespoons olive oil, without chilies

1 1/2 cups white wine

2 teaspoons light brown sugar (optional)

1 teaspoon Hungarian paprika

1. Lay the lamb flat in a shallow roasting pan and score the thickest part of the meat to ensure even cooking. Prick the lamb all over with a fork. Mix together the lemon juice, garlic, spices, and salt to taste. Rub the marinade over the lamb. Turn to coat well. Cover and marinate for at least 4 hours at room temperature or refrigerate for 2 days (let the lamb stand at room temperature for 30 minutes before cooking).

2. Preheat a charcoal grill or an oven broiler.

3. Remove the meat from the marinade, scraping off and reserving the excess marinade. Brush the lamb with half the chili oil and, if barbecuing, arrange the lamb on the grill. If broiling, put the lamb on the broiler pan and place it under the broiler, 4 to 5 inches from the heat. Grill or broil the lamb, turning, for 20 minutes for rare lamb. Cook longer for medium or well-done meat. Place the lamb on a carving board and let it rest for 5 minutes. Make the sauce while the lamb is resting.

4. Stir the wine into the reserved marinade, then transfer the mixture to a small saucepan. Add the brown sugar, if using, and the paprika and boil until the sauce is reduced by half.

5. Cut the meat across the grain into thin slices and arrange on a platter. Brush with the remaining oil and serve with the sauce.

Serving Suggestions: Serve the lamb with Brussels Sprouts with Fennel (page 206), Roasted Sweet Potatoes with Cloves (page 218), and Avocado, Onion, and Cilantro Relish (page 231), accompanied with a basket of bread, including Currant and Mace Puffs (page 242), Cumin Rolls (page 246), and Dill Tortilla Bread (page 240).

annatto oil

Annatto oil is an intrinsic part of the cooking of Latin America and the Spanish-speaking Caribbean islands. This orange-colored oil is what gives Arroz con Pollo (page 93) its characteristic yellow color. Annatto seeds (see page 33) are cooked in oil just until they release their rich orange color, then the oil is strained. Annatto Oil is wonderful to baste white fish, shrimps, and scallops and to flavor soups and vegetables, as in Sofrito Green Beans and Potatoes (page 179). It is the cooking medium for Sofrito (page 92), the vegetable and herb base of many Caribbean dishes.

annatto oil

MAKES 1 CUP

1 cup olive oil   ½ cup annatto seeds

Heat the oil in a heavy skillet over low heat until medium-hot. Add the annatto seeds and cook over low heat, stirring, for 10 minutes, or until the seeds release their color. Be careful not to overcook the seeds or there will be a loss of color and flavor. Turn off heat. Let the seeds stay in the oil until it cools completely. Strain and pour the oil into a jar; discard seeds. (*May be stored, tightly covered, for up to 3 months in the refrigerator.*)

seared red chicken

The chicken in this recipe is marinated in annatto oil and herbs. For a change of pace, you can eliminate the peas from the recipe and grill or broil the chicken instead of cooking it in a pan.

2 whole boneless and skinless chicken breasts (about 1½ pounds each)

2 tablespoons Annatto Oil

1 teaspoon minced garlic

1 teaspoon cumin seeds, crushed

½ teaspoon anise or fennel seeds, crushed

2 teaspoons dried marjoram or oregano

½ teaspoon ground red pepper, or more to taste

½ teaspoon grated tangerine or orange zest

1 cup green peas, fresh or frozen

1 to 2 tablespoons fresh tangerine or orange juice

Tangerine segments or orange slices, for garnish

MAKES 8 SERVINGS

1. Cut the chicken breasts in half and trim all visible fat. Place the chicken in a shallow dish. Add the oil, garlic, cumin, anise, marjoram, ground red pepper, and tangerine zest. Rub the mixture over the chicken and set aside for 15 minutes.

2. Heat a heavy nonstick skillet over high heat until very hot. Add the chicken with the spices and pan-grill, turning once, for 5 minutes, or until firm to the touch. Remove the chicken to a cutting board and cover loosely with aluminum foil. Add the peas to the pan. Sprinkle with 1 tablespoon of the tangerine juice and toss, adding more juice if necessary to glaze the peas. Turn off the heat.

3. Slice the chicken on the bias and arrange one chicken breast on each of 4 plates. Add the peas, garnish with tangerine slices, and serve.

Serving Suggestions: Serve with Pan-grilled Pineapple with Young Ginger (page 222), Pumpkin with Allspice (page 216), Mango-Mint Salsa (page 231), Parsley Rice (page 192), and Five Pepper Rolls (page 247). Saffron Cream (page 261) with Ginger Crisps (page 274) would make a fine ending for this meal.

sofrito

Just as all New Orleans soups, sauces, and stews begin with a cooked mixture of onion, green bell pepper, garlic, and celery scented with thyme, Spanish Caribbean dishes begin with a mixture of onion, green bell pepper, garlic, and tomato flavored with oregano. This Sofrito is the underpinning of all dishes of the islands; it gives the dishes their characteristic color, aroma, and taste. And unless the vegetables are cooked in Annatto Oil, it is not the real thing. My friend Brunilda Mesa from Puerto Rico taught me that principle—and many wonderful dishes—over a quarter of a century ago.

In the old days, Sofrito was cooked in lard, but most people now use olive or corn oil. While some cooks add ham to the Sofrito mixture, I prefer mine plain, just with vegetables. Ham can always be sautéed with the vegetables in those recipes calling for ham. Sofrito is aromatic and slightly sweetish tart. Think of it as a warm salsa and use it to season rice, eggs, stews, soups, and vegetables, as in the vegetable stew Sofrito Green Beans and Potatoes (page 179).

sofrito

MAKES 1 ¼ CUPS

2 tablespoons Annatto Oil (page 90) or 2 tablespoons olive oil and 1 teaspoon annatto seeds

1 tablespoon finely chopped garlic

1 cup finely chopped onions

¾ cup finely chopped green bell pepper

1 cup chopped peeled tomatoes, fresh or canned

1 teaspoon minced cilantro

½ teaspoon minced fresh oregano or ¼ teaspoon dried oregano

1 fresh chili, stemmed, seeded, and minced (optional)

¼ cup finely diced smoked ham (optional)

Freshly ground black pepper and Kosher salt

If you are using Annatto Oil, proceed directly to the next paragraph. If you are using olive oil, heat the oil in a heavy skillet over low heat until medium-hot. Add the annatto seeds and cook over low heat, stirring, for 10 minutes, or until the seeds release their color. Let stand until cool, then strain the oil and discard the seeds.

Pour the oil into the skillet and add the garlic, onions, and bell pepper. Sauté, stirring, over medium-high heat until the vegetables look soft, about 5 minutes. Add the tomatoes, cilantro, oregano, chili, and ham if using. Bring to a boil. Reduce the heat and simmer, covered, stirring occasionally, until the vegetables are very soft and the sauce is thick, about 30 minutes. Turn off the heat. When completely cool, transfer the sauce to a jar, cover tightly, and refrigerate. Sofrito may be made ahead; the flavor seems to improve when it stands for 1 or 2 days in the refrigerator. (*May be stored, tightly covered, for up to 5 days in the refrigerator.*)

arroz con pollo

This chicken and rice casserole is the soul food of Puerto Rico. There is no fixed recipe for the dish, but basic guidelines are fairly clear. You need Sofrito, rice, and chicken, in that order of importance. Aside from that, it doesn't matter if you add green peas, pigeon peas, or fava beans to the dish.

1 fryer chicken (3½ to 4½ pounds)

Freshly ground black pepper and kosher salt

2 tablespoons Annatto Oil (page 90) or olive oil

2 ¾ cups chicken stock, low-sodium canned broth, or water

1¼ cups Sofrito

1 bay leaf

1 tablespoon chopped fresh oregano or 1 teaspoon dried oregano

¼ cup chopped pitted black olives

1 cup green peas, fresh or frozen

1½ cups long-grain rice

Sprigs of parsley, for garnish

MAKES 4 SERVINGS

1. Cut the chicken into 8 serving pieces. Remove the skin and trim all visible fat. Sprinkle with pepper and salt.

2. Preheat the oven to 350°F.

3. Heat the oil in a large heavy ovenproof casserole. Add the chicken pieces and sear over medium heat, turning, until nicely browned and partly cooked, about 10 minutes. If desired, cover the pot to hasten cooking. Remove the chicken to a plate. Add the stock, Sofrito, bay leaf, oregano, olives, peas, and rice. Season to taste with salt. Add the chicken pieces, gently pushing them into the sauce. Bring to a boil and cover the casserole. Turn off the heat.

4. Bake in the middle level of the oven for 50 minutes, or until the rice is tender and the liquid is fully absorbed. To serve, remove the chicken pieces and divide among 4 plates. Fluff the rice, spoon some next to the chicken, and garnish with parsley.

Serving Suggestions: Serve accompanied with Pan-grilled Plantains with Ginger (page 223), Pumpkin with Allspice (page 216), and Yellow Tomato and Green Peppercorn Salsa (page 235). A nice dessert to follow is Mango Sauce with Nutmeg (page 259) spooned over Old-fashioned Vanilla Ice Cream (page 266).

green curry paste

Green curry paste is called curry not because it contains curry powder but because the dishes it is used to season are called curries. It is a combination of citrus-floral ingredients—cilantro, basil, citrus zest, ginger—and a few highly aromatic spices—toasted cumin and coriander. Green chilies and black pepper are added for heat and the mixture is pureed into an emerald green paste. Green Curry Paste, a popular seasoning of Thailand, lends a lovely herbal flavor to salad dressings, soups, and stews.

green curry paste

MAKES ⅓ CUP

4 teaspoons coriander seeds

1 teaspoon cumin seeds

1 teaspoon black peppercorns

¼ cup chopped shallots

2 tablespoons finely chopped garlic

1 tablespoon finely chopped young ginger (see page 38) or very fresh juicy ginger

1 tablespoon finely minced lime zest

1 tablespoon finely minced lemon zest

3 tablespoons chopped cilantro

3 tablespoons chopped basil

4 fresh green chilies, stemmed, seeded, and cut up

Kosher salt

Toast the coriander seeds, cumin seeds, and peppercorns in a small ungreased frying pan over medium-high heat, shaking and tossing, until the cumin turns a few shades darker and gives off an aroma. Remove to a plate. When completely cool, grind until fine, using an electric spice/coffee grinder.

Transfer the spice mixture to a food processor. Add the shallots, garlic, ginger, lime zest, lemon zest, cilantro, basil, and chilies and process to a smooth puree. Season to taste with salt. Transfer the paste to a jar, cover tightly, and refrigerate. (*May be stored, tightly covered, for up to 1 week in the refrigerator.*)

green mussels curry

Fragrant with herbs, this curry is very refreshing in summer, when plump mussels are plentiful. At other times, you may substitute shrimps or scallops or any nonoily white fish. The curry is best served as soon as it is made since the beautiful green color will dull with reheating.

4 pounds mussels, scrubbed clean (about 48 mussels)

1 tablespoon canola oil

⅓ cup Green Curry Paste

1 red bell pepper, stemmed, seeded, and julienned

1 cup unsweetened coconut milk (see Note), white wine, chicken stock, low-sodium canned broth, or water

Kosher salt

2 tablespoons chopped cilantro

Sprigs of basil, for garnish

Cooked rice, for serving

MAKES 4 SERVINGS

1. Place the mussels in a large pot over high heat. Cover and steam, shaking the pot occasionally, until the mussels open, about 5 minutes. Transfer the mussels to a large shallow dish. When cool enough to handle, remove the mussels from the shells and put into a small bowl. Discard the shells. Strain the liquid through a double layer of dampened cheesecloth and reserve. You should have about 2 cups.

2. Heat the oil in a large saucepan over medium-high heat. Add the curry paste and cook, stirring, for 3 minutes, or until lightly fried. Add the mussels liquid and the bell pepper and gently boil for 2 minutes. Add the coconut milk and mussels and cook until piping hot. Season to taste with salt. Spoon the curry into 4 plates, sprinkle with cilantro, and garnish with basil. Serve with cooked rice.

Note: Unsweetened coconut milk is available canned in Asian markets. If only coconut cream is available, dilute it half and half with water. Frozen coconut milk is also sometimes available. Do not use a sweetened product.

Serving Suggestions: Serve the curry with Tomato-Cumin Rice (page 193), Curried Rice (page 194), or Summer Peach Pilaf with Bay (page 197); Turmeric Cauliflower (page 209), or Glazed Cucumbers with Sesame (page 212); and Cranberry Relish with Apricots, Walnuts, and Cinnamon (page 237). For dessert serve raspberries with Saffron Cream (page 261).

appetizers

flavorful dried tomatoes

Dried vegetables and fruits are not simply vegetables and fruits whose moisture has been removed. Some kind of chemical change takes place during drying that gives them a unique flavor. I have loved this intense flavor since childhood, when my grandmother would prepare countless batches of cumin-scented green peppers, cinnamon-flavored plums, and chili-laced tiny eggplants and lay them out on the slopes of Blue Mountain to dry in the eucalyptus-scented air under the tropical Indian sun.

What makes this recipe special is the unusual combination of spices and herbs which—everyone who has tasted it agrees—is exquisite. The tomatoes are slightly moist and far more flavorful than commercial varieties, but they are perishable. The spices help the tomatoes keep longer. The recipe comes from Alice Ross, a food historian, teacher, and gifted cook.

4 pounds firm ripe tomatoes, preferably Italian plum tomatoes from the garden

¼ teaspoon kosher salt

¼ teaspoon sugar

1 teaspoon coarsely ground black pepper

2 teaspoons crushed red pepper

1 teaspoon fennel seeds

1 bay leaf, coarsely crushed

4 sprigs of thyme or 1 teaspoon dried thyme

3 tablespoons chopped garlic

1 tablespoon fresh lemon juice

Olive oil spray

Olive oil

MAKES 1 PINT

1. Preheat the oven to 225°F.

2. Cut the tomatoes lengthwise in half. Seed and squeeze out the excess juice without crushing the tomatoes.

3. Lay the tomatoes in a snug single layer, cut side up, on a 10 x 15-inch baking sheet. Sprinkle with salt, sugar, black and red pepper, fennel, bay, thyme, garlic, and lemon juice. Spray with olive oil and bake in the middle level of the oven for 8 hours or overnight, or until the tomatoes are medium-dry.

4. Remove from the oven, cool completely and serve. (*To store, transfer the tomatoes together with the spices into a jar, making sure there are no trapped air bubbles. Pour over a thin layer of olive oil to seal the top. Cover tightly with the jar lid. The tomatoes will keep for up to 3 weeks in the refrigerator.*)

Serving Suggestions: Arrange the tomatoes on a plate, garnish with sprigs of thyme, and serve accompanied with a basket of bread, including Parmesan-Chive Puffs (page 243), Five Pepper Rolls (page 247), Thyme Pita Bread (page 248), and an Italian country loaf. For the main course, serve Risotto of Cauliflower with Oregano (page 198).

spicy tomato spread

The anise and hot peppers in Harissa combine with the thyme and other flavors in the Flavorful Dried Tomatoes and lift them to new heights.

MAKES 2 CUPS

1 recipe Flavorful Dried Tomatoes (page 98), cooled

¼ cup finely chopped pine nuts or walnuts

¼ cup finely chopped dried cranberries

1 tablespoon Harissa (page 78) or 1 teaspoon minced fresh chili

Olive oil

Crackers or bread, for serving

Place the tomatoes together with the accumulated spices in a food processor and process until coarsely pureed. Transfer to a bowl and fold in the nuts, cranberries and Harissa. Serve on crackers or as a dip. (*To store, transfer the tomato spread to a jar making sure there are no trapped air bubbles. Pour over a thin layer of oil to seal the top. Cover tightly with the jar lid. The spread will keep for up to 3 weeks in the refrigerator.*)

Serving Suggestions: Serve the spread on Cumin Crackers (page 111) or Ajowan Crackers (page 112) or as a dip with flat breads such as Stuffed Sage Roti Bread with Olives (page 251) and Stuffed Tarragon Roti Bread with Ham and Mushrooms (page 252). Follow it with Chicken Braised in Cardamom Sauce (page 147), Orange-Cinnamon Pilaf (page 196), and Cumin Potatoes (page 215).

goat cheese spread with dried tomatoes and juniper berries

The juniper in the spread cuts the heavy taste of goat cheese and adds a sweet piney scent. In addition, the recipe combines some of my favorite seasonings—jalapeño chilies, niçoise olives, and cilantro. Instead of Cumin Crackers, you can serve the spread on bagel thins or Belgian endive leaves.

1 cup (8-ounce container)
  nonfat sour cream

4 juniper berries, well crushed

2 tablespoons minced red
  onion

4 pickled chilies, such as
  jalapeños, drained and
  chopped

$\frac{1}{2}$ cup chopped cilantro

8 ounces fresh goat cheese

1 ripe Haas avocado, peeled,
  pitted, and diced

12 niçoise or similar black
  olives, pitted and chopped

10 Flavorful Dried Tomatoes
  (page 98) or storebought
  sun-dried tomatoes, thinly
  sliced

Cumin Crackers (page 111),
  for serving

MAKES ABOUT 3 CUPS

Combine the sour cream, juniper berries, onion, chilies, and cilantro in a bowl and whip until thoroughly blended. Carefully fold in the goat cheese so that it retains some texture. Fold in the avocado, olives, and tomatoes. Cover and refrigerate for several hours to allow the flavors to blend. Serve with Cumin Crackers. (*The spread keeps well, tightly covered, for up to 1 day in the refrigerator.*)

Serving Suggestions: To complete the meal, serve Steamed Fish with Ginger Essence (page 131), Polenta with Green Peppercorns (page 191), and Glazed Carrots with Cloves (page 208). Blueberry-Cinnamon Sauce (page 257) over Old-fashioned Vanilla Ice Cream (page 266) is the perfect dessert.

spinach with chili cheese on endive boats

This recipe is an adaptation of an Ethiopian spinach and cheese preparation that was introduced to me by my friend Philippe LeBel, an economist who spends much of his time in East and West Africa. What I love about this saladlike preparation is the fusion of three sensations—warm herbal spinach with cool creamy cheese against hot peppery chilies. The dish is eaten while the spinach is piping hot, by spooning cheese on the endive leaf, then topping it with spinach. You'll be surprised how mild the Harissa feels on the palate.

1 pound fresh spinach, trimmed and washed, or 1 package (10 ounces) frozen spinach

1 cup (8-ounce container) lowfat small-curd cottage cheese

1 tablespoon Harissa (page 78)

3 heads Belgian endive, leaves separated, for serving

MAKES 6 SERVINGS

1. If using fresh spinach place it in a large sauté pan over high heat. When the spinach begins to sizzle, reduce the heat slightly and cover the pan. Cook until the spinach is wilted, about 5 minutes. Plunge the spinach in cold water and drain it. Working quickly, finely chop the spinach. If using frozen spinach, cook, drain, and chop it.

2. Transfer the warm spinach to a shallow bowl, spreading it slightly to make a crater. Heap the cheese in the center and drizzle with Harissa. Serve immediately, accompanied with endive leaves for scooping.

Note: The appetizer can be assembled in advance. Spoon Harissa-drizzled cheese and spinach in endive boats. It will not, of course, be hot when served.

Serving Suggestions: To complete the meal, serve Milk-marinated Grilled Pork Chops with Ajowan (page 161) or Island Vegetable Stew with Thyme (page 177), or Sofrito Green Beans and Potatoes (page 179) with Mango-Mint Salsa (page 231), and Stuffed Tarragon Roti Bread with Ham and Mushrooms (page 252).

marinated mozzarella with thyme

When fresh mozzarella is available, I marinate it with herbs. You can use any herb or combination of herbs but I find chives and the strong balmy fragrance of thyme best offset the creaminess of the cheese. Broccoli florets, lightly steamed, can be added.

1 pound whole milk or part-skim milk mozzarella, preferably fresh, cut into ¾-inch cubes

2 tablespoons plain nonfat yogurt, water from yogurt, or buttermilk

2 teaspoons minced Flavorful Dried Tomatoes (page 98) or storebought sun-dried tomatoes

1 tablespoon chopped fresh chives or 1 teaspoon dried chives

½ teaspoon finely chopped garlic

½ teaspoon minced thyme

½ teaspoon crushed red pepper

Freshly ground black pepper

MAKES 2 CUPS

Combine all the ingredients in a bowl. Cover and refrigerate for at least 2 hours, preferably overnight. To serve, mound the mozzarella cubes in a shallow bowl. (*Marinated mozzarella keeps well for up to 3 days in the refrigerator.*)

Serving Suggestions: To complete the meal, serve Barbecued Tarragon Game Hens with Quick Cherry Coulis (page 152), Smothered Cabbage with Caraway (page 207), and Cumin Rolls (page 246). Serve Chocolate-Cinnamon Ice (page 270) as dessert.

broiled vegetables with oregano

I like to spread these vegetables out on a large ceramic platter alongside rustic country breads. Almost all vegetables work well in this preparation. Serve the vegetables with grilled fish or chicken or in pita pocket sandwiches.

½ pound carrots

1 pound turnips

1 pound Japanese eggplant

1 pound zucchini

1 tablespoon fresh lemon juice

¼ cup fresh sprigs of oregano or 2 teaspoons dried oregano

2 tablespoons chopped basil or cilantro

1 teaspoon ground coriander

Vegetable or olive oil spray

1 tablespoon fresh lime juice

MAKES 12 SERVINGS

1. Peel the carrots and turnips and trim the eggplant and zucchini. Slice the vegetables paper thin using a mandoline, vegetable slicer, or knife and place in a bowl. Add enough water to cover the vegetables completely. Stir in the lemon juice and soak for 30 minutes. Drain well and pat dry on paper towels. Return the vegetables to the bowl and toss with the oregano, basil, and coriander.

2. Preheat the broiler.

3. Spread the vegetables in a single layer on a 10 x 15-inch baking sheet. Spray lightly with oil and place under the broiler about 4 to 5 inches from the heat source. Broil for 6 minutes, or until vegetables are lightly charred and cooked al dente. Remove the pan and immediately cover with aluminum foil. (The smoky steam will further cook the vegetables and lend flavor.) When completely cool, uncover and sprinkle with lime juice. Serve at room temperature or refrigerate and serve chilled. (*The vegetables keep well, tightly covered, for 1 day, at room temperature, or for 2 days in the refrigerator.*)

Serving Suggestions: To complete the meal, serve Tarragon Scallops Kedgeree (page 201) or Marjoram Risotto with Water Chestnuts (page 200) and Blueberry Tart with Saffron Cream (page 262) for dessert.

chili-stuffed prawns

A great dish for outdoor entertaining. Stuffed shrimps in the shell are laid out in a platter and guests grill their own. You do not need any sauce with these grilled shrimps—the shell and the chili paste keep them from drying during grilling. Choose the variety of chilies according to how hot you want the dish to be.

2 pounds jumbo shrimps, shell on (8 to 10 per pound)

4 tablespoons red wine vinegar

3 tablespoons olive oil

1 1/2 teaspoons kosher salt

1 1/2 tablespoons minced garlic

2 tablespoons minced fresh chili

1/3 cup minced cilantro

1/3 cup minced chives or scallion greens

Lemon slices, for garnish

MAKES 8 FIRST COURSE SERVINGS, 4 MAIN COURSE SERVINGS

1. Hold each shrimp underside down. Using a sharp knife, slice through the shell down along its length, almost 1/2 inch deep. Devein and rinse in cold water. Dry thoroughly on paper towels and put the shrimps in a bowl. Add the vinegar, oil, and 1/2 teaspoon salt and toss. Cover and marinate for 15 minutes or refrigerate for 2 hours.

2. Light a charcoal grill or preheat a broiler. Soak as many bamboo skewers in water as there are shrimps.

3. Combine the garlic, chili, cilantro, chives, and the remaining salt in a small bowl. Stuff the cavity of each shrimp with the minced herbs. Thread the shrimps lengthwise on the skewers, one per skewer, and arrange them on a platter. Charcoal grill or broil the shrimps, turning once and brushing with any remaining marinade in the bowl, until they are just cooked, 6 to 7 minutes. Serve immediately with lemon slices.

Serving Suggestions: To complete the meal, serve Pepper-rubbed Rack of Lamb (page 159) or Escabeche of Chicken in Allspice Sauce (page 105), Carrot Salad with Coriander Vinegar (page 166), Brown Rice Salad with Basil Dressing (page 174), and Mango-Mint Salsa (page 231), with a basket of breads, including Chili Tortilla Bread (page 241) and Ham Puffs with Black Pepper (page 244).

escabeche of chicken in allspice sauce

Escabeche is a Spanish technique in which fish or meat is cooked and then marinated in an oil-vinegar mixture. There are many versions of this dish, but the spicy ones with an allspice accent from Jamaica are truly exceptional. Besides adding flavor, the spice has a preserving effect on the chicken. This is a splendid party dish. Serve the escabeche on a lipped platter that can hold the marinade comfortably without overflowing.

2 ½ to 3 pounds chicken drumsticks (12 drumsticks)

Freshly ground black pepper and kosher salt

1 teaspoon minced garlic

¼ cup fresh lemon juice

4 tablespoons olive oil

2 medium onions, sliced (1½ cups)

2 large carrots, sliced (1½ cups)

1 cup wine vinegar

2 bay leaves, split in half

1 tablespoon allspice berries, lightly crushed

½ to 1 teaspoon crushed red pepper

1 teaspoon grated lemon zest

MAKES 12 SERVINGS

1. Remove the skin from the drumsticks and put them in a bowl. Prick the meat with a fork and rub with garlic, pepper, and salt to taste, and the lemon juice. Cover and marinate for 30 minutes at room temperature or for 2 hours to overnight in the refrigerator.

2. Heat 2 tablespoons of the oil in a nonstick pan over medium-high heat. Add the drumsticks and cook, turning, until the meat is tender and the juices run clear when pierced with a skewer, about 20 minutes. Add the onions and carrots and continue to cook until the vegetables lose their raw look, 5 to 10 minutes.

3. Stir in the vinegar, bay leaves, allspice, and red pepper and bring to a boil. Lower the heat and cook, basting the chicken, until most of the vinegar is absorbed, about 10 minutes. Stir in the lemon zest and the remaining oil and turn off the heat. When completely cool, cover tightly and refrigerate. Let the drumsticks marinate for at least 4 hours, preferably for a day, before serving. (*The escabeche keeps well, tightly covered, for 2 days in the refrigerator.*)

Serving Suggestions: Accompany the dish with a basket of breads, including Parmesan-Chive Puffs (page 243), Thyme Pita Bread (page 248), Raisin and Caraway Rolls (page 245), and country loaves. Follow the escabeche with a main course like Savory Millet Cake with Rosemary (page 181), Island Vegetable Stew with Thyme (page 177), or Scrod Ragout with Fragrant Spices (page 137); accompany with Parsley Rice (page 192) and Avocado, Onion, and Cilantro Relish (page 231). Serve Raspberry Yogurt Bavarian with Mace and Pistachio (page 265) for dessert.

turmeric escabeche of vegetables

This is a vegetarian version of escabeche, the traditional Spanish way of pickling food in a spicy oil and vinegar marinade. Turmeric gives the sauce a lovely golden hue and woodsy scent. A spectacular dish for parties and picnics.

2¼ to 2½ pounds vegetables, such as a combination of broccoli and cauliflower florets, and carrots, kohlrabi, and celery, cut into bite-size pieces

Kosher salt

4 tablespoons light vegetable oil

1 teaspoon turmeric

2 medium onions, cut into ¼-inch slices

1 teaspoon minced garlic

1 cup wine vinegar

2 bay leaves, split in half

8 fresh sprigs of thyme or 1 teaspoon dried thyme

6 whole cloves, crushed

1 tablespoon black peppercorns, crushed

4 fresh chilies, stemmed, seeded, and thinly sliced (optional)

1½ teaspoons kosher salt

MAKES 8 SERVINGS

1. Trim, peel, and cut the vegetables into bite-size pieces. Bring a large pot of salted water to a boil. Add the vegetables, bring back to a boil, and cook for 3 minutes. Drain and pat dry on paper towels.

2. Transfer the vegetables to a large heavy skillet. Add 2 tablespoons of the oil, the turmeric, onions, and garlic and cook, stirring occasionally, over medium-high heat until the vegetables look cooked but are still crisp, about 6 minutes.

3. Combine the vinegar, bay leaves, thyme, cloves, peppercorns, and chilies, if using, in a small saucepan and bring to a boil. Pour the spiced vinegar on the vegetables and continue to cook until the vegetables absorb most of the vinegar. Stir in the remaining oil and the salt and turn off the heat. When completely cool, transfer the vegetables and sauce to a dish. Cover tightly and refrigerate. Let the vegetables marinate for 4 hours or overnight before use. To serve, pile the vegetables in a shallow bowl and accompany them with a basket of rustic breads. (*The marinated vegetables keep well, tightly covered, for 1 week in the refrigerator, with the flavor peaking on the third day.*)

Serving Suggestions: To complete the meal, serve Jerk Chicken (page 61), Arroz con Pollo (page 93), or Seared Red Chicken (page 91) accompanied with Curried Rice (page 194) or Summer Peach Pilaf with Bay (page 197). Banana-Ginger Cream (page 258) would be a suitable dessert.

peppery squid puffs

Meaty squid nuggets in a spicy crisp batter can be served as an appetizer or a main course. For those wary of squid, clams, bay scallops, and small or medium shrimps can be substituted; the results are just as good. These puffs are fairly hot. For a milder taste, reduce the pepper to one teaspoon.

2 pounds smallest possible
squid, cleaned

2 teaspoons minced garlic

1 teaspoon grated lemon zest

1 tablespoon fresh lemon
juice

2 teaspoons freshly ground
white pepper

4 cups all-purpose flour

1 teaspoon baking powder

1 teaspoon kosher salt

2 tablespoons light
vegetable oil

4 large eggs, separated

1/2 cup and 2 tablespoons dry
white wine or water

Oil, for deep-frying

**MAKES 4 FIRST COURSE SERVINGS,
2 MAIN COURSE SERVINGS**

1. Cut each squid body into 3/8-inch-wide rings and the tentacles into 2 bunches. Put the squid in a bowl, add the garlic, lemon zest, lemon juice, and pepper, and toss well. Marinate the squid for 15 minutes.

2. Combine 3 cups of the flour, the baking powder, and salt in a bowl. Mix the oil, egg yolks, and wine in a measuring cup and pour over the flour. Mix only until blended. Do not overmix. Beat the egg whites in a clean bowl until stiff. Fold into the batter. Place the bowl near the deep-fryer.

3. Heat the oil in the deep-fryer until hot (365°F.). Put the remaining 1 cup flour in a shallow bowl and keep it close by. Dip the squid pieces first in the flour and then in the batter. Drop by the tablespoonful into the hot oil. Make a few puffs at a time so as not to crowd them in the oil. Fry the puffs, turning once, for 2 minutes or until golden. Remove with a slotted spoon and drain on paper towels. Make all the puffs the same way, bringing the oil back up to 365°F. before frying a new batch. Serve immediately.

Serving Suggestions: Serve the squid puffs hot with Sweet Sesame Dipping Sauce (page 227), Yogurt Dip with Herbs (page 230), or Mango-Mint Salsa (page 231) accompanied with Peach Cooler with Sage (page 282). To complete the meal, serve a hearty soup such as Fragrant Fish Chowder with Celery Seed (page 123) or Bean and Pasta Soup with Oregano (page 116) accompanied with Ham Puffs with Black Pepper (page 244), Parmesan-Chive Puffs (page 243), and Raisin and Caraway Rolls (page 245). For dessert, serve Baked Saffron Custard (page 263).

fried clams with barbecue spices

Serve mild and fragrant clam fritters as an appetizer or as a main course. For best results, use plump, ocean-fresh clams, shucked just before use.

2 cups all-purpose flour, or more as needed

1 tablespoon Barbecue Spice Blend (page 70)

½ teaspoon baking powder

½ teaspoon kosher salt

2 large eggs, separated

2 cups shucked littleneck or cherrystone clams, juices reserved, or 2 cans (10 ounces *each*) whole baby clams, drained with juice reserved

About ⅔ cup white wine or water

¾ cup chopped scallions, white and green parts

Oil, for deep-frying

MAKES 6 SERVINGS

1. Combine the flour, Barbecue Spice Blend, baking powder, and salt in a bowl. Mix the egg yolks, juices from the clams, and ⅓ cup wine in a measuring cup and pour over the flour. Mix, adding more wine as necessary to make a thick batter, as for muffins. Stir in the clams and scallions and mix only until blended. Beat the egg whites in a clean bowl until stiff. Fold into the batter.

2. Heat the oil in a deep-fryer until hot (375°F.). Scoop out rounded spoonfuls of batter and drop into the hot oil. Make several fritters at a time without crowding. Fry the fritters, turning, for 2 minutes, or until golden. Remove with a slotted spoon and drain on paper towels. Make all the fritters the same way, bringing the oil back to 375°F. before frying a new batch. Serve immediately.

Serving Suggestions: Serve the clams hot with Hot Wasabi Dipping Sauce (page 229), Cilantro-Walnut Dip (page 229), or Apple-Mustard Salsa (page 233) accompanied with Raspberry Tea with Sage (page 283). To complete the meal, serve a soup and rice or vegetable main course, such as Chilled Borscht with Caraway (page 121) or Red Lentil Soup with Bay Leaf and Pepper Cream (page 120) with Tarragon Scallops Kedgeree (page 201) or Risotto of Cauliflower with Oregano (page 198). For a more elaborate meal, add a vegetable, such as Roasted Sweet Potatoes with Cloves (page 218), and Basil-Pineapple Ice (page 269) for dessert.

white pepper cashew nuts

These nuts taste hotter at first bite than they really are. This is because the white pepper blends in with the color of the cashew nuts, catching the nibbler totally off guard. For a milder taste, reduce the pepper to two teaspoons.

MAKES 3 CUPS

¼ cup sugar

¼ cup water

2 tablespoons fresh lemon juice

1½ pounds roasted cashew nuts, salted or unsalted

1½ tablespoons freshly ground white pepper

1. Heat the sugar and water in a small pot over low heat until the sugar is fully dissolved. Add the lemon juice, increase the heat, and bring to a boil. Rapidly boil the syrup for 3 minutes. Add the nuts and cook, stirring, until nuts absorb the syrup, about 1 minute.

2. Immediately transfer the nuts to a nonstick or lightly greased baking sheet, spreading them in a single layer. Sprinkle with pepper and gently mix to coat evenly. Cool completely before serving. (*May be stored, tightly covered, for up to 3 months in a cool dark place, for up to 6 months in the refrigerator, and for up to 1 year in the freezer.*)

Note: Blanched almonds, brazil nuts, or macadamia nuts may be substituted for the cashews.

Serving Suggestions: For a main course, serve Bluefish with Tomato-Coriander Sauce (page 130) or Salmon Steamed in Bay Leaf Vapor (page 136) with a vegetable such as Cucumber with Toasted Cumin Seeds (page 211) and a condiment like Fresh Fig Salsa with Sesame (page 234).

pepper sticks

You can control the heat of your Pepper Sticks by altering the amount of salt in them. To increase the heat, decrease the salt. For a very spicy batch, eliminate the salt altogether. Serve the sticks before dinner—they are an appetite stimulant—with a cool beverage, like Peach Cooler with Sage (page 282) or Cardamom-Citrus Tea (page 286).

2 cups unbleached all-purpose flour

1 tablespoon black peppercorns, cracked

1 teaspoon kosher salt

3 large eggs

2 tablespoons unsulphured molasses

Vegetable oil, for deep-frying

MAKES 8 SERVINGS

1. Mix the flour, pepper, and salt in a large bowl. Make a well in the center and add the eggs and molasses. Using your hand or a fork, mix until the flour is incorporated into the eggs and a rough, hard dough is formed. Turn out onto a floured work surface. Knead until the dough is smooth and silky. Or make the dough in a food processor: Process all the ingredients at once until a rough dough ball forms on top of the blade. Knead briefly by hand. (*The dough may be set aside, wrapped in plastic, for up to 8 hours at room temperature, or kept, tightly covered, for up to 5 days in the refrigerator, or for up to 3 months in the freezer. Defrost the dough before rolling out.*)

2. Divide the dough into 4 portions. Working with 1 portion at a time, roll out the dough into a thin 5- x 10-inch rectangle, dusting often with flour. Cut the dough into short $1/2$-inch-wide strips. Dust lightly with flour. Roll out and cut the remaining 3 portions the same way. Or roll out the dough with a pasta machine.

3. Heat 2 inches of oil in a deep saucepan over medium-high heat. When the oil is hot (375°F.), add the strips, a few at a time, and fry until light golden, about $1^1/2$ minutes. Remove with a slotted spoon and drain on paper towels. Serve warm or at room temperature. When completely cool, transfer to a covered container. (*May be stored, tightly covered, for up to 3 weeks in a cool dark place or for up to 3 months in the refrigerator.*)

Serving Suggestions: To complete a grand meal, serve Mild Indian Chile with Paprika (page 163), Cilantro-Walnut Dip (page 229), Mango-Mint Salsa (page 231), Pan-grilled Plantains with Ginger (page 223), and Parsley Rice (page 192). Blueberry-Cinnamon Sauce (page 257) over Old-fashioned Vanilla Ice Cream (page 266) makes a fine ending.

cumin crackers

Cumin contributes flavor and also lightens these crackers, making them all the more enjoyable. Serve the crackers with tea or coffee, at a cocktail party or at a picnic. Attractively packaged, these crackers make a lovely holiday gift.

1 cup unbleached all-purpose flour

¹/₄ cup rice flour, or Cream of Wheat cereal, or chick pea flour, or ¹/₄ cup additional all-purpose flour

1 teaspoon kosher salt

¹/₄ teaspoon baking soda

³/₄ teaspoon cumin seeds

3 tablespoons unsalted butter or canola oil

5 tablespoons plain nonfat yogurt

MAKES 3 DOZEN CRACKERS

1. Mix together both flours, the salt, baking soda, and cumin seeds in a medium bowl. Add the butter and yogurt and mix until the flour can be gathered into a mass. Lightly knead the dough until smooth. (*The dough may be wrapped in plastic and set aside for up to 8 hours at room temperature or kept, tightly covered, for up to 5 days in the refrigerator, or it may be frozen. Defrost the dough before use.*)

2. Preheat the oven to 375°F.

3. Divide the dough into 2 portions. Working with 1 portion at a time, dust the dough with flour and roll it out into a circle about ¹/₈ inch thick. Cut crackers, using a 1¹/₂-inch cookie cutter. Prick the crackers with a fork to prevent them from puffing. Continue with the remaining dough. Finally, gather the scraps, press them into a ball, and roll and cut more crackers.

4. Place the crackers ¹/₂ inch apart on an ungreased baking sheet. Bake in the middle level of the oven for 13 to 15 minutes, or until they are lightly browned. Cool the crackers on racks. Serve hot or at room temperature. (*May be stored, tightly covered, in a cool dark place for up to 3 weeks.*)

variation Add ¹/₂ teaspoon coarsely ground black pepper or ¹/₄ teaspoon ground red pepper to the flour mixture.

Serving Suggestions: For an afternoon tea, accompany these crackers with Anise Cookies (page 277), Ginger Crisps (page 274), Saffron Scones (page 275), and Cardamom Cookies (page 279). As a beverage, serve Raspberry Tea with Sage (page 283), Chilled Anise Tea (page 285), or Mogul Spice Tea (page 284). For cocktails, serve the crackers with Spicy Tomato Spread (page 99), Goat Cheese Spread with Dried Tomatoes and Juniper Berries (page 100), Avocado Spread with Tahini (page 81), or Lima Bean Spread with Cumin Vinaigrette (page 83).

ajowan crackers

These are similar to Cumin Crackers but sweeter and more herbal, as good with tea as they are with cocktails. Pack them in festive boxes for holiday gift giving.

1¼ cups unbleached all-purpose flour

1 teaspoon kosher salt

½ teaspoon baking powder

¼ teaspoon ajowan seeds

3 tablespoons unsalted butter, chilled

5 tablespoons plain nonfat yogurt

MAKES 3 DOZEN CRACKERS

1. Mix together the flour, salt, baking powder, and ajowan seeds in a medium bowl. Add the butter and yogurt and mix until the flour can be gathered into a mass. Lightly knead the dough until smooth. (*The dough may be set aside in plastic wrap for up to 8 hours at room temperature or kept, tightly covered, for up to 5 days in the refrigerator, or it may be frozen. Defrost the dough before use.*)

2. Preheat the oven to 375°F.

3. Divide the dough into 2 portions. Working with 1 portion at a time, dust the dough with flour and roll it out into a circle about ⅛ inch thick. Cut crackers, using a 1½-inch cookie cutter. Prick the crackers with a fork to prevent them from puffing. Continue with the remaining dough. Finally, gather the scraps, press them into a ball, and roll and cut more crackers.

4. Place the crackers ½ inch apart on an ungreased baking sheet. Bake in the middle level of the oven for 13 to 15 minutes, or until they are lightly browned. Cool the crackers on racks. Serve them hot or at room temperature. (*May be stored, tightly covered, in a cool dark place for up to 3 weeks.*)

Note: Substitute 1 teaspoon dried thyme if ajowan is not available.

variation For a spicier version, add ½ teaspoon ground red pepper to the flour mixture.

Serving Suggestions: With cocktails, serve these crackers with Spicy Tomato Spread (page 99), Avocado Spread with Tahini (page 81), Marinated Mozzarella with Thyme (page 102), and Turmeric Escabeche of Vegetables (page 106), and beverages like Peach Cooler with Sage (page 282) and Raspberry Tea with Sage (page 283). The crackers are perfect served with such stews and soups as Black Bean Soup with Epazote (page 115), Chile con Carne (page 55), or Vegetarian Pumpkin, Eggplant, and Lima Bean Chile (page 180).

above: lobster sandwich on arugula with curry mayonnaise

left: sage, star anise, mace, saffron, turmeric

left: garlic chives, star anise, green cardamom, dried coriander berries

below: pepper-rubbed rack of lamb with acorn squash

above: savory millet cake with rosemary

left: peach cooler with sage and cumin crackers

above: barbecued tarragon game hens with quick cherry coulis

right: pan-grilled plantains with ginger

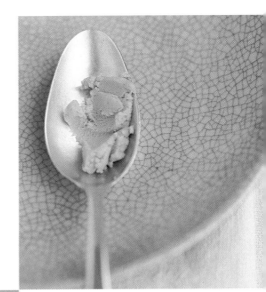

right: wasabi

below: clear mushroom and shrimp soup with wasabi

above: saffron scones with tomato jam

right: candied fennel seeds with cup of coffee

below: saffron

above: mogul potpourri

left: anise–pistachio crêpes with fruit

below: basil–pineapple ice

above: zaatar dip with spices

right: green chili vinegar

below: annatto seeds and oil

soups

green beans and potatoes in paprika broth

Delicately tinged with paprika, this mild and rather filling soup is at its best when made with garden-fresh beans and tiny new potatoes. Besides the brilliant red color, paprika has a unique smokiness; it also gives body to the soup.

2 teaspoons canola oil

1 teaspoon caraway seeds, crushed

2 teaspoons minced garlic

1/2 cup finely chopped onion

1/2 pound green beans, trimmed and cut into bite-size pieces

1 pound potatoes, peeled and cut into bite-size pieces

1/8 teaspoon freshly grated nutmeg

4 teaspoons Hungarian paprika

4 cups chicken stock or low-sodium canned broth

Freshly ground black pepper and kosher salt

1/4 cup finely chopped parsley

MAKES 6 SERVINGS

1. Heat the oil in a saucepan over medium-high heat and add the caraway seeds. When the seeds turn a few shades darker and give off aroma, about 30 seconds, add the garlic and onions. Cook, stirring, until the onions are soft, about 2 minutes.

2. Add the green beans, potatoes, nutmeg, paprika, and stock and bring to a boil. Lower the heat and simmer until the vegetables are tender, about 25 minutes. Season with pepper and salt to taste. Ladle the soup into deep soup bowls. Garnish with parsley and serve.

Note: Substitute ancho chili powder for some of the paprika.

Serving Suggestions: Follow the soup with Steamed Sea Bass with Dill (page 138) or Shrimp Sauté with Bay (page 141) and Polenta with Green Peppercorns (page 191) or Orange-Cinnamon Pilaf (page 196) with Apple-Mustard Salsa (page 233) on the side.

black bean soup with epazote

A very filling soup that can also be served as a main course. The soup is best the day it is made while the vegetables still retain their texture and fresh flavor. Just about any bean soup benefits from the use of epazote, which has the propensity to break down hard-to-digest proteins such as those present in beans.

1 pound dried black beans

2 tablespoons chopped fresh epazote or 1 tablespoon dried epazote

1 tablespoon chopped fresh oregano or 1 teaspoon dried oregano

1 piece (3 inches) lemon zest

2 medium onions, chopped

2 large green bell peppers, stemmed, seeded, and finely chopped

1 large red bell pepper, stemmed, seeded, and finely chopped

1 medium zucchini, scrubbed and finely chopped

½ cup chopped parsley

3 cloves garlic, finely chopped

Olive oil spray

1 teaspoon sugar

3 tablespoons wine vinegar, or more to taste

Freshly ground black pepper and kosher salt

1 cup (8-ounce container) plain nonfat yogurt, lightly beaten with a fork or whisk

2 tablespoons minced parsley, for garnish

MAKES 6 SERVINGS

1. For an overnight soak, soak the beans in water to cover overnight. For a short soak, place the beans in a large pot, add 8 cups of water, and bring to a boil. Cook, uncovered, for 2 minutes. Remove from the heat and let stand, covered, for 2 hours.

2. Drain and rinse the beans. Place in a large pot and add enough water to cover by 1 inch. Add the epazote, oregano, lemon zest, half the onion, and half the green peppers and bring to a boil. Reduce the heat and simmer, covered, for 2 hours, or until the beans are very soft, adding additional water as needed.

3. While the beans are cooking, place a large nonstick frying pan over high heat. Add the remaining onions, the remaining green pepper, the red pepper, zucchini, parsley, and garlic. Spray lightly with oil to coat the vegetables evenly. Pan-roast the vegetables over medium-high heat until tender and streaked browned. Stir the roasted vegetables into the soup. Stir in the sugar. Mix thoroughly, crushing some of the beans to thicken the soup. Cook for 5 minutes, or until the vegetables are soft. Remove and discard the lemon zest.

4. Stir in the vinegar and season to taste with pepper and salt. Ladle the hot soup into soup bowls, top with the yogurt, garnish with minced parsley, and serve.

Note: Substitute all or some of the black beans with kidney, pinto, or navy beans.

Serving Suggestions: Serve the soup accompanied with Parmesan-Chive Puffs (page 243) and Parsley Rice (page 192). To complete the meal serve Arroz con Pollo (page 93) with Pan-grilled Plantains with Ginger (page 223) and Avocado, Onion, and Cilantro Relish (page 231).

bean and pasta soup with oregano

This soup is wonderful at any time of the year but particularly when fresh herbs are available. Oregano and rosemary both mellow the starchy quality of the soup and render it surprisingly light.

1⅓ cups (8 ounces) dried white cannellini beans

¼ cup olive oil

1½ cups finely chopped onions

1 tablespoon finely chopped garlic

6 cups water

1 pound Italian plum tomatoes, peeled and chopped, or 1 can (14½ ounces) plum tomatoes, drained and coarsely chopped

4 ounces spaghetti, broken into 1-inch pieces, or other very small pasta shapes

1 tablespoon chopped fresh oregano or 1 teaspoon dried oregano

1 teaspoon fresh rosemary or ½ teaspoon dried rosemary

Freshly ground black pepper and kosher salt

4 tablespoons chopped flat-leaf parsley

1 cup (4 ounces) grated parmesan

1. For an overnight soak, soak the beans in water to cover overnight. For a short soak, place the beans in a large pot, add 8 cups of water, and bring to a boil. Cook, uncovered, for 2 minutes. Remove from the heat and let stand, covered, for 2 hours. Drain and rinse the beans. Set aside.

2. Combine the olive oil, onions, and garlic in a deep pot. Cook, stirring, over medium heat until the onions are soft. Add the beans and 4 cups of the water. Simmer, covered, for 1 hour, or until the beans are very soft. Crush some of the beans with the back of the spoon. Or transfer 2 cups of the beans to a food processor and process to a coarse puree; return the puree to the soup.

3. Add the tomatoes and the remaining 2 cups of water and bring to a boil. Cook until the tomatoes lose their raw flavor and collapse about 2 minutes. (*The soup may be made ahead to this point. It keeps well, tightly covered, for up to 5 days in the refrigerator. Bring the soup to a boil before proceeding.*)

4. Add the pasta, oregano, and rosemary. Simmer, uncovered, over low heat until the pasta is soft, about 15 minutes. Check the consistency, adding water as necessary. Season to taste with pepper and salt. Stir in half of the parsley and half of the parmesan. Ladle hot soup into bowls, garnish with the remaining parsley and serve immediately. Pass the remaining parmesan at the table.

Serving Suggestions: This is a very filling main-course soup. Accompany it with salad greens tossed in Cumin Vinaigrette (page 82) or Carrot Salad with Coriander Vinegar (page 166). Cardamom Cookies (page 279) with Cinnamon Coffee (page 288) are soothing at the end of the meal.

winter bean soup with bay leaf

Enriched with squash and other winter vegetables, a hearty bean soup can take the chill off cold winter days. Bay leaves and fennel seeds are added to the soup for their delicate floral aroma as well as to lighten it. You can make the soup with any combination of winter squash and cabbage-family vegetables. Stir the soup carefully—cooked squash disintegrates with the lightest of touch.

1 pound dried navy beans

1 tablespoon olive oil

2 bay leaves

1 teaspoon fennel seeds

1 tablespoon finely chopped garlic

2 large onions, chopped (2 cups)

1 large carrot, chopped (1 cup)

1 teaspoon sugar

1 rutabaga or 2 kohlrabi, cubed (1 cup)

6 cups ham stock, chicken stock, or low-sodium canned broth, or more as needed

½ medium butternut squash or 2 large sweet potatoes, cubed (2 cups)

½ small cabbage, chopped (2 cups)

2 tablespoons tomato paste or 1 tablespoon tomato paste and 1 tablespoon paprika

Freshly ground black pepper and kosher salt

⅓ cup minced parsley

2 tablespoons red wine vinegar

MAKES 8 SERVINGS

1. For an overnight soak, soak the beans in water to cover overnight. For a short soak, place the beans in a large pot, add 8 cups of water, and bring to a boil. Cook, uncovered, for 2 minutes. Remove from the heat and let stand, covered, for 2 hours. Drain and rinse the beans. Set aside.

2. Heat the oil in a heavy pot over medium-high heat and add the bay leaves, fennel seeds, garlic, onions, carrots, and sugar. Cook the vegetables, stirring, until lightly browned, 8 to 10 minutes. Add the stock, beans, rutabaga, squash, cabbage, and tomato paste and bring to a boil.

3. Lower the heat and simmer, covered, for 2 hours, or until the beans are very soft, adding broth or water as needed. Remove and discard the bay leaves. Crush some of the beans and squash with the back of the spoon. Season to taste with pepper and salt. Stir in 4 tablespoons of the parsley and the vinegar. Ladle the soup into bowls. Garnish with the remaining parsley and serve.

Serving Suggestions: This soup can be served in a deep bowl as a meal in itself, accompanied with Cumin Crackers (page 111) or Stuffed Sage Roti Bread with Olives (page 251) and Celery Root Salad with Celery Seeds (page 167).

lentil soup with smoked turkey and tarragon

Heady with floral tarragon and smoky turkey aromas, this lentil soup is surprisingly filling and very refreshing. The soup is easy to make, and you can put it aside for several days in the refrigerator.

1½ cups (10 to 12 ounces) brown lentils, picked clean, rinsed, and drained

6 cups boiling water

8 cups beef or chicken stock or low-sodium canned broth

6 ounces white button mushrooms, sliced

4 stalks celery, cut into ¼-inch dice

3 carrots, cut into ¼-inch dice

1 large onion, cut into ¼-inch dice

1 teaspoon minced garlic

¼ teaspoon ground allspice

½ pound smoked turkey breast, cut into ¼-inch dice

3 tablespoons chopped fresh tarragon or 2 teaspoons dried tarragon

2 tablespoons chopped parsley

¼ teaspoon grated lemon zest

1 tablespoon fresh lemon juice

Freshly ground black pepper and kosher salt

MAKES 6 SERVINGS

1. Place the lentils in a large heavy pot. Add the boiling water and let stand for 2 hours at room temperature.

2. Drain the lentils and return them to the pot. Add the stock, mushrooms, celery, carrots, onion, and garlic and bring to a boil. Reduce the heat and simmer, covered, for 40 minutes, or until the lentils are very soft, stirring occasionally.

3. Mash the soup with a potato masher to crush some of the lentils. Add the turkey and cook for 5 minutes more. (*The soup may be made ahead to this point. It keeps well, tightly covered, for up to 3 days in the refrigerator.*)

4. Just before serving, bring to a simmer and stir in the tarragon, parsley, lemon zest and juice. Season to taste with pepper and salt. Ladle into bowls and serve.

Note: Smoked chicken or smoked trout can be substituted for the turkey.

Serving Suggestions: Follow the soup with Penne with Broccoli and Turmeric (page 187) or Bulgur Salad with Allspice (page 173) and such breads as Parmesan-Chive Puffs (page 243) and Currant and Mace Puffs (page 242).

chilled carrot soup with mace

Make this soup when garden-fresh carrots are available. The sweetness of the soup is heightened by mace, which draws out and concentrates the sugar in the carrots. The soup can be served hot or chilled. To add more depth to the soup, garnish each bowl of soup with a tablespoon of Spicy Tomato Spread (page 99) or Pesto (page 232).

1½ pounds carrots, sliced

1 large onion, sliced

1 small baking potato, peeled and sliced

1 pound Italian plum tomatoes, peeled and chopped

6 scallions, green and white parts, sliced

¼ teaspoon ground red pepper

¼ teaspoon ground mace

½ teaspoon ground ginger

1 teaspoon kosher salt

3 cups skim milk or water

2 cups lowfat (2%) milk

¼ cup sliced almonds, toasted

2 tablespoons minced basil or cilantro

MAKES 8 SERVINGS

1. Combine the carrots, onion, potato, tomatoes, scallions, ground red pepper, mace, ginger, salt, and skim milk in a large pot and bring to a boil. Lower the heat and simmer, covered, for 30 minutes, or until the carrots are soft. Transfer the soup in batches to a blender or a food processor and process in batches until smoothly pureed.

2. Return the soup to the pot and stir in the lowfat milk. Reheat the soup until very hot or cover and refrigerate until thoroughly chilled, at least 4 hours. (*The soup keeps well, tightly covered, for up to 3 days in the refrigerator.*)

3. To serve cold, taste and add salt if needed. To serve hot, reheat the soup, taste, and add salt if needed. Either way, ladle the soup into bowls, garnish with toasted almonds and basil, and serve.

Serving Suggestions: For a light summer meal, follow the soup with Roasted Chicken Legs with Sage (page 149) or Grilled Mustard Tuna (page 133), Curried Rice (page 194), and Mango-Mint Salsa (page 231).

red lentil soup with bay leaf and pepper cream

Bay leaf goes with lentils. It gives a lemon accent, and it helps with the digestion of beans. Turmeric also aids digestion as well as lending color and flavor. Without the pepper cream, this is one of the most delicate of all lentil soups, red lentils having a very nutty flavor. The pepper cream adds bite and perks up the flavor. If you prefer a mild soup, omit the pepper cream.

1½ cups (10 to 12 ounces) red lentils, picked clean, rinsed, and drained (see Note)

1 cup chopped onions

2 bay leaves

½ teaspoon turmeric

4 cups rich chicken stock or low-sodium canned broth

1 cup lowfat (2%) milk

Freshly ground white pepper and kosher salt

Pepper Cream

1 tablespoon canola oil

1 teaspoon mustard seeds, crushed

2 tablespoons thinly sliced garlic

1 to 4 fresh chilies, steamed, seeded, and minced

2 red bell peppers, stemmed, seeded, and chopped (2 cups)

2 tablespoons tomato paste

½ cup water

1 tablespoon wine vinegar

Sprigs of cilantro, for garnish

MAKES 6 SERVINGS

1. For the soup, combine the lentils, onions, bay leaves, turmeric, and broth in a medium saucepan and bring to a boil. Lower the heat and simmer, partly covered, for 30 minutes, or until the lentils are soft. Remove and discard the bay leaves.

2. Transfer to a food processor or blender and process in batches until smoothly pureed. Return the soup to the saucepan and stir in the milk. The consistency should be like light cream; add water if necessary. Season to taste with pepper and salt. (*The soup may be made ahead to this point. It keeps well, tightly covered, for up to 3 days in the refrigerator.*)

3. For the pepper cream, place the oil, mustard seeds, garlic, chilies, and red bell pepper in a large heavy frying pan. Cook the vegetable mixture over medium-high heat, stirring, for 10 minutes, or until the peppers are soft. Stir in the tomato paste and water. Lower the heat and cook, covered, for 5 minutes. Turn off the heat.

4. Transfer the vegetable mixture to a food processor or blender and process until smoothly pureed, adding water as necessary. The pepper cream should be the consistency of pancake batter. Return the pepper cream to the pan and stir in the vinegar. Keep warm.

5. Just before serving, reheat the soup. Ladle it into bowls. Top with a generous tablespoonful of pepper cream, garnish with cilantro, and serve.

Note: Red lentils are available in Indian markets and health-food stores.

Serving Suggestions: Follow the soup with Steamed Fish with Ginger Essence (page 131), Parsley Rice (page 192), Mango-Mint Salsa (page 231), and Glazed Carrots with Cloves (page 208).

chilled borscht with caraway

For decades, one of my favorite summer soups has been borscht, the Russian beet, cabbage, and beef soup that is thickened with caraway-studded rye bread. Besides giving the soup a hint of licorice flavor, the caraway makes the cabbage easy to digest. Borscht can be as light and refreshing as a gazpacho or as heavy as a hearty stew. Dora Zhivotensky, a fine cook from the Ukraine, taught me to make borscht the light way. This soup, the color of crushed raspberries, is elegant yet very simple to make.

2 medium onions, chopped
(1¼ cups)

2 large carrots, sliced
(1¼ cups)

4 medium beets, peeled and
chopped (2½ cups)

3½ cups water

1 tablespoon unsalted butter
or margarine

½ small cabbage, chopped
(3 cups)

1½ cups rich beef stock or
low-sodium canned broth

1 slice rye bread with caraway
seeds, toasted and broken
into pieces, or 1 slice
toasted seedless rye bread,
crumbled, and ⅛ teaspoon
toasted caraway seeds

Freshly ground black pepper
and kosher salt

Nonfat sour cream or plain
nonfat yogurt, for serving

MAKES 6 SERVINGS

1. Combine the onions, carrots, beets, and water in a deep pot over medium-high heat and bring to a boil. Lower the heat and simmer, covered, for 20 minutes. Add the butter, cabbage, and broth. Simmer, uncovered, for 20 minutes, or until the cabbage is cooked. Turn off the heat.

2. Stir in the bread pieces. Process the soup in batches in a blender or food processor until well pureed. The soup will never be a smooth puree because of the cabbage; it should have some texture. Season to taste with pepper and salt. Cover and refrigerate for at least 4 hours, or until well chilled. (*The soup keeps well, tightly covered, for up to 5 days in the refrigerator.*)

3. To serve, taste and adjust the seasoning if necessary. Ladle the soup into bowls and top with a dollop of sour cream.

Serving Suggestions: For a light summer meal, follow the soup with Steamed Lobster in Juniper Berry Vapor (page 142) or Steamed Sea Bass with Dill (page 138), Parsley Rice (page 192), and Cucumber with Toasted Cumin Seeds (page 211).

fennel, green bean, and cauliflower soup with celery seed

This soup is a light broth full of floating vegetables. The beauty of it is that you can distinguish the flavor and texture of each vegetable while simultaneously enjoying the fusion created by the citrus accents of celery seed. You can use any combination of summer vegetables, even greens, in place of fennel, beans, and cauliflower as long as they hold their shape when cooked.

1 medium fennel bulb, sliced (1 cup)

¼ pound green beans, trimmed and cut into bite-size pieces (1 cup)

1 cup cauliflower florets

1 large baking potato, peeled and cut into bite-size pieces (1 cup)

1 pound Italian plum tomatoes, peeled and chopped, or 1 can (14½ ounces) plum tomatoes, drained and coarsely chopped

1 teaspoon celery seeds

1 tablespoon ground coriander

2 teaspoons ground cumin

2 tablespoons tomato paste

4 cups chicken stock or low-sodium canned broth, or more if needed

Freshly ground black pepper and kosher salt

1 tablespoon minced cilantro or parsley

MAKES 6 SERVINGS

1. Combine the fennel, green beans, cauliflower, potato, tomatoes, celery seeds, coriander, cumin, tomato paste, and chicken stock in a large pot and bring to a boil. Lower the heat and simmer, covered, for 30 minutes, or until the vegetables are very soft.

2. Crush some of the potatoes with the back of the spoon to thicken the soup slightly. Do not overcrush or the soup will cloud. Check the consistency and add more stock if necessary. Season to taste with pepper and salt. Ladle the hot soup into bowls, garnish with cilantro, and serve.

Serving Suggestions: This soup can be a complete meal when served with a filling bread like Stuffed Tarragon Roti Bread with Ham and Mushrooms (page 252) and a salad like Warm Potato Salad with Caraway Dressing (page 168).

fragrant fish chowder with celery seed

A unique chowder contains no salt pork or bacon, no heavy cream, not even butter. Instead, flavor is achieved though a combination of spices and herbs. The result is every bit as chowderlike as a fish soup made with the classical enrichments, but it is delicate and smoky-sweet. You can make the chowder with any white nonoily fish as long as it's fresh, as sweet smelling as an ocean breeze.

2 stalks celery, sliced (1 cup)

3 medium onions, chopped
(1½ cups)

1 pound potatoes, peeled and
cut into bite-size pieces
(2 cups)

1 tablespoon canola or
olive oil

¼ teaspoon celery seeds

⅛ teaspoon fennel seeds

1 teaspoon fresh thyme or
½ teaspoon dried thyme

2 cups chicken stock or low-
sodium canned broth

1 quart skim milk

1 pound scrod or cod fillet, cut
into 1-inch pieces

2 tablespoons minced celery
leaves

1 teaspoon lemon juice

Freshly ground black pepper
and kosher salt

2 tablespoons minced parsley

MAKES 6 SERVINGS

1. Toss the celery, onions, and potatoes in oil in a deep pot. Cook the vegetables over medium-high heat until they are slightly soft, about 5 minutes. Add the celery seeds, fennel seeds, thyme, and chicken stock and bring to a boil. Lower the heat and simmer, covered, over low heat for 20 minutes, or until the potatoes are tender.

2. Add the milk. When the soup comes to a boil, slip in the fish. Cook for 1 minute and turn off the heat. Stir in the celery leaves and lemon juice and season to taste with pepper and salt. Ladle the soup into bowls, sprinkle with parsley, and serve.

Serving Suggestions: Follow the soup with a light dish like Linguine with Cilantro Sauce (page 186) or Lentil and Endive Salad with Juniper Berries (page 171), and Parmesan-Chive Puffs (page 243) or Mini Pita with Basil and Dried Tomatoes (page 250).

kale soup with crabmeat and thyme

Kale soup, called *caldo verde* in Portuguese, is made with kale greens thickened with potatoes. Every former Portuguese colony, of which are many around the globe, has a version of *caldo verde* it calls its own. In the hands of local cooks, each one is metamorphosed to yet another form. This unusual rendition is from Mozambique. There pureed kale is accented with fresh chilies, coriander seeds, and thyme. The sharpness of the soup is balanced with sweet juicy crabmeat. For best results use fresh lump crabmeat.

4 medium onions, chopped (2 cups)

1 tablespoon minced garlic

1 pound baking potatoes, peeled and chopped (2 cups)

2 tablespoons canola oil

1 tablespoon chopped fresh thyme or 1 teaspoon dried thyme

2 teaspoons ground coriander

1 to 2 teaspoons minced fresh chilies

6 cups chicken stock or low-sodium canned broth, or more as needed

2 pounds kale greens, stemmed and roughly chopped

Kosher salt

3 Italian plum tomatoes, peeled, seeded, and diced (1 cup)

1 pound cooked lump crabmeat, picked over for cartilage

Sprigs of thyme

MAKES 6 SERVINGS

1. Combine the onions, garlic, potatoes, and oil in a deep pot over medium-high heat. Cook, stirring occasionally, until the onions are wilted and begin to brown, about 7 minutes. Stir in the thyme, coriander, and chilies and cook until they give off an aroma, about 2 minutes. Add the stock and kale and stir until the greens wilt and the liquid comes to a boil. Lower the heat and simmer, covered, until the potatoes are soft, about 20 minutes. Turn off the heat.

2. Puree the soup in batches using a food processor or food mill. Return the soup to the pot. The soup should be the consistency of heavy cream. Add more stock or water, if necessary. Season to taste with salt. (*The soup may be made ahead to this point. It keeps well, tightly covered, for up to 3 days in the refrigerator.*)

3. Just before serving, reheat the soup to piping hot. Pour the soup into soup bowls. Sprinkle the diced tomatoes and the crabmeat on top. Garnish with thyme sprigs and serve.

Serving Suggestions: For an elegant meal, follow the soup with Pepper-rubbed Rack of Lamb (page 159) or Roast Duck with Hot Pepper and Plums (page 155), Saffron Pilaf with Peas and Almonds (page 199) or Summer Peach Pilaf with Bay (page 197), Green Beans in Mustard Sauce (page 204), and Sesame Pita Bread (page 249).

clear mushroom and shrimp soup with wasabi

Clear soups are esteemed in every cuisine for their lightness and elegance and for the soothing effect they have on the palate and on the psyche. This Japanese-inspired soup is subtly flavored with wasabi.

4 Chinese dried mushrooms

4 cups chicken stock or low-sodium canned broth

1 tablespoon light (low-sodium) soy sauce

8 ounces fresh fancy mushrooms, such as shiitakes, oyster mushrooms, or cremini, or a combination, thinly sliced (1½ cups)

4 scallions, green and white parts, thinly sliced or julienned (½ cup)

¾ pound medium shrimps, shelled and deveined

8 to 12 spinach leaves

½ teaspoon dark sesame oil

Freshly ground white pepper and kosher salt

2 tablespoons shredded basil, cilantro, and mint

1 teaspoon wasabi paste (see page 49), for serving (see Note)

MAKES 4 SERVINGS

1. Soak the dried mushrooms in warm water to cover for 30 minutes. Drain and rinse the mushrooms. Discard stems and cut the caps into thin slices.

2. Bring the stock to a boil in a sauté pan. Add the soy sauce, fresh mushrooms, and soaked mushrooms. Simmer for 5 minutes, or until the mushrooms are cooked. Add the scallions, shrimps, and spinach and cook just until the shrimps turn pink, 2 minutes. Turn off heat.

3. Stir in the sesame oil and pepper and salt to taste. Divide the herbs among the bowls and ladle piping hot soup on top. Serve immediately. Pass the wasabi paste in a small bowl.

Note: If only wasabi powder is available, mix ½ teaspoon powder with enough water to make a paste.

Serving Suggestions: For a light lunch, serve the soup with the Lobster Sandwich with Curry Mayonnaise (page 85) and Mango-Mint Salsa (page 231) or Fresh Fig Salsa with Sesame (page 234) and Raspberry Tea with Sage (page 283).

iced pear soup with mint

This cooling soup is one of the simplest to make—all you need to do is combine and puree the ingredients. For best results, make the soup several hours, even a day ahead, before serving to allow the mint to mellow and the flavors to fuse harmoniously.

2 ripe Bartlett pears, peeled, cored, and chopped

1 pound yellow tomatoes, peeled, seeded, and chopped

1 pound yellow bell peppers, stemmed, seeded, and chopped

2 tablespoons minced fresh mint or 2 teaspoons dried mint

2 tablespoons balsamic vinegar

Freshly ground white pepper and kosher salt

1/3 cup sliced almonds, toasted

Sprigs of mint

MAKES 6 SERVINGS

1. Process the pears, tomatoes, peppers, and mint in batches in a food processor or blender until smoothly pureed. Transfer the soup to a bowl and stir in the vinegar and pepper and salt to taste. Cover and refrigerate for at least 4 hours, or overnight, or until well chilled. (*The soup keeps well, tightly covered, for up to 5 days in the refrigerator.*)

2. To serve, taste and adjust the seasoning if necessary. Ladle the soup into soup plates, garnish with almonds and mint, and serve.

variations Add one of the following as a garnish: 1/2 recipe Seared Pears with Cloves (page 219) or 1/3 cup Warm Tomato Butter with Paprika (page 236) or 1/3 cup Spicy Tomato Spread (page 99).

Serving Suggestions: To complete the meal, serve Savory Millet Cake with Rosemary (page 181) accompanied with Warm Tomato Butter with Paprika (page 236) or Curry-grilled Scallops (page 57) with Parsley Rice (page 192), Chick Pea Salad with Cumin (page 172), and Avocado, Onion, and Cilantro Relish (page 231).

tomato soup with basil cream

A soup to make only when vine-ripened tomatoes are plentiful; the flavor of the soup is a direct reflection of the quality of the tomatoes. Basil bonds naturally with tomatoes. The colors complement each other and basil tempers the acidity of the tomatoes. The soup may be served hot or chilled.

Basil Cream

1 cup (8-ounce container) nonfat sour cream or plain nonfat yogurt

1 cup (packed) basil leaves

1/3 cup pistachio nuts or walnuts

1 to 2 teaspoons Tabasco

Tomato Soup

4 large ripe red tomatoes, peeled, seeded, and chopped (3 cups)

2 leeks, white parts only, or 1 small onion, finely chopped (1/2 cup)

2 large cloves garlic

1 teaspoon powered dry mustard

1 tablespoon Curry Powder (page 56)

1 cup chicken stock, low-sodium canned broth, or water

2 1/2 cups skim milk

2 teaspoons maple syrup

1 tablespoon fresh lemon juice

6 sprigs of basil, for garnish

MAKES 6 SERVINGS

1. For the basil cream, combine all the ingredients in a food processor or blender and process until smoothly pureed. Transfer to a bowl, cover, and refrigerate until needed. (*The basil cream keeps well, tightly covered, for up to 4 days in the refrigerator.*)

2. For the tomato soup, combine the tomatoes, leeks, garlic, mustard, curry powder, and chicken stock in a deep pot and bring to a boil. Lower the heat and simmer, covered, for 20 minutes, or until the vegetables are soft. Transfer to a food processor or blender and process in batches until smoothly pureed. Return the soup to the pot.

3. Add the milk and cook until heated through. Stir in the maple syrup and lemon juice. Serve soup immediately or refrigerate for at least 4 hours or overnight. (*The soup keeps well, tightly covered, for up to 2 days in the refrigerator. Reheat if serving hot.*)

4. To serve, taste and adjust the seasoning if necessary. Ladle the soup into soup plates. Spoon or pipe the basil cream decoratively on top. Garnish with sprigs of basil and serve.

Serving Suggestions: For an elegant meal, follow the soup with Rosemary-crusted Veal Chops (page 160), Brussels Sprouts with Fennel (page 206), Parsley-Garlic Noodles (page 184), Green Beans in Mustard Sauce (page 204), and Fresh Fig Salsa with Sesame (page 234). Old-fashioned Vanilla Ice Cream (page 266) with Mango Sauce with Nutmeg (page 259) will make a grand finale to this meal.

cool yogurt soup with toasted cumin seeds

A creamy, minty soup, perfect for hot summer days. It is fairly mild, so if you would like a hotter flavor, grate in two red radishes. Toasted cumin seeds give the soup a delicate smoky aroma. Toasted Coriander Seeds (page 35) may be substituted for the cumin.

1 teaspoon cumin seeds, toasted

2 medium cucumbers, peeled, seeded, and chopped

¼ cup (lightly packed) mint leaves

1 clove garlic

1 tablespoon sugar

1 cup chicken stock or water

3 cups plain nonfat yogurt

Freshly ground white pepper and kosher salt

4 sprigs of mint

MAKES 4 SERVINGS

1. Place the cumin seeds in an ungreased skillet. Toast over medium-high heat until the seeds turn a few shades darker. Remove from the heat and cool completely. Set aside.

2. Place the cucumbers, mint leaves, garlic, sugar, and stock in a food processor or a blender. Process until the contents are smoothly pureed. Do this in batches if necessary. Pour the cucumber puree into a bowl.

3. Add the yogurt and pepper and salt to taste and whisk until blended. Cover and refrigerate to chill thoroughly, at least 8 hours. (*The soup keeps well, tightly covered, for up to 3 days in the refrigerator.*)

4. To serve, taste and adjust the seasoning if necessary. Ladle the soup into bowls. Sprinkle the cumin seeds on top and garnish with sprigs of mint. Serve immediately.

Serving Suggestions: Follow the soup with Jerk Chicken (page 61) or Grilled Leg of Lamb with Smoked Chili Pepper Oil (page 88), Mango-Mint Salsa (page 231), and Summer Peach Pilaf with Bay (page 197). You can also serve Mini Pita with Basil and Dried Tomatoes (page 250) and Thyme Pita Bread (page 248) with the soup.

fish and shellfish

bluefish with tomato-coriander sauce

Quickly sautéed in the barest amount of oil, bluefish fillets retain all their wonderful moistness and aroma. They are dressed with a piquant tomato sauce. Coriander adds a floral touch and serves to bind the sauce. The fava beans give the sauce a meaty bite.

2 tablespoons olive oil

1½ teaspoons ground coriander

2 pounds fresh young fava beans, shelled, or 1 package (10 ounces) frozen baby lima beans (about 2 cups) (see Note)

2 Italian plum tomatoes, fresh or canned, peeled, seeded, and chopped (½ cup)

¼ cup white wine, chicken stock, or water

Freshly ground black pepper and kosher salt

¼ cup skim milk

¼ cup all-purpose flour

2 bluefish fillets (about 6 ounces each)

Lemon slices

MAKES 2 SERVINGS

1. Heat 1 tablespoon of the oil in a medium saucepan over medium heat. Add the coriander and cook until the spice gives off an aroma and is lightly fried, about 1 minute. Stir in the fava beans and continue to cook for 2 minutes, or until the beans begin to fry. Add the tomatoes and wine and increase the heat. Boil the sauce until the moisture evaporates and the beans are glazed, about 8 minutes. Season to taste with pepper and salt. Cover and keep warm.

2. Pour the milk into a shallow soup bowl and spread out the flour on a plate. Place the remaining tablespoon of oil in a large nonstick frying pan over medium-high to high heat. When the oil is hot, dip the fillets, one at a time, first in the milk and then in the flour, coating them lightly, and put them in the oil. Lower the heat to medium and cook, undisturbed, for 2 minutes, or until nicely browned and almost cooked. Turn carefully with a wide spatula and cook the second side for 1 minute, or until fully cooked. Serve fillets topped with the sauce and garnished with lemon slices.

Note: Fresh fava beans are available in the spring in specialty food shops and many ethnic markets, which also carry frozen favas year round. Baby lima beans are an acceptable substitute.

Serving Suggestions: A nice appetizer to precede the fish is Spinach with Chili Cheese on Endive Boats (page 101). To complete the meal, serve Parsley Rice (page 192), Glazed Carrots with Cloves (page 208), and Currant and Mace Puffs (page 242).

steamed fish with ginger essence

This steamed fish is an easy and elegant choice for entertaining since everything can be done in advance, and the fish can be served at room temperature or cold as well as hot. In this dish the fish is smothered with a herb paste and steamed wrapped in lettuce. Then it is served with a fresh ginger and shallot topping. The ginger helps the fish retain its fresh ocean fragrance longer. Paired with a sauce like Hot Wasabi Dipping Sauce (page 229), it can be served as a first course instead of a main course.

¼ cup shredded young ginger (page 38) or very fresh juicy ginger

1 tablespoon finely slivered shallots

2 tablespoons fresh lemon juice

2 tablespoons pineapple juice or fresh orange juice

8 romaine lettuce leaves, steamed

1½ pounds Hawaiian mahi-mahi, sole, or salmon fillets, cut into 4 serving pieces

⅓ cup Green Curry Paste (page 94) (see Note)

Kosher salt

**MAKES 8 FIRST COURSE SERVINGS
4 MAIN COURSE SERVINGS,**

1. Combine the ginger, shallots, lemon juice, and pineapple juice in a small bowl. Cover and refrigerate.

2. Trim off the hard portion of the lettuce leaves. Lay 2 pieces leaves, overlapping, on the work counter. Place 1 piece of fish on top and sprinkle with salt. Spread one-quarter of the curry paste on top and enclose the fish completely with the lettuce. Prepare the remaining 3 pieces the same way. (*The packets may be made ahead and refrigerated, tightly covered, for up to 1 day.*)

3. When ready to cook, bring water to a boil in a steamer. Place the wrapped fish on the steaming rack and steam for 7 to 8 minutes, or until the fish feels firm to the touch. Serve immediately while hot, let stand at room temperature, or cover and refrigerate for at least 4 hours to serve cold. Place the fish whole or sliced with the lettuce wrapping on a plate. Top with the ginger, shallots, and juices and serve.

Note: If Green Curry Paste is not available, use a mixture of 3 tablespoons minced cilantro, 2 teaspoons minced garlic, 2 teaspoons minced fresh chilies, and 1 teaspoon grated lemon zest.

Serving Suggestions: For a complete seafood meal, start with Clear Mushroom and Shrimp Soup with Wasabi (page 125) or Kale Soup with Crabmeat and Thyme (page 124). Then serve Angel Hair with Olives, Basil, and Chilies (page 188) and Seared Pears with Cloves (page 219) wrapped in Savory Herb Crêpes (page 253).

flash-grilled flounder with ajowan

Light fillets of flounder, buttery in texture, are flavored with ajowan, which has a thymelike fragrance. Ajowan also has a preserving effect on the fish, preventing it from spoiling, and a binding property. So while the lemon juice in the marinade "cooks" the fish, the ajowan prevents it from disintegrating. In this recipe the fish is pan-grilled to retain maximum juices; it can also be grilled under the broiler. The recipe works equally well with sole, sea bass, kingfish, shrimps, and bay scallops as with flounder. You can serve the fish hot, at room temperature, or cold.

2 fillets of flounder (about ³/₄ pound)

1 teaspoon minced garlic

¹/₈ teaspoon ajowan seeds (see Note)

1 teaspoon fresh lemon juice

¹/₄ cup all-purpose flour

1 tablespoon light vegetable oil, or more if needed

MAKES 2 SERVINGS

1. Lay fish in a shallow dish. Add the garlic, ajowan, and lemon juice and rub over the fillets. Set aside until needed. (*The fish may be refrigerated, covered, for up to 1 day.*)

2. Add the oil, barely enough to coat the bottom of a large nonstick frying pan, and heat over medium-high heat. When the oil is hot, dust the fish lightly with flour and put it in the pan. Cook for 1 minute, or until brown. Turn carefully and continue to cook for a few seconds, or until the fish is lightly browned. Remove the fish with a spatula and serve hot. The flounder may also be served at room temperature or cold. (*The fish may be kept, tightly covered, for up to 2 days in the refrigerator.*)

Note: If not available, substitute ¹/₂ teaspoon dried thyme.

Serving Suggestions: Start the meal with a starchy soup like Red Lentil Soup with Bay Leaf and Pepper Cream (page 120). To complete the meal, serve the fish with Tomato-Cumin Rice (page 193) and Green Beans in Mustard Sauce (page 204).

grilled mustard tuna

Since ancient times, mustard rubs have been used for fish not only to add mustard's characteristic piquant flavor but to cure the fish. Tuna can stand up well to the mustard sauce in this recipe. Arugula and fennel tops are particularly good in the salad greens paired with the grilled tuna.

¼ cup red wine vinegar

¼ cup white wine

2 tablespoons olive oil

1 tablespoon honey, maple syrup, or dark corn syrup

3 tablespoons coarse-grain mustard

2 teaspoons minced garlic

1 teaspoon grated orange zest

¾ pound tuna steak

3 cups baby salad greens

2 tablespoons minced basil or Italian flat-leaf parsley

1 tablespoon currants or minced dried cranberries

MAKES 2 SERVINGS

1. Combine the vinegar, wine, oil, honey, mustard, garlic, and orange zest in a small bowl. Place the tuna in a shallow dish. Add one-third of the dressing or enough to coat the tuna well. Cover and refrigerate the dressing and the fish. (*The fish may be left in the marinade for 1 day.*)

2. When ready to cook, light a charcoal grill or preheat the broiler.

3. Remove the tuna and the dressing from the refrigerator. If barbecuing, lightly brush the rack with oil and place the tuna on top. If broiling, lightly oil the pan and put the tuna on it. Place it under the broiler, 4 to 5 inches from the heat. Cook, turning once and brushing with some of the dressing, until the tuna is lightly charred and seared on the outside but still a little rare on the inside, about 7 minutes. Transfer the tuna to a cutting board and slice it across the grain.

4. Place the salad greens in a shallow bowl. Add the basil, currants, and the remaining dressing and toss. Divide the salad and tuna between 2 plates and serve.

Serving Suggestions: Start the meal with an appetizer like Avocado Spread with Tahini (page 81) or Barbecued Chicken Wings (page 71). To complete the meal, serve Yellow Tomato and Green Peppercorn Salsa (page 235) and Penne with Mushrooms and Crushed Red Pepper (page 189) or Cumin Potatoes (page 215).

tuna and grape salad in celery seed–curry dressing

The thought of canned tuna, or for that matter anything canned, usually brings to mind convenience, not great flavor. But that opinion will change once you've tasted this tuna salad. Celery seeds are an essential feature in the salad; they add an herbal touch and smooth out flavors.

2 cans (6½ ounces each) chunk light tuna in water

1 cup thinly sliced tender celery

1 cup red or white small seedless grapes

¼ cup finely chopped onion

2 teaspoons Curry Powder (page 56)

½ teaspoon celery seeds

2 cloves garlic

8 ounces nonfat cottage cheese

¾ cup skim milk

4 tablespoons fresh lemon juice

Freshly ground black pepper and kosher salt

¼ cup chopped toasted walnuts (optional)

MAKES 4 SERVINGS

1. Drain the tuna and place it in a shallow bowl. Add the celery, grapes, and onion, and lightly toss.

2. Toast the Curry Powder in a heavy skillet over medium heat until the aroma rises, about 3 minutes. Using a spatula, remove immediately to a bowl and let cool. Combine the celery seeds, garlic, cottage cheese, skim milk, and lemon juice in a food processor. Add the Curry Powder. Process until thoroughly liquefied. Season generously with pepper and salt to taste.

3. Pour the dressing over the tuna and toss. Sprinkle with toasted walnuts, if desired, and serve.

Serving Suggestions: For a summer luncheon, precede the salad with a cool soup like Iced Pear Soup with Mint (page 126) or Chilled Borscht with Caraway (page 121). To complete the meal, serve Polenta with Green Peppercorns (page 191), Mango-Mint Salsa (page 231), and Thyme Pita Bread (page 248).

black pepper–rubbed salmon

I often use this way of cooking salmon to have it for salads, soup garnishes—it is wonderful flaked and sprinkled on cream soups such as Iced Pear Soup with Mint (page 126)—and stuffing as well as for serving it hot. It is imperative to get the freshest possible salmon since this recipe has just two flavors: salmon and black pepper. For best results, use a highly fragrant black pepper, Tellicherry pepper, for example.

¾ to 1 pound salmon fillet, cut into 2 serving portions

2 teaspoons black peppercorns, cracked

1 tablespoon unsalted butter or olive oil

MAKES 2 SERVINGS

1. Just before cooking, place the fish fillets on a plate and rub with pepper and oil.

2. Heat a large heavy nonstick frying pan over high heat until very hot. Reduce the heat to medium and put the fish in the pan. Cook until lightly seared, about 1 minute. Turn the fish and cover with a piece of aluminum foil.

3. Cook the fish, steaming in pepper vapor, until it feels firm to the touch and is opaque, about 6 minutes. Do not cook to the point of flaking. The fish should be medium-rare, slightly darker and very moist in the center. Remove the fish to serving plates. Scrape the juices from the pan and brush them over the fish. Serve immediately. (*The salmon keeps well, tightly covered, for up to 4 days in the refrigerator.*)

Serving Suggestions: Serve the salmon with Apple Compote with Fennel (page 221), Linguine with Cilantro Sauce (page 186), and Dill Tortilla Bread (page 240).

salmon steamed in bay leaf vapor

Cooking fish wrapped in bay is an old Mediterranean technique. The bay leaves lend a spicy lemon aroma and also cure the salmon. You can also use sole, sea bass, kingfish, shrimps, and bay scallops in place of salmon. The fish can be served hot, at room temperature, or cold.

2 bay leaves

¹/₂ teaspoon black peppercorns

1¹/₂ pounds salmon fillets, cut into 4 serving portions

¹/₂ cup white wine

1 tablespoon chopped garlic

¹/₂ teaspoon dried thyme

¹/₂ teaspoon grated lemon zest

MAKES 4 SERVINGS

1. Preheat the oven to 350°F.

2. Combine the bay leaves and black pepper in an electric spice/coffee grinder, and grind until coarsely powdered. Rub the spice mixture over the fish and place the pieces in a single layer in a baking dish. Pour the wine over the fish and sprinkle with garlic, thyme, and lemon zest. Cover tightly with foil.

3. Bake in the middle level of the oven for 10 minutes, or until the fish is firm to the touch. Do not overcook. If desired, open the foil and check after 8 minutes. Remove the dish from the oven and let it stand, covered, for 2 minutes to allow the vapors to settle on the fish, making it more flavorful. Serve with the accumulated juices spooned on top. (*The fish keeps well, tightly covered, for up to 4 days in the refrigerator.*)

Serving Suggestions: Serve the salmon with Cucumber with Toasted Cumin Seeds (page 211), Risotto of Cauliflower with Oregano (page 198) or Parsley Rice (page 192), and Chili Tortilla Bread (page 241).

scrod ragout with fragrant spices

Coconut milk mellows the pungent spices and harmonizes them with the fish in this seafood dish, which is permeated with Caribbean flavors. Although I have used scrod, you can make the ragout with any lean fish, or combination of fish, such as sea bass, red snapper, catfish, halibut, swordfish, or turbot. For a spicier flavor, substitute Smoked Chili Pepper Oil (page 88) for some of the canola oil.

2 tablespoons canola oil

2 cups finely chopped onions

1 tablespoon minced garlic

2 tablespoons Fragrant Spice Rub (page 62)

1 cup bottled clam broth or water

1 large (8 ounce) sweet potato, peeled and cut into 1-inch cubes

1 cup unsweetened coconut milk (see Note)

2 pounds scrod fillets, cut into 1½-inch pieces

1½ teaspoons kosher salt, or to taste

2 tablespoons chopped Italian flat-leaf parsley

MAKES 6 SERVINGS

1. Heat the oil in a heavy-bottomed pan. Add the onions and cook over medium-high heat, stirring occasionally, until soft and glazed, about 5 minutes. Stir in the garlic and Fragrant Spice Rub and cook 2 minutes more.

2. Add the broth and sweet potato and bring to a boil. Lower the heat and simmer, covered, for 15 minutes, or until the sweet potato is tender. Add the coconut milk and scrod and bring to a boil. Turn off the heat and season with salt. Ladle the ragout into deep plates and serve garnished with parsley.

Note: Unsweetened coconut milk is available canned in Asian markets. If only coconut cream is available, dilute it half and half with water. Frozen coconut milk is also sometimes available. Do not use a sweetened product.

Serving Suggestions: For an appetizer, serve Escabeche of Chicken in Allspice Sauce (page 105) or Turmeric Escabeche of Vegetables (page 106). To complete the meal, serve Brown Rice Salad with Basil Dressing (page 174), Pan-grilled Plantains with Ginger (page 223), and Chili Tortilla Bread (page 241).

steamed sea bass with dill

This is a very light and clean tasting fish dish from the Mediterranean. Although the fish is called steamed, it is, in fact, poached. Since the poaching liquid is kept to a minimum, it gets to be served as a sauce. The best part is that the fish stays incredibly moist and fragrant with dill. This recipe works equally well with salmon.

2 sea bass fillets (6 to 8 ounces each)

Freshly ground white pepper and kosher salt

1 tablespoon olive oil

2 cloves garlic, thinly sliced

4 scallions, green and white parts, thinly sliced (½ cup)

2 tablespoons chopped fresh dill or 1 tablespoon dried dillweed

⅓ cup fruity white wine

¼ cup sliced almonds, toasted

Lemon slices and sprigs of dill, for garnish

MAKES 2 SERVINGS

1. Rub the fish with pepper and salt. Heat the oil in a heavy non-stick sauté pan. Add the garlic and cook over medium-high heat until pale gold. Add the scallions and continue to cook until wilted and slightly seared, about 2 minutes. Push the seasonings to the side of the pan and add the fish fillets in a single layer. Scatter the dill on top and pour the wine on and around the fish.

2. Lower the heat, cover the pan, and steam the fish until it turns opaque and feels firm to the touch, about 7 minutes. Uncover the pan and carefully transfer the fish, using a wide spatula, to individual plates. Stir the almonds into the juices remaining in the pan and spoon over the fish. Garnish with dill and serve.

Serving Suggestions: Start the meal with Chilled Borscht with Caraway (page 121) or Broiled Vegetables with Oregano (page 103). To complete the meal, serve Polenta with Green Peppercorns (page 191), Chili Hash-Brown Potatoes (page 214), Parmesan-Chive Puffs (page 243), and Five Pepper Rolls (page 247).

fish fillet braised in vanilla sauce

In many classic cuisines, sweet spices play a pivotal role in flavoring savory dishes. Such spices mellow and round off flavors as well as lending a more aristocratic appeal to the dish. Moroccan *bisteeya* (pigeon pie with saffron, cinnamon, almonds, and powdered sugar), Mexican *mole poblano* (turkey in a sauce of cinnamon, anise, chocolate, raisins, and almonds), and the Indian *mogul raan* (lamb with saffron, cardamom, rose water, cherries, and raisins) are just a few examples.

During my travels through East Africa I encountered a unique flavoring technique using the vanilla bean in a savory dish. This vanilla-scented fish, which bears a vague resemblance to the French Mediterranean fish stew *bouillabaisse,* is believed to have originated with the French in Madagascar. They seem to have found vanilla a good stand-in for saffron.

In this recipe, vanilla brings out the sweetness in the fish and balances the heat of the chilies. Surprising as it may seem, the flavors are extremely compatible. Depending upon your preference, use more or less crushed red pepper.

1 tablespoon olive oil

¹/₂ cup sliced onions

¹/₄ teaspoon fennel seeds, lightly crushed

¹/₄ to 1 teaspoon crushed red pepper

1 cup white wine, chicken stock, or water

1 vanilla bean or ¹/₄ teaspoon pure vanilla extract

¹/₂ cup peeled, seeded, and chopped tomatoes with juices

1 teaspoon minced fresh oregano or ¹/₂ teaspoon dried oregano

1 pound skinless scrod or sea bass fillets, cut into 2 serving portions

1 teaspoon fresh lime or lemon juice

Kosher salt

2 teaspoons minced Italian flat-leaf parsley

MAKES 2 SERVINGS

1. Heat the oil in a saucepan over medium-high heat and add the onions, fennel, and red pepper. Cook, stirring, until the onions are wilted and the spices give off fragrance, about 3 minutes. Add the wine and vanilla bean and bring contents to a boil. Simmer the sauce, uncovered, for 4 minutes.

2. Remove the vanilla bean and add the tomatoes and oregano. Cook for 3 minutes, or until the sauce is slightly reduced. Add the fish and cook, basting with the sauce, for 2 minutes, or until the fish is barely white and opaque. Turn off the heat. Add the lemon juice and season with salt to taste.

3. Remove the fish to serving plates. Spoon the sauce over, garnish with parsley, and serve.

Serving Suggestions: Start the meal with Chilled Borscht with Caraway (page 121) or Iced Pear Soup with Mint (page 126). Serve the fish with Parsley Rice (page 192), Curried Rice (page 194), or Cumin Potatoes (page 215). Peach Ice Cream with Marjoram (page 267) will make a fine ending to this meal.

red snapper with anise-tomato sauce

A very common way to sauce fish in the eastern Mediterranean region is with anise and olives. The play of sweet licorice anise and saline olives on the distinct flavor of red snapper is indeed magical. For the best flavor, use Greek kalamata or French niçoise olives. You can also make this dish with catfish or sea bass.

2$\frac{1}{2}$ tablespoons olive oil

1 tablespoon thinly sliced garlic

$\frac{1}{4}$ cup minced shallots

$\frac{1}{4}$ teaspoon anise seeds, lightly crushed

1 tablespoon capers, drained and rinsed

1 cup peeled, seeded, and chopped tomatoes with juices

$\frac{1}{4}$ cup white wine, chicken stock, or water

1 teaspoon grated orange zest

2 tablespoons finely chopped pitted black olives

Freshly ground black pepper and kosher salt

4 red snapper fillets, boneless with skin (about 6 ounces each)

2 tablespoons all-purpose flour

Sprigs of cilantro or parsley, for garnish

MAKES 4 SERVINGS

1. Heat 1 tablespoon of the oil in a saucepan over medium-high heat. Add the garlic and shallots and cook for 3 minutes, or until soft. Stir in the anise, capers, tomatoes, and wine. Increase the heat and boil until the excess moisture evaporates and the sauce thickens, about 5 minutes. Turn off the heat and stir in the orange zest and olives. Season to taste with pepper and salt. Cover and keep warm while you fry the fish.

2. Heat the remaining 1$\frac{1}{2}$ tablespoons oil in a nonstick frying pan over high heat. When the oil is hot, dust the fish lightly with flour and put in the pan, skin side down. Reduce the heat to medium and cook until the fish is browned and almost opaque, about 4 minutes. Turn and cook for 1 minute more. Remove the fish to a serving plate. Spoon the sauce over and serve garnished with cilantro or parsley.

Serving Suggestions: For a complete seafood meal, start with Peppery Squid Puffs (page 107) or Kale Soup with Crabmeat and Thyme (page 124). To complete the meal serve Parsley Rice (page 192), Linguine with Cilantro Sauce (page 186) or Pumpkin with Allspice (page 216), and Sesame Pita Bread (page 249).

shrimp sauté with bay

This is an old Bengal Lancers recipe from the East India Company. It is an incredibly simple sauté of shrimps in bay-infused oil. Bay leaves lend a balmy, springlike flavor to shrimps. These are good hot, at room temperature, and cold. For best results use tiny shrimps; they are more flavorful than the larger more impressive-looking ones.

3 bay leaves

1 tablespoon canola or olive oil

1 tablespoon finely chopped garlic

¼ cup white wine or chicken stock

1 small Italian plum tomato, unpeeled and minced, or 1 tablespoon tomato paste

2 pounds small shrimps, shelled and deveined, with or without the tails left on

Freshly ground black pepper and kosher salt

Grated zest of 1 small lemon

2 teaspoons fresh lemon juice

¼ cup finely chopped parsley

MAKES 4 TO 6 SERVINGS

1. Cook the bay leaves in the oil in a large heavy skillet over medium-high heat, stirring, until the spice gives off fragrance and turns brown. Add the garlic and cook just until it turns pale gold. Mix the wine and minced tomato and stir in. Cook until the sauce reduces to a paste, about 3 minutes.

2. Increase the heat to high and add the shrimps, stirring to coat evenly with the spice mixture. Sauté, stirring, until the shrimps turn pink and curl up, about 2 minutes. Season to taste with pepper and salt. Remove the bay leaves and discard. Add lemon peel, lemon juice, and parsley. Toss well and serve hot or at room temperature. Or refrigerate for at least 4 hours and serve cold. (*The shrimps keep well, tightly covered, for up to 2 days in the refrigerator.*)

Serving Suggestions: Start the meal with Tomato Soup with Basil Cream (page 127). Complete the meal with Curried Rice (page 194), Green Beans in Mustard Sauce (page 204), and Cranberry Relish with Apricots, Walnuts, and Cinnamon (page 237).

steamed lobster in juniper berry vapor

In a new twist on an old summertime favorite, juniper lends a very delicate, spicy scent to the lobsters while they steam in its vapor. Even more wonderful—the aroma is not lost when the lobsters cool. They stay fresh and sweet tasting for several days in the refrigerator. You can have cooked lobster on hand for, for example, Lobster Sandwich with Curry Mayonnaise (page 85). Some great hot condiments to serve alongside the steamed lobster are Hot Wasabi Dipping Sauce (page 229), Green Chili Vinegar (page 76), Smoked Chili Pepper Oil (page 88), or Harissa (page 78), thinned with water.

1 teaspoon juniper berries, crushed

2 live lobsters (about 1½ pounds each)

MAKES 2 SERVINGS

Bring a large pot of water, enough to fully submerge both lobsters, to a boil. Add the juniper berries and let the water boil, covered, for 2 minutes. Add the lobsters and cover the pot. Cook, rapidly boiling, for 10 minutes. Remove the lobsters from the pot and serve immediately. Or when the lobsters are cool enough to handle, shell them and remove the meat in large chunks. (*Lobster meat keeps well, tightly covered, for 3 days in the refrigerator. Chop the lobster meat, according to need, only when ready to use.*)

Serving Suggestions: Begin the meal with an appetizer like Marinated Mozzarella with Thyme (page 102) or Spicy Tomato Spread (page 99) served with Thyme Pita Bread (page 248). To finish the meal, serve Mushrooms with Nutmeg (page 213) with Parsley Rice (page 192).

cajun shrimp boil

Less hot and more fragrant than the classic New Orleans crawfish boil, but like the original, great for entertaining a crowd outdoors, especially in summer. The shrimps are cooked with vegetables, so all you need to round off the meal is bread and a couple of dipping sauces.

MAKES 4 SERVINGS

¼ cup Cajun Spice Blend
(page 58)

3 quarts water, light chicken
stock, or a combination of
low-sodium canned broth
and water

3 cups white wine or more of
the water and/or stock

Kosher salt

¼ cup finely chopped cilantro

1 pound very small red
potatoes, preferably all the
same size, scrubbed

½ pound green beans, tipped

2 pounds jumbo shrimps shell
on, scrubbed and deveined

1 pound spinach leaves,
rinsed and cut into
chiffonade, shredded or
finely cut (optional)

2 lemons, cut into wedges

1. Combine the Cajun spices, water, and wine in a deep pot and bring to a boil. Reduce the heat and simmer for 10 minutes, or until the spices are cooked and give off a mellow aroma. Stir in salt to taste and the cilantro and potatoes. Cover and cook for 15 minutes. Add the green beans and continue to cook, covered, until the vegetables are soft, about 10 minutes.

2. Add the shrimps and continue to cook, stirring, until the liquid comes to a boil. If you are not using the spinach, turn off the heat. If you are using it, fold it in and as soon as it wilts, turn off the heat. Drain the shrimps and vegetables and arrange on a large platter with the lemon wedges. Serve.

Note: If you like spicy flavors, reserve the broth and use it to thin sauces or vinegar, or even cook sausages and hot dogs. It is also a very good base for making tomato sauce. (*The broth may be strained and stored, tightly covered, indefinitely in the refrigerator s long as it is brought to a full boil every 24 hours, or indefinitely in the freezer.*)

cajun lobster boil: Substitute 2 small live lobsters, about 1½ pounds each, for the shrimps. Cook lobsters for 10 minutes after the liquid comes to a boil. Omit the spinach. Makes 2 servings. Follow the same serving suggestions as for Cajun Shrimp Boil.

Serving Suggestions: For dipping sauces, serve Tahini Dip (page 80), Cilantro-Walnut Dip (page 229), Sweet Sesame Dipping Sauce (page 227), and Cool Yogurt Dill Sauce with Dried Cranberries and Almonds (page 230). For bread, serve Parmesan-Chive Puffs (page 243), Currant and Mace Puffs (page 242), Raisin and Caraway Rolls (page 245), and Mini Pita with Basil and Dried Tomatoes (page 250).

poultry and meat

pot roast of chicken with rosemary, figs, and pine nuts

Pot-roasting, or braising, is one of the most popular ways of cooking poultry and meat all over the world. It is a hassle-free, ingenious method of transforming ordinary poultry and tough cuts of meat into mouth-watering delicacies. In this dish, a whole skinned chicken is pot-roasted with rosemary and garlic. Fresh figs add more flavor and also diffuse the intense perfume of rosemary. Use fresh figs if possible: They fall apart easily, thus enhancing and thickening the sauce. Although not essential, pine nuts lend a creamy mellowness to the dish.

1 pint fresh figs or ³/₄ cup (8 ounces) dried California mission figs

1 fryer chicken (about 3¹/₂ pounds)

6 sprigs of fresh rosemary

6 large cloves garlic, mashed

2 tablespoons canola oil

³/₄ cup chopped onions

6 whole cloves, crushed

1 tomato, finely chopped

²/₃ cup white wine or water

Freshly ground black pepper

1 teaspoon kosher salt

¹/₄ cup pine nuts, toasted (optional)

MAKES 6 SERVINGS

1. Preheat the oven to 350°F.

2. Cut half of the figs into small dice and leave the rest whole. Skin the chicken and remove all visible fat. Rinse and pat the chicken dry. Stuff the rosemary and 4 cloves of the garlic into the cavity and truss the chicken.

3. Heat 1 tablespoon of the oil in a Dutch oven or heavy lidded casserole over high heat until very hot. Place the chicken, breast side down, in the oil and let it brown for 2 minutes. Turn the chicken over, breast side up, and continue to brown for 1 minute more. Place the chicken on its side and brown for 2 minutes, turn it over to brown the other side for 2 minutes, and remove it to a plate.

4. Add the remaining tablespoon of oil to the pan. Add the onion and the remaining 2 cloves of garlic. Cook over medium–high heat for 4 minutes, or until the onions are lightly colored. Add the cloves, figs, both whole and chopped, tomato, and wine. Place the chicken, breast side down, in the casserole. Cover the casserole with a piece of aluminum foil and secure tightly with the lid.

5. Bake in the middle level of the oven for 50 minutes, or until the chicken is tender and the juices run clear when the thigh is pierced. Remove from the oven, uncover, and transfer the chicken to a cutting board. Remove and discard the trussing string, rosemary, and garlic cloves. (If you like garlic, do not discard it.) Cover with foil and keep warm. Boil the fig sauce until thick, like gravy. Carve the chicken and place on a heated platter. Spoon the sauce over the chicken and scatter the pine nuts, if using, on top. Serve immediately

Serving Suggestions: Serve the pot roast with Orange-Cinnamon Pilaf (page 196), Brussels Sprouts with Fennel (page 206), and Apple-Mustard Salsa (page 233).

chicken braised in cardamom sauce

Cardamom is one of those special spices that combines well in both sweet and savory dishes. In this dish, chicken is braised in a cardamom-flavored sauce. The cardamom heightens the sweetness of the onions and almonds in the sauce.

2 tablespoons oil

1 fryer chicken, skinned and cut into 4 pieces (about 3¹/₂ pounds)

1 cup thinly sliced onions

2 teaspoons ground cardamom

2 tablespoons ground coriander

1 teaspoon ground black pepper

¹/₄ cup sliced blanched almonds

1¹/₂ cups plain nonfat yogurt

Kosher salt

¹/₄ cup sliced almonds, toasted

MAKES 4 SERVINGS

1. Preheat the oven to 350°F.

2. Heat 1 tablespoon of the oil in a nonstick sauté pan over medium-high heat. Add the chicken pieces and cook, turning often, for 5 minutes, or until the chicken turns opaque. Remove and arrange the pieces in a small Dutch oven or ovenproof casserole.

3. Add the remaining tablespoon of oil and the onions to the sauté pan. Cook for 3 minutes, or until the onions are wilted. Stir in the cardamom, coriander, black pepper, and blanched almonds and cook until the nuts are pale gold, about 2 minutes. Turn off the heat.

4. Transfer the mixture to a food processor. Add yogurt and process until smoothly pureed. Season to taste with salt and pour over the chicken. Bake, covered, in the middle level of the oven for 50 minutes, or until chicken is tender and the juices run clear when the thigh is pierced. Garnish with toasted almonds, and serve with sauce.

Serving Suggestions: Accompany the chicken with Orange-Cinnamon Pilaf (page 196), Seared Pears with Cloves (page 219), and Fresh Tomato-Ginger Sauce (page 227).

chicken with basil

The strong penetrating aroma of basil complements chicken in this adaptation of the famous Thai dish, chicken with basil. Use holy basil, also called Thai basil or licorice basil (see page 8), in this dish if you can find it. It has an extra layer of anise and pepper that sweet basil lacks. Coconut milk fuses the many flavors in the sauce and enriches it. It is not necessary to make coconut milk from scratch; canned coconut milk from Thailand works very well. You need to check its consistency, however, since some are coconut cream, thick as heavy cream, and have to be diluted with an equal amount of water. If you like, you can make this dish with vegetables instead of chicken, a combination of small eggplants, zucchini, pumpkin, sweet potatoes, and green beans, for example.

2 whole boneless and skinless
  chicken breasts (about
  1 pound each)

1 cup chicken stock or low-
  sodium canned broth

1 cup coconut milk, freshly
  made or canned (see Note)

1 teaspoon minced fresh
  chilies

1 star anise

1 teaspoon ground coriander

Kosher salt

1 tablespoon canola oil

1 teaspoon minced garlic

1 cup (packed) basil leaves

1/3 cup unsalted peanuts

MAKES 4 SERVINGS

1. Trim the chicken of all visible fat and cut, lengthwise, in half. Cut each half on the diagonal into 1-inch-wide strips.

2. Combine the chicken stock, coconut milk, chilies, star anise, and coriander in a medium saucepan over medium heat and bring to a boil. Boil the sauce, covered, for 7 minutes, or until reduced to 1 cup. Stir in the chicken. Cook, stirring, for 4 minutes, or until the chicken turns white. Turn off the heat. Add salt to taste.

3. Heat the oil in a frying pan over medium–high heat. When the oil is hot, add the garlic. When the garlic begins to turn golden, about 2 minutes, add the basil. Reduce the heat and sauté, turning with tongs, until all the basil leaves wilt. Turn off the heat.

4. Add the basil mixture to the chicken, scraping with a rubber spatula. Mix well. Transfer the chicken to a platter, garnish with peanuts, and serve.

Note: To make 1 cup of fresh coconut milk, start by piercing the "eyes" of a coconut and pouring out the liquid. Bake the coconut at 375°F. for 25 minutes, or until the shell cracks. Tap it all around, then give it a hard whack. The meat should fall away from the shell; if not, loosen it with a knife. Peel off the skin and cut the meat into 1-inch pieces. Grate as much as you need in a food processor or blender. Combine 1 cup (tightly packed) grated coconut with 1 cup of boiling water or milk. Cover and soak for 30 minutes. Pour into a food processor or blender and puree. Strain through a double layer of dampened cheesecloth, squeezing the pulp as much as possible.

Serving Suggestions: Accompany the chicken with Curried Rice (page 194) and Pumpkin with Allspice (page 216) and, if desired, serve a condiment like Cranberry Relish with Apricots, Walnuts, and Cinnamon (page 237).

roasted chicken legs with sage

The thought alone of sage-rubbed chicken conjures up memories of autumn wind and winter holidays. Sage lends a fresh aroma, reminiscent of mountain breezes, that I so love. You can cook as few as one chicken leg or as many as fit in your oven. Just increase or decrease the ingredients proportionally; the cooking time remains the same. Since the chicken is skinned before roasting, it is very light tasting. Misting keeps it moist.

2 whole chicken legs, skinned and trimmed of all visible fat

2 teaspoons olive oil

2 teaspoons minced garlic

8 large fresh sage leaves, minced, or ¹⁄₂ teaspoon dried ground sage

1 teaspoon minced fresh thyme or ¹⁄₂ teaspoon dried thyme

¹⁄₄ teaspoon ground cinnamon

¹⁄₂ teaspoon freshly ground black pepper

¹⁄₄ teaspoon kosher salt

Water-oil mist (see Note)

2 sprigs of sage, for garnish

MAKES 2 SERVINGS

1. Preheat the oven to 375°F.

2. Place the chicken legs in a shallow dish. Combine the olive oil, garlic, sage, thyme, cinnamon, pepper, and salt and rub the mixture over the chicken. Set aside for 15 minutes.

3. Place the legs on a rack in a roasting pan. Roast in the middle level of the oven for 40 minutes, or until the chicken is tender and the juices run clear when the thigh is pierced at the thickest part. Spray with water-oil mist 2 times during roasting. Remove from the oven and serve warm or at room temperature.

Note: Combine equal amounts of olive oil and water in a spray bottle and shake well before each use. To add sage aroma to the mist, pour ¹⁄₂ cup boiling water over 2 tablespoons minced fresh sage leaves in a small bowl. Cover and set aside to cool. Strain the sage water into the bottle and add ¹⁄₂ cup olive oil.

Serving Suggestions: To complete the meal, serve Curried Rice (page 194), Smothered Cabbage with Caraway (page 207), and Cranberry Relish with Apricots, Walnuts, and Cinnamon (page 237).

pomegranate braised chicken

One of the finest ways to cook chicken is to braise it in a walnut-pomegranate sauce like this one of royal Persian origin. The piquant pomegranate contrasts with the sweet rich walnuts, and together they lend the dish extraordinary texture and flavor. Ideally, freshly pressed pomegranate juice should be used, but pomegranate molasses works well here.

1 large fryer chicken (3½ to 4¼ pounds)

Freshly ground black pepper and kosher salt

1 cup walnuts

4 pitted dates

2 cups fresh tart pomegranate juice or 3 tablespoons pomegranate molasses (see page 42) mixed with 2 cups chicken stock or low-sodium canned broth

1 tablespoon Hungarian paprika

3 tablespoons light vegetable oil

2 cups finely chopped onions

Juice of ½ lemon

1 cup fresh pomegranate seeds (optional)

MAKES 4 SERVINGS

1. Skin the chicken and remove all visible fat. Cut the chicken into 4 serving pieces. Sprinkle with pepper and salt. Set aside.

2. Place the walnuts, dates, and ½ cup pomegranate juice in a food processor and process until pureed, adding more liquid as needed. Transfer the sauce to a bowl and stir in the remaining pomegranate juice and the paprika. Set aside.

3. Heat 1 tablespoon of the oil in a large nonstick sauté pan over high heat. Add the chicken and sear, turning the pieces often, until lightly colored, about 3 minutes. Remove to a platter. Add the remaining oil and the onions to the pan. Cook, stirring, for 10 minutes or until the onions are browned. Return the chicken to the pan. Add the pomegranate mixture and bring to a boil.

4. Cook, covered, over medium-low heat for 15 minutes, or until the chicken is almost tender. Uncover and continue to cook, basting the chicken, until the sauce is thick and shiny, about 5 minutes. To serve, transfer the chicken to a bowl. Taste the sauce and adjust the seasoning. Divide among 4 dinner plates. Arrange 1 piece of chicken on each plate, sprinkle with lemon juice, and scatter pomegranate seeds, if using, over the top. Serve immediately.

pomegranate braised quail: Substitute 8 ready-to-cook skinless quails for the chicken and proceed as directed.

pomegranate braised duck: Substitute one 5-pound duck, skin removed and all visible fat trimmed, for the chicken and proceed as directed.

Serving Suggestions: Serve the chicken with Mint Pilaf (page 195), Turmeric Cauliflower (page 209), and Apple-Mustard Salsa (page 233).

thyme roasted chicken

One of the most straightforward ways that I know of to cook chicken. An herb paste is rubbed directly on the chicken meat—under the skin—for maximum infusion of favor, and during and after roasting, the chicken is kept breast side down so that the fragrant juices flow right into the white meat. As a result, the chicken is very moist and flavorful. I usually peel off the skin, which is saturated with fat, before serving; therefore sogginess due to moisture is of no concern. You will get much finer results with fresh and free-range chicken than with frozen chicken.

1 large fryer chicken (3½ to 4½ pounds)

1 tablespoon chopped fresh thyme or 2 teaspoons dried thyme

2 teaspoons minced garlic

1 teaspoon grated lemon zest

1 tablespoon unsalted butter

1 tablespoon fresh lemon juice

1 tablespoon olive oil

½ teaspoon fennel seeds

¼ teaspoon ground red pepper

MAKES 4 SERVINGS

1. Rinse and pat the chicken dry. Remove all visible fat. Cut off the wing tips. Combine the thyme, garlic, lemon zest, and butter. Loosen the skin and insert the herb mixture under it, spreading the mixture over the breast and thigh.

2. Combine the lemon juice, oil, and fennel and rub the chicken inside and out. Sprinkle with red pepper and set aside for 15 minutes.

3. Preheat the oven to 425°F.

4. Place the chicken, breast side down, on a rack in a roasting pan. Roast in the middle level of the oven for 15 minutes. Turn the chicken on the side and roast for 15 minutes more. Turn the chicken on the other side and roast for 15 minutes more. Finally, place the chicken on its back and roast for 20 to 25 minutes, or until the chicken is tender and the juices run clear when the chicken is pierced between the thigh and the drumstick.

5. Remove the chicken from the oven and let stand, breast side down, for 10 minutes. Turn the chicken over on its back. If desired, remove the skin. Scrape off any herb mixture that clings to it and spread it over the chicken. Discard the skin. Carve the chicken and serve.

Serving Suggestions: Precede the chicken with Black Bean Soup with Epazote (page 115) or Chilled Carrot Soup with Mace (page 119). To complete the meal, serve Green Beans in Mustard Sauce (page 204), Yellow Tomato and Green Peppercorn Salsa (page 235), and Tomato-Cumin Rice (page 193).

barbecued tarragon game hens with quick cherry coulis

Rock Cornish game hens stuffed with tarragon are great cooked on the grill. Because they are stuffed under the skin, the herbs remain moist and fragrant without getting charred and the hens stay juicy. Although they are delicious by themselves, a special cherry coulis, prepared quickly on the side, adds special flair. The recipe works extremely well for entertaining a large crowd outdoors since all the preparations are done in advance.

3 tablespoons chopped fresh tarragon leaves or a pinch of ground star anise

3 tablespoons chopped parsley

1 tablespoon minced garlic

1 tablespoon minced fresh chilies, seeds discarded

2 tablespoons Tomato-Ginger Jam (page 271), or apricot jam

4 Rock Cornish game hens, halved (1½ pounds each)

¾ cup dry white wine

¾ cup fresh lemon juice

2 tablespoons minced shallots

Olive oil spray

1 cup Quick Cherry Coulis (recipe follows)

MAKES 8 SERVINGS

1. Combine the tarragon, parsley, garlic, chilies, and jam in a small bowl.

2. Rinse and pat the hens dry. Loosen the skin and insert about 1 tablespoon of the herb mixture under the skin of each half-hen, spreading the mixture over the breast and thigh.

3. Combine the wine, lemon juice, and shallots in a large glass baking dish. Place the hens in the marinade and let marinate for at least 4 hours or overnight in the refrigerator, turning once. Take the hens out of the refrigerator 30 minutes before cooking.

4. Preheat the grill. Adjust the rack about 5 inches from the heat source and brush the rack with oil.

5. Remove the hens from the marinade, spray with oil, and place on the rack. Cook, turning a few times, for about 10 to 15 minutes on each side, or until the juices run clear when the thigh is pricked with a fork. Serve garnished with Quick Cherry Coulis.

Serving Suggestions: A nice appetizer with the game hens is Chili-stuffed Prawns (page 104). Serve the hens with Summer Peach Pilaf with Bay (page 197), Avocado, Onion, and Cilantro Relish (page 231), Lentil and Endive Salad with Juniper Berries (page 171), Mini Pita with Basil and Dried Tomatoes (page 250), and a beverage like Raspberry Tea with Sage (page 283).

quick cherry coulis

MAKES 1 CUP

1 cup chopped pitted fresh or frozen cherries

1 tablespoon fresh lemon juice

2 tablespoons sugar

1 teaspoon ground ginger

1/4 cup white wine

1 teaspoon cornstarch

Combine all the ingredients in a small saucepan over medium-low heat. Bring to a boil, stirring constantly, until the sauce thickens. Turn off the heat. Cool completely, then cover and refrigerate until needed. Reheat at serving time.

chicken and papaya salad with pomegranate dressing

2 cups cooked chicken, cut into 1/2-inch pieces

1/2 cup walnuts or peanuts, coarsely chopped

1 ripe papaya, peeled, seeded, and cut into 1/2-inch dice pieces

1/3 cup minced red onion

1 head radicchio, leaves separated and shredded

1/3 cup fresh tart pomegranate juice or 2 teaspoons pomegranate molasses (see page 42) mixed with 3 tablespoons orange juice

2 teaspoons finely chopped garlic

2 teaspoons finely chopped fresh ginger

1/4 cup finely chopped cilantro

1 to 2 teaspoons minced fresh chilies

1 teaspoon cumin seeds, toasted and crushed

Kosher salt (optional)

Although the idea of this dish is to use up leftover cooked chicken, I often roast a whole chicken just so I can make this wonderful salad. It is perfect for a buffet or picnic. The list of ingredients may seem intimidating, but all you have to do is combine them. The complexity of flavors heightens the effect on the palate. Once assembled, the salad must be eaten right away. The pomegranate juice draws moisture out of the ingredients, and the papain in the papaya breaks down the chicken if the salad is left to stand for any length of time.

MAKES 4 MAIN COURSE SERVINGS, 8 BUFFET SERVINGS

Just before serving, combine the chicken, walnuts, papaya, onion, radicchio, pomegranate juice, garlic, ginger, cilantro, chilies, and cumin in a large shallow ceramic bowl and toss. Taste for seasoning and add salt, if desired, and serve.

Serving Suggestions: This salad is a meal in itself accompanied with an assortment of breads, including Stuffed Sage Roti Bread with Olives (page 251), Parmesan-Chive Puffs (page 243), Cumin Crackers (page 111), and Raisin and Caraway Rolls (page 245).

grilled chicken kabobs with anise

These chicken kabobs are of Lebanese origin. In that part of the world, simple lemon-onion marinades are often infused with one or two spices, which lend a delicate flavor and also help tenderize the meat. You can make these kabobs with beef, lamb, or a firm fish like sea bass, turbot, or monkfish.

1 whole skinless and boneless
chicken breast (about
1½ pounds)

1 teaspoon ground anise
seeds

1 tablespoon minced fresh
mint or 2 teaspoons dried
mint, crushed

½ cup fresh lemon juice

½ cup grated or pureed onion

Freshly ground black pepper
and kosher salt

1 large red bell pepper,
stemmed, seeded, and cut
into 1½-inch pieces

1 portobello mushroom, cut
into ¼-inch slices, or 6 small
white button mushrooms

1 large onion, cut into
1½-inch pieces

Olive oil spray

MAKES 4 SERVINGS

1. Trim any visible fat from the chicken. Cut the meat into 1½-inch pieces and place in a bowl. Add the anise, mint, lemon juice, grated onion, and pepper and salt to taste. Toss to coat the meat. Cover and set aside for 30 minutes or refrigerate overnight.

2. Preheat a charcoal grill or an oven broiler. Soak 8 bamboo skewers in water.

3. Add the pepper, mushroom, and cut-up onion to the chicken. Toss to coat the vegetables with the marinade. Alternating vegetables with chicken, thread pieces on the skewers. Reserve the marinade. Spray with olive oil.

4. If barbecuing, arrange the skewers on the rack. If broiling, put the skewers on the broiler pan and place it under the broiler, 4 to 5 inches from the heat. Cook for 8 minutes, turning and basting with the marinade. Do not overcook as the chicken dries out easily. Serve 2 skewers per person on individual plates. Serve immediately.

Serving Suggestions: For starters, serve Avocado Spread with Tahini (page 81) and Marinated Mozzarella and Carrots in Harissa Sauce (page 79). Serve the kabobs accompanied with Tahini Dip (page 80), Cool Yogurt Dill Sauce with Dried Cranberries and Almonds (page 230), Glazed Carrots with Cloves (page 208), Orange-Cinnamon Pilaf (page 196), and a basket of Sesame Pita Bread (page 249).

roast duck with hot pepper and plums

Glazed to a rich red-brown, peppery sweet duck can form the centerpiece of any holiday table. The recipe is very versatile. In place of plums, you can substitute any other sweet-sour fruit, such as peach, apricot, orange, nectarine, persimmon, pear, or raspberries. For the duck, you can substitute chicken, squab, or quail. The fruity-floral accents of the sauce complement all poultry.

1 duck, skin and all visible fat removed, cut in half (4 to 5 pounds)

8 pearl onions, peeled and cut in half

Olive oil spray

1½ pounds purple plums

1 teaspoon ground cinnamon

1 teaspoon dried ginger

1 teaspoon ground red pepper

2 tablespoons sugar

1 teaspoon grated lemon zest

¼ cup dried cranberries or golden raisins

2 sprigs of mint

MAKES 2 SERVINGS

1. Preheat the oven to 425°F.

2. Heat a nonstick frying pan over high heat. Spray the duck and pearl onions lightly with oil and place in the frying pan. Cook until the duck is seared and the onions are brown. Remove the duck and place in a small baking dish that will hold the 2 halves snugly in a single layer. Scatter the onions over them.

3. Reserve 2 plums for garnish. Pit and slice the remaining plums. Puree to a smooth sauce in a food mill. Stir in cinnamon, ginger, red pepper, sugar, lemon zest, and dried cranberries. Pour the sauce over the duck.

4. Cover the dish loosely with foil and bake in the middle level of the oven for 30 minutes. Reduce the heat to 350°F. and bake for 30 minutes more, or until the juices run clear when the thigh is pierced. While the duck is cooking, pit and slice the remaining 2 plums.

5. Serve the duck and onions with the sauce spooned over. Garnish each plate with plum slices and mint.

Serving Suggestions: Begin with a soup such as Winter Bean Soup with Bay Leaf (page 117). Accompany the duck with Seared Pears with Cloves (page 219), Brussels Sprouts with Fennel (page 206), Polenta with Green Peppercorns (page 191), and Currant and Mace Puffs (page 242).

steamed duck with star anise

This is my version of the classic anise-flavored steamed duck so popular in Chinese cooking. The meat is fat-free yet moist, and the prolonged marinating and steaming allow the flavor of star anise to penetrate the meat so thoroughly that you don't even need a condiment to enjoy the dish—though I do suggest wasabi sauce for those who want one. In addition to lending its lovely sweet licorice scent, star anise helps the duck stay fresh tasting longer. To prevent the star anise from overpowering the flavor of the duck, be sure to remove the spice from the duck cavity before refrigerating. The duck can be served hot, at room temperature, or cold.

1 orange

1 duck (4 to 5 pounds)

1 teaspoon black
   peppercorns, crushed to a
   coarse powder

1 teaspoon whole allspice,
   crushed to a coarse powder

3 star anise, broken into
   chunks

1 teaspoon kosher salt

MAKES 2 TO 4 SERVINGS

1. Grate the zest of the orange and put it in a bowl. Squeeze the juice and strain it into the bowl. Stir in the peppercorns, allspice, star anise, and salt and set aside. Save the orange halves.

2. Trim all the excess fat off the duck and discard. Place the duck in a baking dish and rub the orange-pepper-allspice mixture, reserving the star anise, over and under the skin by sliding your fingers between the skin and the meat. Add orange pulp and stuff the cavity with the orange halves and star anise. Sew or skewer closed. Loosely cover the duck with plastic wrap and refrigerate for 8 hours or overnight.

3. Bring water to a boil in a steamer large enough to hold the duck. Place the duck on the steamer rack and steam for 2 to 2½ hours, or until the juices run clear when the thigh is pierced. Remove the duck from the steamer. Scoop out the stuffing and discard. Serve hot, at room temperature, or refrigerate for at least 4 hours and serve cold. (*Let the duck cool thoroughly, wrap in aluminum foil, and refrigerate. The duck may be kept, well wrapped, for up to 2 days in the refrigerator.*)

4. When ready to serve, place the duck on a cutting board. Remove the skin and, if desired, the bones and discard. Cut the duck into 4 to 6 serving pieces, arrange on a platter, and serve.

Serving Suggestions: Serve with Sweet-and-Hot Wasabi Sauce (page 86) or Hot Wasabi Dipping Sauce (page 229). To complete the meal, serve Glazed Cucumbers with Sesame (page 212) and Penne with Mushrooms and Crushed Red Pepper (page 189).

lamb shanks in black pepper sauce

A hearty lamb stew, warm with the heat of black pepper, is very welcome on cold winter days. I like to make it with lamb shanks, stewing them slowly (a crock pot works very well) so that the flavors mellow and the meat develops buttery tenderness. Lamb shank is a fatty cut of meat; trim off the fat as carefully as possible, leaving the parchmentlike covering so that the meat doesn't fall apart. Black pepper is added to the dish at the very last minute to keep its pungent aroma and flavor highly pronounced.

1 piece (2 inches) fresh ginger

6 large cloves garlic

3 ripe tomatoes (about 1 pound), peeled and chopped

2 lamb shanks, trimmed of fat (about 1 pound each)

1 cup chicken stock, low-sodium canned broth, or water

Kosher salt

1 tablespoon vegetable oil

1 cup thinly sliced onions

1 to 2 teaspoons freshly cracked black pepper

$^1/_2$ cup chopped cilantro, leaves and tender stems

MAKES 2 SERVINGS

1. Combine the ginger, garlic, and tomatoes in a food processor and process to a smooth puree. Pour the sauce into a large heavy-bottomed pan. Add the lamb shanks and stock and bring to a boil. Lower the heat and cook, covered, until the lamb is very tender, at least $1^1/_2$ hours. If the moisture evaporates too fast, add more stock. Taste and add salt to taste.

2. Heat the oil in a frying pan over medium-high heat. Add the onions, stirring until lightly browned, about 7 minutes. Stir in the pepper and cilantro. Pour the onion mixture over the lamb shanks, mix well, and serve.

Serving Suggestions: Accompany the lamb shanks with Saffron Pilaf with Peas and Almonds (page 199), Lentil and Endive Salad with Juniper Berries (page 171), and Green Beans in Mustard Sauce (page 204).

ginger ragout of lamb

A great dish to make for entertaining, especially for a large crowd. Simply multiply all the ingredients, proportionally, except the stock. (With larger amounts of meat, you can use less stock, relatively speaking.) And, you can make the ragout several days ahead. Besides lending a floral touch, the ginger in the ragout helps the lamb stay fresh longer. I prefer to make the dish with lamb shoulder, which is juicier and more flavorful than leg of lamb in a sauce—and much cheaper. On the other hand, lamb shoulder takes almost twice as long to cook. Choose the cut according to what suits your needs.

2 cups finely chopped onions

2 tablespoons canola oil

1 tablespoon minced garlic

2 tablespoons Curry Powder (page 56)

1/3 cup finely julienned fresh ginger

2 cups pureed tomato, fresh or canned

1 tablespoon tomato paste

3 pounds boneless lean lamb, shoulder or leg, cut into 1-inch pieces

1 cup chicken stock or low-sodium canned broth

Kosher salt

1/2 cup finely chopped mixed herbs (a combination of mint, basil, and cilantro)

MAKES 8 SERVINGS

1. Combine the onions and oil in a large heavy-bottomed saucepan and cook, stirring, over medium-high heat. When the onions are very soft, about 8 minutes, stir in the garlic and Curry Powder and cook for 5 minutes, or until the curry loses its raw aroma. Add the ginger, tomato, tomato paste, lamb, and stock. Mix well and bring to a boil.

2. Lower the heat and simmer, covered, for 2 1/2 hours for lamb shoulder, 1 1/2 hours for leg of lamb, or until the lamb is fork tender. Check and stir often during cooking, adding more liquid if necessary. Turn off the heat and season to taste with pepper and salt. (*The ragout keeps well, tightly covered, for up to 5 days in the refrigerator. Reheat before proceeding. Taste and adjust the seasoning if necessary.*) Fold in half the herbs and serve garnished with the rest.

Serving Suggestions: Accompany the ragout with Saffron Pilaf with Peas and Almonds (page 199), Pan-grilled Pineapple with Young Ginger (page 222), Chick Pea Salad with Cumin (page 172), and Apple-Mustard Salsa (page 233).

pepper-rubbed rack of lamb

Here is an elegant and beautifully flavored dish that takes very little time to cook. All you do is coat the lamb with the pepper-herb mix and roast it. Be careful not to overcook the meat: It should remain slightly pink in the center. A rack of lamb consists of several loin chops. It is the most delicate and tender piece of lamb but also an expensive cut. Save this recipe for a special occasion or a celebration.

1 trimmed rack of lamb
(1½ to 1¾ pounds)

2 teaspoons olive oil

2 tablespoons prune butter
(lekvar) or pureed
apricot jam

1 tablespoon coarse-grain
mustard

2 tablespoons Five Pepper Mix
(page 68)

2 tablespoons minced parsley

½ cup freshly made fine
bread crumbs

MAKES 2 SERVINGS

1. Rub the lamb evenly with the oil. Heat a heavy skillet over high heat until very hot. Place the lamb in the skillet and sear, turning, until browned all over, about 2 minutes. Remove and let cool completely.

2. Preheat the oven to 450°F.

3. Combine the prune butter and mustard in a small bowl and spread it evenly over the lamb. In another small bowl, combine the Five Pepper Mix, parsley, and bread crumbs. Coat the lamb with the seasoned bread crumbs, pressing to ensure they adhere to the meat.

4. Arrange the lamb on a rack placed in a baking pan. Roast in the middle level of the oven for 20 minutes for medium-rare. Cook longer for well done. Remove from the oven, carve into separate chops, and serve.

Serving Suggestions: Start the meal with a soup like Red Lentil Soup with Bay Leaf and Pepper Cream (page 120). Accompany the lamb with Orange-Cinnamon Pilaf (page 196), Apple Compote with Fennel (page 221), and Yellow Tomato and Green Peppercorn Salsa (page 235).

rosemary-crusted veal chops

I cook veal chops in the oven because I find that open grilling dries out this very lean—and pricy—cut of meat. A crumb coating further helps seal in the moisture. Rosemary's piney aroma blends well with veal. The dish can be served hot, at room temperature, or cold.

6 thick veal loin or rib chops, bone in (about 8 ounces each)

1 tablespoon olive oil

1 tablespoon milk

¾ teaspoon ground black pepper

Kosher salt

2 teaspoons minced garlic

1½ cups freshly made fine bread crumbs

2 tablespoons almond flour or ground blanched almonds

2 teaspoons minced fresh rosemary or ½ teaspoon dried rosemary

1. Preheat the oven to 425°F.

2. Place the veal chops in a shallow bowl. Combine the oil, milk, pepper, and salt to taste and rub over the chops. Marinate the chops for 15 minutes at room temperature. Combine the bread crumbs, almond flour, and rosemary in a plate and set aside.

3. Coat each chop with the seasoned crumbs, press to coat evenly, and place on a rack in a baking pan. Bake for 20 minutes, or until the veal is fully cooked, with no pink in the middle. Serve hot, at room temperature, or refrigerate for at least 4 hours and serve cold. (*Let the chops cool thoroughly, wrap in aluminum foil, and refrigerate. The chops may be kept, well wrapped, for up to 2 days in the refrigerator.*)

Note: Pork or lamb chops may be substituted for the veal. Use 6 thick pork loin chops or 12 thick lamb loin or rib chops.

Serving Suggestions: Start the meal with an appetizer like Spinach with Chili Cheese on Endive Boats (page 101) or a soup like Fennel, Green Bean, and Cauliflower Soup with Celery Seed (page 122). Serve the veal chops accompanied by Polenta with Green Peppercorns (page 191), Cucumber with Toasted Cumin Seeds (page 211), and Mango-Mint Salsa (page 231).

milk-marinated grilled pork chops with ajowan

Marinating pork in milk concentrates the salt, naturally present in both milk and pork, and the sugar in milk. The result is a delicate balance of savory and sweet sensations. Ajowan (see page 32) both lends a sweet flavor and cures the meat, making it eminently suitable for picnics and buffets. You can make this dish with lamb chops as well.

2 pounds boneless pork chops, ³/₄-inch thick preferably from the center loin, trimmed of excess fat

¹/₂ teaspoon ajowan seeds (see Note)

2 teaspoons black peppercorns, cracked

1 tablespoon minced garlic

¹/₂ cup whole milk

Olive oil spray

MAKES 4 TO 6 SERVINGS

1. Place the pork chops in a shallow dish and rub with ajowan, black pepper, and garlic. Pour the milk over the chops and toss to coat evenly. Marinate the chops for at least 4 hours or overnight in the refrigerator.

2. When ready to cook, light the grill or preheat the broiler.

3. Remove the chops from the marinade and spray with oil. Place on the rack or broiler pan, about 5 inches from the source of heat. Grill or broil, turning and basting with the reserved milk marinade, until fully cooked, about 15 minutes. Serve, thinly sliced, warm or at room temperature.

Note: If ajowan is not available, substitute 2 teaspoons chopped fresh thyme or 1 teaspoon dried thyme.

Serving Suggestions: Serve the chops accompanied with Stewed Apples with White Pepper and Fennel (page 220), Cumin Potatoes (page 215), and Fresh Fig Salsa with Sesame (page 234). A nice soup to start with is Tomato Soup with Basil Cream (page 127).

grilled pork with epazote

Every cuisine around the world has a simple and inexpensive marinade for everyday use. Flavorings in the marinade are kept to a minimum so that the meat's own natural flavor is not masked but can be brought to the fore with subtle sauces and condiments. The purpose of the marinade is, essentially, to tenderize the meat. The spices and herbs that are used vary from one cuisine to another. In Mexico it is epazote (see page 36) that gets added to the marinade. Beef, lamb, and chicken all take well to this marinade.

2 pounds center-cut pork loin, trimmed of all visible fat

Epazote Marinade

1 tablespoon minced fresh epazote or 1 teaspoon dried epazote

2 teaspoons minced fresh chilies

1 tablespoon minced garlic

4 tablespoons fresh lime juice

1 tablespoon Annatto Oil (page 90) or olive oil

1 teaspoon kosher salt

Olive oil spray

MAKES 4 SERVINGS

1. Cut the pork into 4 evenly thick slices and flatten them using a mallet. Put the pork in a shallow bowl and add all the marinade ingredients. Toss well, cover, and refrigerate for at least 2 hours, preferably overnight.

2. When ready to cook, light a charcoal grill or preheat the broiler.

3. Remove the meat from the marinade, scraping off the excess and reserving it. Spray the meat lightly with oil and, if barbecuing, arrange on the rack. If broiling, put the pork on the broiler pan and place it under the broiler, 4 to 5 inches from the heat. Cook, turning and basting with the reserved marinade, for 15 minutes, or until the pork is fully cooked. Serve immediately.

Serving Suggestions: For an appetizer, serve Avocado Spread with Tahini (page 81) and Raisin and Caraway Rolls (page 245). Accompany the pork with Sweet Sesame Dipping Sauce (page 227), Tomato-Cumin Rice (page 193), and Pumpkin with Allspice (page 216).

mild indian chile with paprika

1 pound lean ground beef

½ cup finely chopped onion

1 teaspoon minced garlic

1 tablespoon grated or
crushed fresh ginger

2 teaspoons ground cumin

½ teaspoon turmeric

1 teaspoon ground red pepper

1 tablespoon Hungarian
paprika

1 cup chopped peeled
tomatoes, fresh or canned

2 cups chicken stock, low-
sodium canned broth, or
water

1 cup frozen green peas or
1 can (16 ounces) chick
peas, rinsed and drained

Freshly ground black pepper
and kosher salt

¼ cup chopped cilantro

2 cups Fresh Tomato Relish
(recipe follows)

A simple way to turn inexpensive ground beef into a true delicacy. The dish is similar in appeal to Chile con Carne (page 55) but is milder and lighter tasting. Paprika is an essential ingredient: It gives Indian chile its characteristic brick-red hue and also emulsifies the sauce. Lean ground pork, lamb, venison, or buffalo meat can be substituted for the beef.

MAKES 4 SERVINGS

1. Sauté the meat in a heavy skillet over medium-high heat, stirring, until there is no more pink and the liquid has evaporated, about 5 minutes. Add the onion, garlic, ginger, cumin, and turmeric. Cook for 2 minutes. Add the red pepper, paprika, tomatoes, and stock. Bring to a boil.

2. Lower the heat and cook, covered, for 40 minutes, or until the meat is tender and the chile is thick, checking and stirring occasionally. Add the peas during the last 10 minutes of cooking. Season to taste with pepper and salt. Fold in the cilantro and serve garnished with the tomato relish.

Serving Suggestions: Accompany the chile with Parsley Rice (page 192), Chili Hash-Brown Potatoes (page 214), Apple Compote with Fennel (page 221), Cilantro-Walnut Dip (page 229), and a basket of bread, including Chili Tortilla Bread (page 241), Thyme Pita Bread (page 248), and Raisin and Caraway Rolls (page 245).

fresh tomato relish

MAKES 2 CUPS

1 cup chopped tomatoes, red, yellow, or
a combination

½ cup chopped peeled cucumber

¼ cup chopped red onions

¼ cup sliced radishes

¼ cup chopped cilantro

¼ teaspoon kosher salt

Combine all the ingredients in a bowl. Cover and refrigerate until needed. (*The relish may be made in advance and kept, tightly covered, for up to 2 days in the refrigerator.*)

special salads and vegetarian meals

carrot salad with coriander vinegar

This refreshingly light and moist salad of shredded carrots has a sweetish-sour dressing with smoky coriander seeds. The amount of sugar depends on the natural sweetness of the carrots: The blander they are, the more sugar you will need to heighten their sweetness to the level where it ought to be. You can also make this salad using julienned jícama or kohlrabi or thinly sliced cucumber.

2 pounds carrots, peeled and grated

2 tablespoons minced shallots

¼ cup wine vinegar

1 tablespoon balsamic vinegar

1 teaspoon ground Toasted Coriander Seeds (page 35)

2 teaspoons sugar, or more to taste

Kosher salt

2 tablespoons finely chopped cilantro

Freshly ground black pepper

MAKES 6 SERVINGS

Place the carrots and shallots in a serving bowl. Mix the wine vinegar, balsamic vinegar, and coriander in a cup and pour the mixture over the carrots. Toss well. Season to taste with sugar and salt. Sprinkle with cilantro and grind lots of black pepper over the top. Toss and serve. (*The salad keeps well, tightly covered, for up to 2 days in the refrigerator.*)

Serving Suggestions: This salad pairs well with Polenta with Green Peppercorns (page 191), with a rice dish like Curried Rice (page 194), and with breads such as Stuffed Sage Roti Bread with Olives (page 251).

celery root salad with celery seeds

Celery root, also called celeriac, is the bulbous edible root of a certain variety of celery plant. I prefer celery root to stalk celery because it is more floral in flavor. In this recipe it is combined with carrots and pears and dressed in a delicate, celery-seed dressing, which lends yet another balmy flavor to the salad.

MAKES 6 SERVINGS

½ teaspoon celery seeds

1 pound celery root, peeled and cut into ¼-inch-thick julienne

2 medium-size Asian pears or Anjou pears, peeled, cored, and cut into ¼-inch-thick julienne

1 large carrot, peeled and cut into ¼-inch-thick julienne

1 tablespoon balsamic vinegar

1 or more fresh chilies, minced

2 tablespoons chopped cilantro

⅓ cup toasted pine nuts or peanuts

1. Toast the celery seeds in an ungreased skillet over medium heat, shaking the pan to keep the seeds moving, for 2 minutes. Pour the seeds into a small bowl and let cool.

2. Bring a large pot of water to a boil. Add the celery root, return to a boil, and cook for 1 minute. Drain and plunge the celery root into a bowl of cold water. Drain again and pat dry with a towel. Combine the celery root, pears, carrots, vinegar, chili, and cilantro. Mix to distribute seasoning. (*May be made ahead to this point and stored, covered, for 1 day in the refrigerator.*)

3. When ready to serve, sprinkle with toasted celery seeds and peanuts and toss lightly.

Serving Suggestions: This delightful mélange of vegetables can be served as a light lunch accompanied with a soup like Bean and Pasta Soup with Oregano (page 116) and bread like Parmesan-Chive Puffs (page 243).

warm potato salad with caraway dressing

Although this is called a warm potato salad, it is good at room temperature and straight from the refrigerator. I like to make it when my farmers' market has very small new potatoes that need only to be cut in half. Caraway has a natural affinity to starch; it enhances its flavor and lightens the taste.

1½ pounds whole new potatoes, scrubbed and cut in half if large

Kosher salt

2 tablespoons olive oil

1 teaspoon caraway seeds

2 tablespoons finely chopped shallots

1 teaspoon finely chopped garlic

1 teaspoon prepared hot mustard

2 tablespoons white wine

2 tablespoons red wine vinegar

½ teaspoon sugar

Freshly ground black pepper

¼ cup finely chopped parsley

MAKES 6 SERVINGS

1. Boil the potatoes in salted water until tender yet firm enough to be sliced, about 35 minutes. While still warm, slice the potatoes without peeling them and put them in a bowl.

2. Heat the oil in a large skillet over medium-high heat. Add the caraway seeds and cook until the aroma rises. Add the potatoes and toss to coat evenly. Turn off the heat. Combine the shallots, garlic, mustard, wine, vinegar, sugar, and pepper to taste in a measuring cup. Pour over the potatoes and toss gently until thoroughly mixed. Sprinkle with parsley and serve while still warm. (*The salad keeps well for 6 hours at room temperature or covered, for up to 2 days, in the refrigerator.*)

Serving Suggestions: This is a great salad for a picnic or any outdoor or indoor grilling. It pairs well with Green Beans in Mustard Sauce (page 204), Brussels Sprouts with Fennel (page 206), or Cucumber with Toasted Cumin Seeds (page 211), all of which can be served at room temperature.

mozzarella and fennel with cumin vinaigrette

A simple spring salad of mozzarella, fennel, and fava beans on a bed of young greens dressed with a spicy Cumin Vinaigrette does double duty as an appetizer. The ingredients are very flexible. In place of hard-to-find fava beans, you can use baby lima beans or cooked dried beans such as chick peas, black-eyed peas, mung beans, or pinto beans.

6 cups mixed salad greens, such as romaine, boston, red leaf, arugula, and/or watercress

$1/2$ cup Cumin Vinaigrette (page 82)

$1/2$ pound whole milk or part-skim milk mozzarella, preferably fresh buffalo milk mozzarella, or $10^1/2$ ounces firm tofu, thinly sliced

3 small fennel bulbs, trimmed and sliced

1 cup fresh fava beans, or 1 package (10 ounces) frozen baby lima beans, cooked

3 tablespoons chopped toasted walnuts

MAKES 6 SERVINGS

Place the greens in a bowl. Add half the vinaigrette to the greens and toss to coat. Spread the greens on a platter. Arrange the mozzarella slices alternating with fennel slices in a circle. Distribute the fava beans on top and drizzle with the remaining vinaigrette. Garnish with walnuts and serve immediately.

Note: To toast walnuts, spread the nuts in a single layer on an ungreased baking sheet and toast them in a preheated 325°F. oven for 12 minutes. Cool to room temperature before using. (*Toasted walnuts may be stored in an airtight container for up to 6 months in the refrigerator.*)

Variation: In place of mozzarella, use crumbled feta cheese (about $3/4$ cup) or blue cheese (about $1/2$ cup).

Serving Suggestions: This salad is almost a meal in itself accompanied with a soup like Green Beans and Potatoes in Paprika Broth (page 114) or Chilled Borscht with Caraway (page 121) and bread such as Mini Pita with Basil and Dried Tomatoes (page 250).

black bean and mango salad with herb citrus dressing

All the flavors of the tropics come alive in this delightful salad. It takes only a few minutes to put it together provided you have a batch of cooked black beans. I often cook extra beans when I am making Black Bean Soup with Epazote (page 115). The beans, cooked in a broth flavored with epazote, oregano, lemon, and sweet peppers, are far more flavorful than plain boiled beans. For best results, use medium-ripe sweetish-sour mangos, just tart enough to make you pucker up.

1 cup cooked black beans

1 large medium-ripe mango, peeled, pitted and chopped (2 cups)

1 large red bell pepper, stemmed, seeded and chopped (1 cup)

½ cup finely chopped red onions

¼ cup fresh lemon juice

¼ cup pineapple or fresh grapefruit juice

1 tablespoon Herb Citrus Blend (page 66)

Kosher salt

2 fresh chilies, stemmed, seeded, and finely chopped, or freshly ground black pepper

¼ cup minced cilantro

MAKES 6 SERVINGS

1. Combine the beans, mango, pepper, and onion in a bowl. Mix the lemon juice, pineapple juice, and Herb Citrus Blend in a measuring cup and pour over the vegetables. Toss well. Cover and set aside for 15 to 30 minutes, to allow the flavors to blend. (*The salad may be made ahead to this point and set aside, covered, in the refrigerator for 1 day. It will keep longer, but the color will deteriorate and the mango will begin to turn mushy.*)

2. When ready to serve, remove the salad from the refrigerator and season with salt to taste. Toss in the chilies or black pepper and cilantro and serve.

Serving Suggestions: This bean and mango salad is perfect with Polenta with Green Peppercorns (page 191). For a more elaborate affair, you might start with a soup like Cool Yogurt Soup with Toasted Cumin Seeds (page 128). Blueberry Tart with Saffron Cream (page 262) is a fine dessert to finish the meal.

lentil and endive salad with juniper berries

I like to make lentil salads in summer when it is too hot to cook, period. I cook the lentils in the cool of the evening or in the microwave, assemble the salad, and put it in the refrigerator. It is cool, protein rich, and filling. In this recipe, juniper berry's spicy sweet fragrance accentuates the floral and citrus flavors of the marinade. Juniper also helps lengthen the life of the salad, keeping it fresh tasting longer.

2 cups brown lentils

4 cups water

³/₄ cup fresh orange juice

3 tablespoons wine vinegar

1 tablespoon balsamic vinegar

1¹/₂ teaspoons ground juniper berries

1 tablespoon minced garlic

1 large red bell pepper, stemmed, seeded, and chopped

²/₃ cup thinly sliced scallions, white and green parts

¹/₂ to 1 teaspoon minced fresh chilies

1 teaspoon grated orange zest

3 tablespoons chopped cilantro

Freshly ground black pepper and kosher salt

3 heads Belgian endive, leaves separated, or 4 to 6 attractive lettuce leaves

MAKES 8 SERVINGS

1. Pick the lentils clean, rinse, and put them in a pot. Add the water and bring to a boil. Cook, uncovered, for 2 minutes. Set aside, covered, for 1 hour.

2. Bring lentils to a boil again, and cook, covered, for 15 minutes, or until the lentils are soft but still hold their shape. Drain and let cool, uncovered.

3. Put the lentils in a shallow bowl. Add the orange juice, wine vinegar, balsamic vinegar, ground juniper berries, and garlic and toss well. Cover and set aside for 1 hour at room temperature or for 4 hours or overnight in the refrigerator. This will allow the lentils to absorb the juices.

4. Just before serving, fold in the red pepper, scallions, chilies, orange zest, and cilantro. Sprinkle generously with pepper and season to taste with salt. Arrange the endive leaves around the edge of a platter and mound the lentils in the center.

Serving Suggestions: This hearty salad can be accompanied simply with a bread like Stuffed Sage Roti Bread with Olives (page 251) or a rice pilaf like Summer Peach Pilaf with Bay (page 197). For a more elaborate affair, add Turmeric Escabeche of Vegetables (page 106).

chick pea salad with cumin

Chick peas are an ancient food of the Mediterranean region. In this salad, the peas are first cooked in cumin water to imbue them with a light spicy flavor and, at the same time, render them more digestible. The chick peas are then dressed in a chili-spiked lime and scallion dressing. You can increase or decrease the amount of chilies according to your taste. For a really spicy version, add a tablespoon of Harissa (page 78).

2 cups dried chick peas

1 teaspoon cumin seeds

1 teaspoon minced fresh chilies

2 teaspoons minced garlic

2 tablespoons fresh lime juice, or more if needed

1 cup chopped scallions, white and green parts

¼ cup minced parsley

1 tablespoon canola oil

Kosher salt

8 red leaf lettuce leaves or other similar lettuce leaves

MAKES 8 SERVINGS

1. Place the chick peas in a bowl and add enough water to cover by 1 inch. Soak the peas for 8 hours or overnight.

2. Drain and rinse the peas and put in a deep pot. Add 5 cups water and the cumin seeds and bring to a boil. Simmer, covered, until the peas are soft, adding more water if the peas begin to dry out, about 2 hours.

3. Drain the peas and place in a bowl. Discard the liquid. Add the chilies, garlic, lime juice, scallions, parsley, oil, and salt to taste, and toss well. Cover and let stand for 30 minutes at room temperature. Check the seasoning and add more salt or lime juice if needed. (*The salad keeps for up to 8 hours at room temperature. Do not refrigerate; chilling the chick peas toughens them.*)

4. Arrange the lettuce leaves on a platter, mound the chick peas in the center, and serve.

Serving Suggestions: Serve with a pita bread like Thyme Pita Bread (page 248) or Sesame Pita Bread (page 249). For a more elaborate meal, include Glazed Carrots with Cloves (page 208) and Cauliflower with Sumac (page 210).

bulgur salad with allspice

This is one of the simplest main course salads ever. All you need to do is soak the cracked wheat in boiling water, which cooks it, drain, and combine it with all the other ingredients. Allspice, a spice with complex aromas, gives the grain a meaty flavor.

1 cup finely ground bulgur

3 cups boiling water

1/4 cup fresh lemon juice

1 teaspoon ground allspice

1 cup chopped cilantro

1/2 cup chopped scallions, white and green parts

1/2 cup chopped mint

1/2 cup chopped pitted olives, black or green, preferably Mediterranean varieties

1/2 cup finely shredded arugula or Belgian endive

Freshly ground black pepper and kosher salt

1 cup chopped ripe red tomatoes

6 radicchio leaves

MAKES 4 SERVINGS

1. Place the bulgur in a large bowl. Add the boiling water and stir well. Cover and soak for 45 minutes. Drain bulgur through a double layer of dampened cheesecloth, pressing and squeezing to extract as much moisture as possible. Return bulgur to the bowl.

2. Add the lemon juice, allspice, cilantro, scallions, mint, olives, and arugula and toss well. Season to taste with pepper and salt. Cover and refrigerate for at least 1 hour before serving. (*The salad keeps well, tightly covered, for up to 5 days in the refrigerator.*) Just before serving, fold in the tomatoes. Sprinkle generously with pepper and season to taste with more salt. Serve spooned in radicchio cups.

Serving Suggestions: Serve this very filling grain salad as an appetizer or as a complete meal accompanied with Thyme Pita Bread (page 248). For a more elaborate meal, add Avocado Spread with Tahini (page 81) and Green Beans with Sichuan Peppercorns (page 205).

brown rice salad with basil dressing

A great, versatile rice preparation, vibrant with basil and the flavors of summer. In large portions the salad makes a fine entree, yet it pairs well with stewed, steamed, and braised dishes. It is also good as a stuffing for fish, poultry, and tortillas. The moisture in the salad comes from fresh tomatoes, so be sure to choose juicy ones.

1 cup uncooked basmati rice

2 large tomatoes

1 cup corn kernels, cooked

1 green bell pepper, stemmed, seeded, and julienned

1/2 cup chopped red onion

2 fresh chilies, seeded and thinly sliced (optional)

1 teaspoon dark sesame oil

1 tablespoon olive oil

3 tablespoons wine vinegar

1 tablespoon finely chopped garlic

Freshly ground black pepper and kosher salt

1/2 cup shredded large or whole small basil leaves

MAKES 6 SERVINGS

1. Wash the rice well and place in a saucepan. Add 2 cups water and let soak for 30 minutes.

2. Bring to a boil over high heat. Reduce heat to medium and cook, partly covered, for 10 minutes, or until most of the moisture is absorbed and the surface of the rice is covered with steam holes. Cover pan tightly and reduce the heat to low. Steam the rice for 10 minutes. Remove from the heat and let stand, covered, for 5 minutes.

3. Place a strainer over a bowl. Cut the tomatoes in half through the widest part and gently squeeze each half over the strainer. Set aside the juice; you should have 1/4 cup.

4. Remove the rest of the insides of the tomatoes with your fingers or a small knife. Cut the flesh into julienne strips. Set aside.

5. Place rice, corn, tomatoes, peppers, red onion, and chilies, if using, in a large bowl. In a measuring cup, combine the sesame oil, olive oil, vinegar, reserved tomato juice, and garlic. Pour the dressing over the rice and toss thoroughly to distribute the seasonings. Sprinkle generously with pepper and season to taste with salt. Serve right away or cover and refrigerate. (*The salad keeps well for 4 hours at room temperature or for up to 2 days in the refrigerator.*) Just before serving, fold in the basil.

Serving Suggestions: Serve this salad with a soup like Chilled Carrot Soup with Mace (page 119) and Cumin Crackers (page 111). For a more elaborate meal, add a dish like Vegetarian Pumpkin, Eggplant, and Lima Bean Chile (page 180) or Island Vegetable Stew with Thyme (page 177).

potato and cheese croquettes with nutmeg

This is the vegetarian answer to Maryland crab cakes. Cottage cheese not only resembles the crabmeat but also provides protein. Nutmeg draws out the sweetness of potatoes and cheese to give a wholesome flavor to the croquettes.

1¼ cups lowfat large-curd cottage cheese

1¼ cups riced potatoes

1 cup fresh bread crumbs

¼ cup minced scallions, white and green parts

⅓ cup finely chopped parsley

¼ teaspoon freshly grated nutmeg

2 fresh chilies, stemmed, seeded, and chopped

Kosher salt

1 tablespoon olive oil

8 Belgian endive leaves, finely shredded

1 cup watercress leaves and tender stems

MAKES 4 SERVINGS

1. Cream the cottage cheese using a food processor or a sieve. Combine the cheese, potatoes, and bread crumbs in a bowl. Add the scallions, parsley, nutmeg, chilies, and salt to taste. Mix well and divide the mixture into 8 equal portions. Form each portion into a 3-inch round patty.

2. Heat the oil in a large nonstick frying pan over medium-high heat. Place the patties in the pan and cook for 5 minutes, or until the underside has browned. Turn and brown the second side the same way. Divide the greens among 4 plates. Nestle 2 patties on the greens on each plate. Serve immediately.

Serving Suggestions: Start with a soup like Chilled Borscht with Caraway (page 121). Serve the croquettes accompanied with Fresh Tomato-Ginger Sauce (page 227) and Curry Mayonnaise (page 84). For a more elaborate meal, add Pumpkin with Allspice (page 216) and Parsley-Garlic Noodles (page 184).

rolled vegetable-cheese sandwiches with green peppercorns

I used to carry sandwiches similar to these for school lunches. They were lighter, healthier, and, most important, tastier than what I would find at school. But they are not restricted to a children's menu. The mild peppery bite and herbal scent of green peppercorns contrasts nicely with the mellow creaminess of the cheese. You can substitute mild goat cheese for some of the farmer cheese.

Vegetable-Cheese Filling

MAKES 4 SERVINGS

1¼ cups farmer cheese or pot cheese

½ cup plain nonfat yogurt

¼ cup coarsely chopped walnuts

⅓ cup grated carrot

½ cup grated cucumber

⅓ cup chopped plum tomatoes, drained

¼ cup chopped green bell pepper

⅓ cup chopped mixed fresh herbs, such as parsley, basil, dill, mint, and cilantro

2 tablespoons dried cranberries or red currants

1 tablespoon dried green peppercorns, crushed, or green peppercorns in brine, drained, rinsed, and chopped

Kosher salt

8 storebought flour tortillas

1. Combine all the filling ingredients in a bowl until well blended. Taste and add more salt if needed.

2. Place 2 tortillas, slightly overlapping, on a work surface. Add one-quarter of the filling in a line at 1 edge and roll up the tortillas jelly-roll fashion. Cover tightly with plastic wrap and refrigerate for at least 30 minutes. (*The sandwiches keep well, tightly covered, for up to 3 days in the refrigerator.*)

3. Just before serving, unwrap the rolls and, using a serrated knife, slice diagonally into 2-inch pieces and serve.

Note: Use the filling to stuff pita pockets, either storebought white or whole wheat pita or homemade pita (see pages 248–250).

Serving Suggestions: Serve these sandwiches with a soup like Fennel, Green Bean, and Cauliflower Soup with Celery Seed (page 122), Cilantro-Walnut Dip (page 229), and Mango-Mint Salsa (page 231).

island vegetable stew with thyme

All over the Caribbean islands and Central and South America, delicious stews of meaty beans, squash, and spring vegetables are made. They are flavored with unique combinations of spices and herbs. In this version, popular in Trinidad, cranberry beans (borlotti), pumpkin, and several vegetables are stewed with millet and thyme. The stew is sprinkled with Angostura, the aromatic bitters made with a secret blend of spices and herbs, at table.

½ cup dried cranberry beans (borlotti), soaked for 4 hours and drained

½ cup millet

1 small (1 pound) butternut squash, peeled, seeded, and coarsely chopped

½ pound green beans, trimmed and cut into 1-inch pieces

1 large carrot, thickly sliced

1 cup chopped medium-hot chilies, such as poblano or anaheim, or green bell pepper

½ pound ripe tomatoes, pureed

½ teaspoon ground allspice

1 cup corn kernels, cooked

1 cup chopped scallions, white and green parts

1 tablespoon chopped fresh thyme or 1 teaspoon dried thyme

Freshly ground black pepper and kosher salt

Sprigs of thyme, for garnish

Angostura bitters

MAKES 6 SERVINGS

1. Place the beans in a large deep pot along with the millet and 2 cups water and bring to a boil. Simmer the beans, covered, over medium heat, for 45 minutes, or until the beans are fully cooked but still firm.

2. Add the squash, green beans, carrot, chilies, tomatoes, and allspice. Bring soup back to a boil. Lower the heat and simmer the stew for 30 minutes, or until the vegetables are soft, stirring occasionally. Stir in the corn, scallions, and thyme. Cook until heated through, about 5 minutes. Turn off the heat. Sprinkle generously with pepper and season to taste with salt. (*The stew may be set aside, covered, for up to 4 hours at room temperature or kept, tightly covered, for up to 3 days in the refrigerator. Reheat before serving.*)

3. Serve the stew in deep dishes, garnished with thyme. Pass the bitters on the side to sprinkle.

Serving Suggestions: Start the meal with an appetizer like Turmeric Escabeche of Vegetables (page 106). Complete the meal with a rice dish like Curried Rice (page 194). For a more elaborate meal, add Pan-grilled Plantains with Ginger (page 223) and Mango-Mint Salsa (page 231).

split pea and winter vegetable stew with warm spices

Split peas are a popular legume for vegetable stews. In addition to providing high quality vegetarian protein, they add meaty flavor, body, and creamy richness. In this stew split peas are combined with several vegetables, including pumpkin, brussels sprouts, kohlrabi, and mustard greens and seasoned with warm spices, including cinnamon, clove, and ginger.

$1^{1}/_{2}$ cups yellow split peas

$6^{1}/_{2}$ cups water

$1^{1}/_{2}$ cups roughly cut up onions, in 1-inch pieces

2 cups sliced kohlrabi or cauliflower florets

1 cup brussels sprouts, trimmed and scored

$^{3}/_{4}$ pound pumpkin or butternut squash, peeled, seeded, and cut into 2-inch pieces

1 cup (packed) chopped mustard greens, kale, or spinach

$^{3}/_{4}$ pound tomatoes, roughly chopped

$^{1}/_{2}$ to 1 teaspoon crushed red pepper

2 teaspoons grated lemon zest

Juice of $^{1}/_{2}$ lemon

Kosher salt

1 tablespoon olive oil

1 tablespoon minced garlic

2 teaspoons Warm Spice Blend (page 64)

MAKES 6 SERVINGS

1. Combine the split peas and 4 cups of the water in a deep pot and bring to a boil. Reduce the heat to medium and simmer, partly covered, for 40 minutes, or until the peas are fully cooked but still retain their shape.

2. Add the onions, kohlrabi, brussels sprouts, pumpkin, mustard greens, tomatoes, and red pepper. Add $2^{1}/_{2}$ cups water and bring to a boil. Reduce the heat, cover, and simmer the vegetables for 20 minutes, or until soft. The pumpkin will fall apart a little during cooking; it will thicken and enrich the sauce. Stir in the lemon zest, lemon juice, and salt to taste.

3. Heat the oil in a small frying pan until hot. Turn off the heat. Add the garlic and spices and cook, shaking the pan for few a seconds. Mix the spice-infused oil into the stew. (*The stew may be set aside, covered, for up to 4 hours at room temperature or kept, tightly covered, for up to 4 days in the refrigerator. Reheat before serving.*) Serve in large deep plates or shallow bowls.

Serving Suggestions: Top the stew with a scoop of Parsley Rice (page 192) and a spoonful of Cranberry Relish with Apricots, Walnuts, and Cinnamon (page 237). Serve a basket of bread on the side, including Raisin and Caraway Rolls (page 245), Parmesan-Chive Puffs (page 243), and Chili Tortilla Bread (page 241).

sofrito green beans and potatoes

This is an incredibly simple preparation that is very satisfying. The secret flavoring is Sofrito, which is the underpinning of the sauce base. Potatoes are marvelous cooked in Sofrito. You can substitute sweet potatoes for the potatoes.

³/₄ pound green beans, trimmed and cut into ¹/₂-inch pieces

³/₄ pound potatoes, peeled and diced into ¹/₂-inch pieces

1 cup chopped tomatoes

1 cup vegetable stock or water

1 cup Sofrito (page 92)

1 teaspoon dried oregano

Juice of 1 lemon

Freshly ground black pepper and kosher salt

2 tablespoons minced parsley

MAKES 6 SERVINGS

Combine the beans, potatoes, tomatoes, stock, Sofrito, and oregano in a large heavy saucepan over medium-high heat. Cover and cook until the vegetables are soft, about 30 minutes. Check and stir occasionally to ensure they are not sticking. If necessary add more stock. Turn off the heat. Add the lemon juice and season to taste with pepper and salt. Serve the stew sprinkled with parsley.

Serving Suggestions: This is a light but filling dish, suited for lunch or brunch. To complete the meal, use it as a stuffing in Savory Herb Crêpes (page 253) and accompany with a soup like Cool Yogurt Soup with Toasted Cumin Seeds (page 128) and a salad like Carrot Salad with Coriander Vinegar (page 166).

vegetarian pumpkin, eggplant, and lima bean chile

It may be hard to imagine a chile without meat, but if you just think about the spices and herbs in the powder, you will see its affinity to pumpkin, eggplant, and similar earthy vegetables. The level of heat is strictly personal. I tend to keep it moderate because I do not have the palate to eat fire. Adjust the heat to your own taste.

2 tablespoons canola oil

2 cups chopped onions

1 tablespoon minced garlic

3 tablespoons Chili Powder (page 54)

1 teaspoon ground allspice

2 cups fresh or frozen baby lima beans or fava beans

2 cups chopped peeled tomatoes, fresh or canned

3 cups vegetable stock or water

1 pound pumpkin, butternut squash, or acorn squash meat, cut into 1½-inch cubes (2 cups)

¾ pound eggplant, unpeeled, cut into 1½-inch cubes (2 cups)

1 cup corn kernels, cooked

Freshly ground black pepper and kosher salt

2 cups Avocado, Onion, and Cilantro Relish (page 231) or chopped Spanish onion

MAKES 6 TO 8 SERVINGS

1. Combine the oil, onions, and garlic in a heavy saucepan over medium-high heat. Cook, stirring occasionally, until the onions wilt and begin to brown, about 6 minutes. (Do not worry if the onions stick or get a few brown spots as this will lend a nice roasted flavor to the sauce.)

2. Add the Chili Powder, allspice, lima beans, tomatoes, and stock and bring to a boil. Lower the heat and simmer, covered, until the beans are tender and the spices develop depth, about 15 minutes. Fold in the pumpkin and eggplant. Continue to cook, covered, until the vegetables are very tender, about 25 minutes. The pumpkin will fall apart and give body to the sauce.

3. Add the corn and cook until heated through. Turn off the heat. Sprinkle generously with pepper and season to taste with salt. (*The stew may be set aside, covered, for up to 4 hours at room temperature or kept, tightly covered, for up to 5 days in the refrigerator. Reheat before serving.*)

4. Ladle the chile into shallow bowls and serve topped with a spoonful of relish. Pass the remaining relish on the side.

Serving Suggestions: Top the chile with Parsley Rice (page 192) and Yogurt Dip with Herbs (page 230) and accompany it with Chili Tortilla Bread (page 241).

savory millet cake with rosemary

Millet is in a class by itself. A savory millet cake, imbued with rosemary and studded with crunchy bits of vegetables and walnuts, makes the most of millet's blandness. You just pat the ingredients down in a pie plate, and bake the cake. It emerges from the oven lightly puffed and full of fragrance. For a spicier version, add half a teaspoon of ground red pepper and one teaspoon minced fresh chilies to the mix.

³/₄ cup millet

³/₄ cup *each* chopped onion, broccoli, zucchini, and red bell pepper

1 teaspoon minced garlic

¹/₂ cup coarsely chopped walnuts

1 cup fresh bread crumbs

3 large eggs

1 cup tomato juice or tomato sauce, fresh or canned

2 tablespoons tomato paste

1 tablespoon fresh lemon juice

2 tablespoons canola oil

2 teaspoons chopped fresh rosemary or ¹/₂ teaspoon dried rosemary

¹/₂ teaspoon freshly ground black pepper

1 teaspoon kosher salt

¹/₃ cup finely chopped parsley, preferably Italian flat-leaf

MAKES 6 SERVINGS

1. Preheat the oven to 375°F.

2. Place the millet in a saucepan. Add enough water to cover by at least 1 inch and bring to a boil. Cook the millet for 15 minutes, or until the grains are soft but still hold their shape. Drain and put in a bowl.

3. Add all the vegetables, the garlic, walnuts, and bread crumbs. Toss to mix. Mix the eggs, tomato juice, tomato paste, lemon juice, and oil in a bowl and stir it into the vegetable mixture. Add the rosemary, black pepper, salt, and parsley. Mix thoroughly and pack into a 10-inch quiche plate or cake pan.

4. Bake the cake, covered with a piece of foil, for 1 hour. Uncover and continue to bake until the excess moisture is absorbed, the pie looks puffed and browned, and a toothpick inserted in the middle of the cake comes out clean, about 20 minutes. Remove from the oven and cool the cake for 5 minutes. Serve the cake hot or at room temperature, sliced into thin wedges.

Serving Suggestions: Serve the cake with cocktails or at a picnic, for lunch or for a late-night supper, accompanied with a green salad. Garnish with Fresh Tomato-Ginger Sauce (page 227) or Cool Yogurt Dill Sauce with Dried Cranberries and Almonds (page 230).

pastas and pilafs

parsley-garlic noodles

Truly a garlic lover's pasta. In this very simple dish, cooked pasta is tossed in a garlic-infused oil. Parsley not only provides a light herbal touch but acts as a breath freshener. You can use any shape or size of pasta, including the rice-shape pasta called orzo, in this dish. For a spicier pasta, add half a teaspoon crushed red pepper or fresh coarsely ground black pepper to the oil after removing the sautéed garlic.

½ **pound linguine**

2 **tablespoons olive oil**

¼ **cup thinly sliced garlic**

¼ **cup white wine**

¼ **cup minced parsley**

Kosher salt

MAKES 2 SERVINGS

1. Bring 6 quarts of water to a boil in a deep pot. Add the linguine and cook until al dente.

2. Heat the oil in a large sauté pan over medium-low heat. Add the garlic and sauté until garlic releases its fragrance and turns light golden. Carefully remove the garlic with a slotted spoon and set aside. Add the wine and parsley to the oil.

3. Drain the linguine and add, tossing until well coated with oil. Sprinkle with salt and continue to cook, tossing, until the excess moisture is absorbed into the pasta and the parsley wilts. Transfer to a serving dish and spread the garlic on top. Serve immediately.

Serving Suggestions: This dish can be served in small portions as a first course. It pairs well with grilled foods that are accompanied with salsas and sauces. Accompanied with a vegetable like Green Beans in Mustard Sauce (page 204) or a hearty salad like Mozzarella and Fennel with Cumin Vinaigrette (page 169), it makes a light meal.

spaghetti with fennel-tomato sauce

This tomato sauce is unique in that it is cooked without any herbs, so the brilliant red color is not marred by dark specks. Instead, the flavor is achieved through a combination of spices. I always put away a few batches of this all-purpose sauce in the freezer; it has great keeping qualities.

$^1/_2$ cup chopped onions

1 tablespoon chopped garlic

$^3/_4$ teaspoon fennel seeds

$^1/_8$ teaspoon ground cloves

1 tablespoon olive oil

1 pound ripe plum tomatoes, peeled, seeded, and chopped

1 tablespoon tomato paste

1 teaspoon sugar

1 tablespoon unsalted butter

$^1/_2$ teaspoon Hungarian paprika

Freshly ground black pepper and kosher salt

1 pound spaghetti

$^1/_2$ cup basil leaves (optional)

$^1/_4$ cup freshly grated parmesan

MAKES 1 $^1/_2$ CUPS SAUCE, 4 SERVINGS

1. Combine the onions, garlic, fennel, cloves, and oil in a heavy-bottomed pan over medium-high heat. Cook for 10 minutes, or until the onions are soft. Add the tomatoes, tomato paste, sugar, butter, and paprika and bring to a boil. Reduce the heat and simmer, covered, for 30 minutes, or until the vegetables are very soft and the sauce is thick.

2. Transfer contents to a food processor or blender and process until smoothly pureed. Return the sauce to the pan and heat until piping hot. Season with pepper and salt to taste. (*The sauce may be made ahead and kept, tightly covered, for up to 2 days in the refrigerator. It can be frozen for up to 3 months. Reheat to very hot before using.*)

3. Bring 6 quarts of water to a boil in a deep pot. Add the spaghetti and cook until al dente. Drain the pasta and transfer to a warmed serving platter. Pour the sauce on top and garnish, if desired, with basil leaves. Pass the parmesan cheese at table.

Serving Suggestions: Although essentially a pasta sauce, this is nice with all fried and grilled foods, particularly white nonoily fish, shrimps, scallops, and chicken breasts. It can also be used to enrich vegetable soups and salsas.

linguine with cilantro sauce

Although this dish sounds like pasta with pesto sauce, it is a totally different preparation, inspired by an Afghan dish where an herb paste is stuffed into pasta. My adaptation is quicker and simpler, and, I think, produces very tasty results.

½ pound linguine

1 cup (packed) cilantro leaves and tender stems

½ cup white wine, chicken stock, or low-sodium canned broth

2 tablespoons extra-virgin olive oil

1 cup thinly sliced scallions, white and green parts

2 to 4 fresh chilies, stemmed, seeds discarded, and thinly sliced

1 pound tomatoes, peeled, seeded, diced, and drained

Kosher salt

MAKES 2 TO 4 SERVINGS

1. Bring 6 quarts of water to a boil in a deep pot. Add the linguine and cook until al dente.

2. Combine the cilantro and wine in a food processor or blender and process briefly until the mixture is coarsely pureed. Set aside.

3. Heat the oil in a large saucepan over medium-high heat. Add the scallions and chilies. Cook, stirring, for 5 minutes, or until the scallions begin to brown.

4. Drain the linguine. Increase the heat to high and add the linguine, tomatoes, cilantro mixture, and salt to taste and cook, tossing, until most of the moisture is absorbed into the pasta. Transfer to a warm serving platter and serve hot.

Serving Suggestions: The pasta can be served in small portions as a first course. It goes well with all stewed and braised beef and lamb dishes as well as hearty vegetarian stews. To make a meal of it, serve it accompanied with a sauce like Cool Yogurt Dill Sauce with Dried Cranberries and Almonds (page 230).

penne with broccoli and turmeric

Turmeric is a spice that generally turns everything it touches sun gold, except when a pinch is added to a green vegetable. Then it intensifies the green and holds it. Whenever possible, I make this dish with the Italian broccoli called broccoli raab or rappini, slightly bitter greens that are available at supermarkets during the fall and winter months. A quarter of a cup of sliced garlic may seem like a lot, but it's only six cloves. You can use less if you prefer.

1 pound broccoli or ³/₄ pound
   broccoli raab

1 pound penne or fusilli

¹/₄ cup thinly sliced garlic

¹/₄ to ¹/₂ teaspoon crushed
   red pepper

1 tablespoon olive oil

¹/₄ teaspoon turmeric

Kosher salt

¹/₃ cup water

¹/₄ cup white wine or water

1 tablespoon unsalted butter

Freshly grated parmesan
   (optional)

MAKES 6 SERVINGS

1. Cut off the stems of the broccoli, peel, and cut into ¹/₈-inch-thick slices. Cut the broccoli tops into 1¹/₂-inch florets.

2. Bring 6 quarts of water to a boil in a deep pot. Add the pasta and cook until al dente.

3. Place the garlic, pepper, and oil in a large heavy skillet over medium-high heat. Cook, stirring occasionally, until the garlic begins to color, about 2 minutes. Stir in the turmeric and broccoli. Sprinkle with salt and add water. Cover and cook over medium heat until the broccoli is tender but still crunchy, about 5 minutes. Uncover, increase the heat, and stir in the wine and butter. Rapidly boil the liquid until it is reduced to a syrup.

4. Drain the pasta and fold into the broccoli mixture. Check and adjust the seasoning and serve sprinkled with parmesan, if desired.

Serving Suggestions: This dish can be served in small portions as a first course. It pairs well with grilled and roasted meat, poultry, and fish. To make a complete meal, accompany it with a salad, like Carrot Salad with Coriander Vinegar (page 166), or a light soup like Tomato Soup with Basil Cream (page 127).

angel hair with olives, basil, and chilies

This pasta dish takes hardly any time at all to prepare. Just cook pasta and toss it in a chili-spiked garlicky olive oil with basil and olives. The only tricky part is the chili because its heat is often difficult to foretell. To play safe, use a type of chili that is known to be mildly hot, such as anaheim or poblano.

½ pound angel hair pasta

1 tablespoon olive oil

1 tablespoon thinly sliced garlic

¼ cup white wine, chicken stock, or water from cooking the pasta

¼ to ½ cup shredded seeded fresh chilies, such as anaheim or poblano

Kosher salt

¼ cup finely shredded basil leaves

½ cup black olives, preferably Mediterranean, pitted and chopped

MAKES 2 SERVINGS

1. Bring 4 quarts of water to a boil in a deep pot. Add the pasta and cook until al dente.

2. Heat the oil in a large sauté pan until very hot. Lower the heat and add the garlic. When garlic begins to color, about 30 seconds, add the chilies and wine. Boil, stirring occasionally, until most of the moisture evaporates.

3. Drain the pasta and add it to the pan. Add salt to taste. Cook, tossing, until the pasta is coated with oil. Fold in the basil and olives. Add more salt if needed. (*The dish may be made ahead and set aside for 6 hours at room temperature.*)

4. Serve hot or at room temperature.

Serving Suggestions: This pasta dish is good in small portions as a first course or as a side dish. It pairs well with grilled and sautéed fish and poultry, particularly those flavored with herbs.

penne with mushrooms and crushed red pepper

A popular pasta preparation in which shaped pasta, such as penne (quills), conchiglie (shells), lumache (snails), fusilli (twists), and farfalle (butterflies), is tossed with sautéed mushrooms. Traditionally a little crushed red pepper is added for bite since mushrooms tend to sweeten the pasta. You can use any combination of fancy mushrooms in this recipe; cremini have the most natural liaison.

5 ounces penne or other medium pasta shape

2 tablespoons olive oil

1/2 teaspoon crushed red pepper

1 tablespoon chopped garlic

3/4 pound fancy mushrooms, preferably cremini, quartered

1/3 cup dry white wine

4 tablespoons finely chopped parsley

Kosher salt

1/2 cup freshly grated parmesan

Sprigs of parsley, for garnish

MAKES 4 SERVINGS

1. Bring 4 quarts of water to a boil in a deep pot. Add the pasta and cook until al dente.

2. Heat the oil in a heavy-bottomed skillet over medium-high heat. When the oil is hot, add the pepper, garlic, and mushrooms. Cook, stirring, for 4 minutes, or until the mushrooms are lightly browned. Add the wine and cook, covered, until the mushrooms, are tender and the moisture has evaporated, about 5 minutes.

3. Drain the pasta and add to the mushrooms. Add the parsley and sprinkle with salt. Cook, tossing, until the liquid is absorbed. Toss in the parmesan. Transfer the pasta to a heated platter, garnish with parsley, and serve.

Serving Suggestions: This pasta dish can be served in small portions as a first course. It pairs well with grilled foods that are accompanied with salsas and sauces. For a light meal, serve the pasta accompanied with a soup like Fennel, Green Bean, and Cauliflower Soup with Celery Seed (page 122).

pasta with mustard shrimps

When mustard seeds are sautéed in oil, they pop like popcorn. Mustard seed–infused oil, sweet and highly aromatic, is the underpinning of this wonderful dish, a mélange of shrimps, pasta, tomato, and herbs. You can substitute scallops, crabmeat, lobster, or squid for the shrimps.

2 tablespoons olive oil

1 teaspoon mustard seeds, crushed

2 teaspoons thinly sliced garlic

1 tablespoon capers, drained and rinsed

¼ cup white wine

1½ pounds tomatoes, peeled, seeded, and chopped

1 pound small shrimps, peeled

Freshly ground black pepper and kosher salt

½ pound angel hair pasta

2 tablespoons freshly grated parmesan

¼ cup basil leaves, finely shredded

Sprigs of basil, for garnish

MAKES 4 SERVINGS

1. Heat the oil in a large sauté pan over high heat. When the oil is hot, add the mustard seeds and cover the pan. When the seeds stop popping, lower the heat, uncover, and add the garlic and capers. Cook over medium heat until the garlic loses its raw aroma, about 1 minute. Increase the heat and add the wine. Cook until the liquid is reduced to a sauce.

2. Add the tomatoes and cook, undisturbed, for 3 minutes, or until the tomatoes begin to soften. Add the shrimps and cook, stirring, until they curl and turn pink, about 2 minutes. Turn off the heat. Season to taste with pepper and salt. Cover and keep warm.

3. Bring a large quantity of water to a boil in a deep pot and add the pasta. Cook until al dente. Drain and transfer to a bowl. Add the cheese and basil and toss well. Divide the pasta evenly among 4 plates. Spoon shrimps and tomatoes on top. Garnish with basil and serve.

Serving Suggestions: This dish can be served in small portions as a first course, yet it is substantial enough to be served as a complete meal, accompanied with a light soup like Chilled Borscht with Caraway (page 121) and, if desired, a salad like Celery Root Salad with Celery Seeds (page 167).

polenta with green peppercorns

Polenta, or coarsely ground Italian cornmeal, can be served either creamy like grits or spread out into sheet cakes, then sliced and sautéed or grilled. It looks like slightly moist cornbread. I love both kinds. In this version very herbal green peppercorns are folded into the polenta. The "bite" comes as a surprise.

4 cups chicken stock

1½ teaspoons kosher salt

1¼ cups regular yellow polenta

1 to 3 teaspoons finely diced green peppercorns

1 teaspoon minced fresh sage or ½ teaspoon ground dried sage

Olive oil spray

MAKES 24 TRIANGLES, 12 SERVINGS

1. Bring the chicken stock to a rapid boil in a saucepan. Add the salt. Stir the water vigorously to keep it in motion and add the polenta in a stream. Cook, stirring constantly, as it thickens. Stir in the green peppercorns and the sage and continue cooking until the polenta is thick and velvety, about 5 minutes. Season to taste with more salt if needed.

2. Pour the polenta into a greased 9 x 13-inch baking dish or onto a greased baking sheet or a marble slab. Spread with a rubber spatula to an even ½-inch thickness. When completely cool, cut into 3-inch squares. Cut each square diagonally in half. You should have 2 dozen triangles. (*The polenta triangles can be made ahead and kept, tightly covered, in the refrigerator for up to 5 days.*)

3. Heat a heavy nonstick griddle over high heat until very hot. Spray with oil as many polenta pieces as will fit on the griddle in a single layer without crowding and place them on the griddle. Grill, turning once, until nicely browned. Repeat with the remaining pieces. Serve immediately.

Serving Suggestions: Polenta can be served with all dishes with gravies as it nicely soaks up the juices. It is also a good addition to a salad or vegetable dish. Accompanied with a sauce like Warm Tomato Butter with Paprika (page 236), it makes a lovely first course.

parsley rice

When you are having doubts about what rice to pair with a certain dish, this is the one to choose. Subtly flavored and mild, it blends with everything. It is also easy to prepare since parsley is the most widely available fresh herb. Be sure, though, to use Italian flat-leaf parsley, which has more flavor than the curly kind. I add a little lemon peel to the rice; it draws out the flavor of parsley.

1 cup chopped onion

1 tablespoon canola oil

½ cup finely chopped parsley

4 cups chicken stock or water

1 teaspoon grated lemon zest

2 cups uncooked
converted rice

1 teaspoon kosher salt

MAKES 6 SERVINGS

1. Sauté the onion in the oil in a saucepan over medium-high heat, until wilted, about 5 minutes. Stir in the parsley and continue to cook for 1 minute. Add the chicken broth, lemon zest, rice, and salt and bring to a boil, stirring with a fork to prevent the rice from settling. Lower the heat and cook, covered, until the rice is tender, about 25 minutes. (*Covered, the rice will stay warm for 25 minutes.*)

2. Just before serving, fluff the rice with a fork.

Serving Suggestions: Serve this all-purpose rice with any stew, braised dish, or grilled dish. It is particularly well suited to spicy dishes like chile, both with meat and without.

tomato-cumin rice

This very appealing crimson rice, redolent of tomatoes and cumin, is quick and easy to prepare. When possible, use fresh tomatoes in season; they give the rice a summery herbal flavor. You can use brown rice here, in which case allow 45 minutes cooking time.

1 tablespoon olive oil

1 teaspoon cumin seeds, crushed

¼ teaspoon ground red pepper

¼ cup finely chopped onions

1 cup uncooked long-grain rice

1 cup pureed tomatoes, fresh or canned

1 cup water

1 teaspoon kosher salt

MAKES 4 SERVINGS

1. Heat the oil in a nonstick saucepan over medium-high heat. Add the cumin seeds, red pepper, and onions. Cook, stirring, for 3 minutes, or until the onions are limp. Add the rice and sauté until it is coated with seasoned oil. Add the tomato puree, water, and salt. Bring to a boil, stirring with a fork to prevent the rice from sticking. Lower the heat and cook, covered, until all the moisture is absorbed and the rice is tender, about 18 minutes. Turn off the heat. Let the rice rest for 5 minutes, covered. (*Covered, the rice will stay warm for 25 minutes.*)

2. Just before serving, fluff the rice with a fork.

Serving Suggestions: The rice pairs well with fried, grilled, and barbecued foods, particularly pan-grilled fish, shrimps, and scallops, and broiled meats, such as chicken kabobs (see page 154) and Jerk Chicken (page 61).

curried rice

This is not a hot-and-spicy rice. Rather, it is a delicate blend of rice with sweet onions, garlic, and traces of coriander, cumin, and fennel that you can detect in the Curry Powder. The golden yellow color comes from the turmeric in the powder. If you like, add a cup of fresh peas to the rice along with the cooking liquid.

1 tablespoon canola oil

½ cup chopped onions

1 teaspoon minced garlic

2 teaspoons Curry Powder (page 56)

1½ cups uncooked converted rice

3 cups chicken stock, low-sodium canned broth, or water

1 teaspoon kosher salt

3 tablespoons dark raisins, for garnish

2 tablespoons toasted almonds, for garnish

MAKES 6 SERVINGS

1. Heat the oil in a nonstick saucepan over medium-high heat. Add the onions and garlic and cook, stirring, for 3 minutes, or until the onions are limp. Stir in the Curry Powder. Add the rice, chicken stock, and salt. Mix well and bring to a boil, stirring with a fork to prevent the rice from settling. Lower the heat and cook, covered, until all the moisture is absorbed and the rice is tender, about 25 minutes. Turn off the heat. Let the rice rest for 5 minutes, covered. (*Covered, the rice will stay warm for 25 minutes.*)

2. Just before serving, fluff the rice with a fork, transfer to a platter, and garnish with raisins and almonds.

Serving Suggestions: This rice has wide appeal because its spiciness is in the fragrance and not in the taste. It is great served with grilled fish, chicken breast, and meat, or with eggs at breakfast. It can be a complete meal, accompanied with a salad like Lentil and Endive Salad with Juniper Berries (page 171).

mint pilaf

Maybe it's just a coincidence, but when I shift my cooking outdoors to charcoal grilling, my herb patch in the yard simultaneously overflows with sweet fragrant mint. Instinctively, I make this pilaf, which goes harmoniously with all sorts of barbecued chicken and game hens, lamb, fish, and shrimps, and grilled vegetables.

1 cup uncooked basmati rice

2 cups water

2 teaspoons canola oil

1/4 cup minced shallots

2 tablespoons minced mint

1/4 cup pureed cooked
  spinach, drained

3/4 teaspoon kosher salt

MAKES 4 SERVINGS

1. Wash the rice thoroughly, drain, and place in a bowl. Add the water and soak for 30 minutes.

2. Heat the oil in a nonstick saucepan over medium-high heat. Add the shallots and cook, stirring, for 2 minutes, or until limp. Add the mint and sauté for 1 minute more. Add the rice and the water it was soaking in, the salt, and spinach and bring to a boil, stirring with a fork to prevent the rice from settling. Reduce the heat to medium and cook, partly covered, for 10 minutes, or until most of the moisture is absorbed and the surface of the rice is covered with steam holes. Cover the pan tightly and reduce the heat to low. Let the rice steam for 10 minutes. Remove from the heat and let the pilaf rest, covered, for 5 minutes. (*Covered, the pilaf will stay warm for 25 minutes.*)

3. Just before serving, fluff the rice with a fork.

Serving Suggestions: Mint Pilaf has a natural affinity to grilled meat and chicken like Grilled Chicken Kabobs with Anise (page 154) or Pepper-rubbed Rack of Lamb (page 159). The pilaf may be served as a meal, accompanied with Cool Yogurt Dill Sauce with Dried Cranberries and Almonds (page 230).

orange-cinnamon pilaf

The Persians were the ones to elevate cooking rice with fruit to an art. In this interpretation, the rice develops a citrus bouquet from orange juice. Cinnamon not only draws sweetness from the fruit but fuses its flavor together with the starch. You can substitute wild rice or pecan rice for the basmati.

1 cup uncooked brown
   basmati rice

1½ cups water

⅔ cup fresh orange juice

1 stick cinnamon

5 whole cloves

¼ teaspoon ground ginger

¼ cup dark raisins

1 orange peeled, sliced, and
   seeded

MAKES 4 SERVINGS

1. Wash the rice well, drain, and place in a saucepan. Add the water and let soak for 30 minutes.

2. Place the saucepan on the stove and add the orange juice, cinnamon, cloves, and ginger. Bring to a boil over high heat, stirring with a fork to prevent the rice from settling. Reduce the heat to medium and simmer, partly covered, for 15 minutes, or until most of the moisture is absorbed and the surface of the rice is covered with steam holes. Cover the pan tightly and reduce the heat to low. Let rice steam for 10 minutes. Remove from the heat and let the rice rest, covered, for 5 minutes. (*Covered, the pilaf will stay warm for 25 minutes. It may be left for up to 6 hours at room temperature or kept, tightly covered, for up to 5 days in the refrigerator.*) Remove and discard the cinnamon and cloves. Fluff with a fork.

3. Serve, garnished with orange slices, hot, at room temperature, or cold.

Serving Suggestions: Serve the pilaf cold, topped with fish, such as Salmon Steamed in Bay Leaf Vapor (page 136) or Grilled Mustard Tuna (page 133), berries, or Concord grapes.

summer peach pilaf with bay

Beautifully flavored and visually appealing, this pilaf can be made only in summer when fragrant tree-ripened peaches are available. The spicy-lemony bay leaves meld with and heighten the flavor of the peaches. For an interesting change of pace, use pecan rice instead of regular long-grain rice.

2 cups peeled thinly sliced peaches

4 cups chicken stock, low-sodium canned broth, or water

2 bay leaves

³/₄ cup chopped onions

1 tablespoon canola or olive oil

2 cups uncooked long-grain rice

¹/₂ teaspoon ground ginger

2 teaspoons unsalted butter

1 tablespoon fresh lemon juice

MAKES 6 TO 8 SERVINGS

1. Puree ¹/₂ cup of the peach slices with ¹/₂ cup of the chicken stock. Set aside.

2. Sauté the bay leaves and onions in the oil in a medium-size saucepan over medium heat for 4 minutes, or until the onions look wilted. Add the rice, ginger, pureed peaches, and the remaining stock. Stir with a fork to prevent the rice from settling and bring to a boil. Lower the heat and simmer, covered, until all the liquid is absorbed and the rice is tender, about 18 minutes. Remove the bay leaves and set aside. (*Covered, the pilaf will stay warm for 25 minutes. It may be left for up to 6 hours at room temperature or kept, tightly covered, for up to 3 days in the refrigerator.*)

3. Heat the butter in a large nonstick frying pan over high heat. When the butter melts, add the remaining peach slices and cook, shaking and tossing, until they are streaked brown and glazed, about 5 minutes. Sprinkle with lemon juice. Transfer rice to a warm platter. Distribute peaches on top and garnish with bay leaves. Serve hot, at room temperature, or cold.

Serving Suggestions: This pilaf is good served with grilled or sautéed food like Pepper-rubbed Rack of Lamb (page 159) or Potato and Cheese Croquettes with Nutmeg (page 175). It can also make a complete meal, accompanied with a salad like Mozzarella and Fennel with Cumin Vinaigrette (page 169).

risotto of cauliflower with oregano

Writing about risotto brings back memories of my teen years, when during a visit to Parma, Italy, I tasted risotto for the first time. I have never forgotten it. Risotto is a simple yet delicate preparation that requires special care. It is made by braising short-grain rice in a flavored liquid until the rice is cooked al dente and most of the moisture has evaporated. Quality ingredients are what differentiates a great risotto from a so-so one. It should be made with Italian Arborio rice, a variety of short-grain rice. A supermarket cauliflower that has spent most of its life in cold storage will not be as perfumed as a fresh-picked one from the farmers' market. The fragrance of the oregano and the quality of the imported parmesan cheese will make a difference too.

6 cups chicken stock or low-sodium canned broth

2 sprigs of fresh oregano or 2 teaspoons dried oregano

2 tablespoons olive oil

$^1/_2$ cup finely chopped onions

1 teaspoon minced garlic

1 small head cauliflower, florets only, cut into $^3/_4$-inch pieces (about 3 cups)

Kosher salt

1 tablespoon unsalted butter

$1^1/_4$ cups uncooked Arborio rice

$^1/_4$ cup freshly grated parmesan, preferably Parmigiano-Reggiano

Freshly ground white pepper

6 sprigs of oregano, for garnish (optional)

MAKES 6 SERVINGS

1. Bring the stock to a boil in a saucepan. Add the sprigs of the oregano to the stock. Reduce the heat and simmer, covered, over low heat.

2. Heat the oil in a heavy sauté pan over medium-high heat and add the onions. Cook, stirring, until onions look light golden, about 5 minutes. Add the garlic and cook for 1 minute more.

3. Add the cauliflower and mix until well coated with oil. Add $^1/_2$ cup hot stock and sprinkle with salt. Reduce the heat and cook, covered, until the cauliflower is tender when pierced with a fork but not mushy, about 6 minutes. Uncover, increase the heat, and continue to cook, shaking and tossing, until the excess moisture evaporates and the cauliflower looks glazed and begins to brown. Reduce the heat to medium-low and stir in the butter.

4. Add the rice and mix to coat thoroughly. Add a ladleful of simmering stock and cook until the liquid is absorbed. During this time the rice should be stirred constantly, with a slow scraping motion, to prevent sticking and ensure maximum evaporation. Add more ladlesful of stock, one at a time, and continue with the same technique until the rice is cooked, about 20 minutes. Use only as much stock as you need; you may have some left over. The risotto should look creamy soft, but the rice grains should be a little chewy to the bite. Turn off the heat.

5. Fold in the parmesan and a generous sprinkle of white pepper. Check and add salt to taste. Cover and let rest for 5 minutes before serving. Serve risotto garnished with the sprigs of oregano, if using.

Serving Suggestions: Serve risotto in small portions as a first course. Or serve it on its own, accompanied with a vegetable dish like Roasted Sweet Potatoes with Cloves (page 218) or Carrot Salad with Coriander Vinegar (page 166). You can also serve risotto as a side dish with grilled or roasted meats like Roasted Chicken Legs with Sage (page 149) or Rosemary-crusted Veal Chops (page 160).

saffron pilaf with peas and almonds

Like vanilla, saffron has a distinct flowery aroma, considered elegant, even aristocratic. It also tints pilaf a beautiful golden color and gives it a sweet flavor. But saffron is an expensive spice, so save this exceptional pilaf for special occasions.

$^{1}/_{4}$ teaspoon saffron threads

1 cup uncooked basmati rice

2 cups water

1 tablespoon canola oil

$^{1}/_{2}$ cup chopped onions

3 whole cloves

1$^{3}/_{4}$ cups chicken stock, or low-sodium canned broth or water

$^{1}/_{2}$ teaspoon kosher salt

$^{1}/_{2}$ cup frozen peas

2 tablespoons toasted sliced almonds

MAKES 4 SERVINGS

1. Combine the saffron threads with 1 tablespoon water in a small bowl. Set aside. Rinse the rice and soak it in water for 30 minutes. Drain the rice, discarding the soaking water.

2. Heat the oil in a heavy saucepan over medium-high heat. Add the onions and cloves and cook, stirring occasionally, for 7 minutes, or until the onions are light golden. Add the rice and broth and bring to a boil, stirring to prevent rice from settling. Stir in the salt, the saffron mixture, and the peas.

3. Reduce the heat to medium and simmer, partly covered, for 10 minutes, or until most of the moisture is absorbed and the surface of the rice is covered with steam holes. Cover the pan tightly and reduce the heat to low. Let rice steam for 10 minutes. Remove from the heat and let the rice rest, covered, for 5 minutes. (*Covered, the pilaf will stay warm for 25 minutes.*)

4. Just before serving, fluff with a fork, garnish with almonds, and serve.

Serving Suggestions: Accompany this exquisitely flavored pilaf with any braised dish, ragout, or roast, including Pomegranate Braised Chicken (page 150), Barbecued Tarragon Game Hens with Quick Cherry Coulis (page 152), or Lamb Shanks in Black Pepper Sauce (page 157).

marjoram risotto with water chestnuts

The water chestnuts used in this risotto are not the common Chinese kind that you see in cans or sometimes fresh at Asian markets but an Italian variety called *Muzzanensis*. Its crisp flesh is fruity, like a pear, rather than starchy like Chinese water chestnuts. This variety of water chestnut grows wild alongside ponds in northern Italy, northern India, and some parts of China. It is available from time to time at Chinese markets, where it is called *ling kio*. The closest substitute for it is jícama or a tender fennel bulb.

4 cups beef stock or water

1 beef bouillon cube (optional)

6 sprigs of fresh marjoram or 2 teaspoons dried marjoram

2 tablespoons unsalted butter

½ cup finely chopped shallots

1 cup uncooked Arborio rice

½ pound fresh *ling kio* water chestnuts, peeled and thinly sliced, or jícama

¼ cup freshly grated parmesan

Freshly ground white pepper and kosher salt

MAKES 6 SERVINGS

1. Bring the stock or water to a boil in a saucepan. If you are using water, add the bouillon cube. Add 2 sprigs of the marjoram. Reduce the heat and simmer, covered, over low heat.

2. Combine the butter and shallots in a heavy sauté pan over medium-high heat. Cook, stirring, until the shallots look light golden, about 5 minutes.

3. Add the rice and mix to coat thoroughly with butter. Add a ladleful of simmering stock and cook until the liquid is absorbed. During this time the rice should be stirred constantly, with a slow scraping motion, to prevent sticking and ensure maximum evaporation. Add more ladlesful of stock, one at a time, and continue adding stock and stirring for 15 minutes.

4. Add the water chestnuts and continue to cook, adding ladlesful of stock as before, until the rice is cooked, about 10 minutes more. (If you are using jícama, cook it for only 5 minutes.) Use only as much stock as you need; you may have some left over. The water chestnuts should be crunchy, the risotto should look creamy soft, and the rice grains be al dente, a little chewy to the bite. Turn off the heat.

5. Fold in the parmesan, season with pepper, and add salt to taste. Cover and let rest for 5 minutes before serving. Serve garnished with the remaining sprigs of marjoram.

Serving Suggestions: Serve the risotto in small portions as a first course, on its own accompanied with salad greens dressed in Cumin Vinaigrette (page 82), or as a side dish with a grilled dish like Grilled Leg of Lamb with Smoked Chili Pepper Oil (page 88).

tarragon scallops kedgeree

Kedgeree is a traditional English brunch or luncheon dish. It is mild tasting and can be made with many kinds of seafood, but the best choices are scallops, shrimps, or mussels, flounder, haddock, or fresh or smoked salmon.

2 cups water

3 tablespoons unsalted butter or canola oil

1½ teaspoons kosher salt

1 cup uncooked converted rice

1 tablespoon all-purpose flour

1¼ cups skim milk

1 tablespoon chopped fresh tarragon or 1 teaspoon dried tarragon

¾ pound sea scallops, sliced into ¼-inch-thick rounds

3 scallions, trimmed and thinly sliced

Freshly ground white pepper and kosher salt

Lemon slices, for garnish

Sprigs of tarragon, for garnish

MAKES 4 SERVINGS

1. Combine the water, 1 tablespoon of the butter, and 1 teaspoon of the salt in a medium saucepan. Bring to a boil over high heat. Stir in the rice, reduce the heat to medium-low and simmer, covered, for 25 minutes, or until the water is absorbed and the rice is al dente.

2. Melt the remaining 2 tablespoons butter in a large frying pan over medium-high heat. Add the flour and cook, stirring, until it is fried but not brown, about 2 minutes. Add the milk and cook, stirring, until the sauce thickens, about 2 minutes. Reduce the heat and stir in the tarragon and scallops. Cook until the scallops barely turn white, about 1½ minutes.

3. Fold in the rice and scallions. Cook, stirring carefully so as not to break the scallops, until scallions are heated through. Sprinkle generously with pepper and salt to taste. Transfer the kedgeree to a serving platter and garnish with lemon slices and tarragon. (*Kedgeree may be made ahead and kept, tightly covered, for up to 1 day in the refrigerator.*) Serve hot, at room temperature, or chilled.

Serving Suggestions: Serve kedgeree at brunch accompanied with a sauce like Parsley Sauce (page 226) or Warm Tomato Butter with Paprika (page 236). It can be served as a light meal, accompanied with a salad like Celery Root Salad with Celery Seeds (page 167) and a salsa like Mango-Mint Salsa (page 231).

vegetables and fruits

green beans in mustard sauce

Green beans are a delicate vegetable, which should be flavored subtly and sparingly. Mustard is among the spices that enhance the natural qualities of beans. In this very simple dish, blanched beans are tossed in a mustard sauce. Lima, fava, and yard-long beans also work well in this recipe.

1 pound green beans, trimmed

1 tablespoon olive oil

2 teaspoons finely chopped garlic

1/2 teaspoon cornstarch

1/3 cup light cream or fruity white wine

1 teaspoon minced fresh chilies

2 teaspoons coarse-grain Dijon mustard

1 teaspoon powdered dry mustard

1/4 teaspoon ground allspice

Freshly ground black pepper and kosher salt

MAKES 4 SERVINGS

1. Bring a large pot of salted water to a boil and add the beans. Boil, uncovered, until the beans are cooked but still crisp, about 5 minutes. Drain, then shock the beans under cold running water. Set aside.

2. Heat the oil in a large skillet over medium-high heat. Add the garlic and cook until light golden, about 1 minute. Dissolve the cornstarch in the cream and add. Cook, stirring, until the sauce thickens. Stir in the chilies, Dijon mustard, dry mustard, and allspice. Cook until slightly thickened, about 2 minutes. Add the beans and toss until heated through. Turn off heat. Season to taste with pepper and salt. (*The beans may be made ahead and set aside for up to 4 hours at room temperature or kept, tightly covered, for up to 2 days in the refrigerator.*)

3. Serve hot, at room temperature, or chilled.

Serving Suggestions: These beans can be paired with any main dish but they are particularly good with seafood dishes like Black Pepper-rubbed Salmon (page 135) and poultry dishes like Thyme Roasted Chicken (page 151).

green beans with sichuan peppercorns

Sichuan peppercorns, also known as fagara (see page 45), are not pepper at all, though they resemble black pepper corns. Here green beans are sautéed in an oil infused with Sichuan peppercorns, which lend a sweet anise-ginger scent. For a spicier taste, stir half a teaspoon crushed red pepper into the oil before adding the beans.

1 tablespoon olive oil

2 teaspoons Sichuan peppercorns, crushed

2 teaspoons finely chopped garlic

1 pound green beans, trimmed

½ cup water

1½ teaspoons fresh lemon juice

Freshly ground black pepper and kosher salt

MAKES 4 SERVINGS

1. Heat the oil in a large skillet over medium-high heat. Add the pepper and garlic and cook until the garlic turns light golden, about 1 minute. Add the beans and toss until the spices are well distributed.

2. Add the water and cover the pan. Lower the heat and cook until the beans are tender, about 15 minutes. Uncover and continue cooking until all the moisture evaporates, about 2 minutes. Sprinkle with lemon juice. Season with pepper and salt to taste. (*The beans may be made ahead and set aside for up to 4 hours at room temperature or kept, tightly covered, for up to 2 days in the refrigerator.*)

3. Serve hot, at room temperature, or cold.

Serving Suggestions: These beans are good with steamed and sautéed poultry and seafood dishes like Steamed Duck with Star Anise (page 156) and Red Snapper with Anise-Tomato Sauce (page 140). To make a complete meal, add a rice dish such as Curried Rice (page 194) and a salsa such as Mango-Mint Salsa (page 231).

brussels sprouts with fennel

Brussels sprouts, which look like miniature cabbages, are inherently sweet. A little fennel draws out that sweetness. It also aids digestion. The almonds add yet another layer of sweetness.

1 tablespoon canola oil

1 teaspoon fennel seeds, lightly crushed

3 tablespoons slivered almonds

1 pint (³/₄ pound) brussels sprouts, trimmed and scored

¹/₄ to ¹/₂ teaspoon crushed red pepper

Kosher salt

¹/₂ cup water

Juice of ¹/₂ small lemon

MAKES 4 SERVINGS

1. Heat the oil over medium-high heat in a frying pan until hot. Add the fennel seeds and almonds. Cook, stirring, for a few seconds or until the fennel exudes its aroma. Do not let the nuts get brown. Add the brussels sprouts, red pepper, and salt to taste. Turn the brussels sprouts to coat with oil. Add the water and bring to a boil. Lower the heat and cook, covered, for 15 minutes, or until the brussels sprouts are very tender and the liquid is absorbed. Sprinkle with lemon juice and more salt and toss well. (*The brussels sprouts may be made ahead and set aside for up to 6 hours at room temperature or kept, tightly covered, for up to 3 days in the refrigerator.*)

2. Serve hot, at room temperature, or cold, straight from the refrigerator.

Note: For a more elegant presentation, omit the crushed red pepper and sprinkle an equal amount of Hungarian hot paprika on top at the end.

Serving Suggestions: Serve the brussels sprouts on a salad platter with Warm Potato Salad with Caraway Dressing (page 168) or Chick Pea Salad with Cumin (page 172). They make a lovely side dish with a stewed or braised entree like Ginger Ragout of Lamb (page 158).

smothered cabbage with caraway

These moist glazed shreds of cabbage, with slivers of carrot and crisp walnuts, are rendered sweet and fragrant with caraway. Caraway has a preserving effect on the vegetables; as a result, the dish keeps well without any change of flavor.

1½ teaspoons caraway seeds

1 tablespoon canola or olive oil

1 large carrot, julienned (1 cup)

1 teaspoon sugar

1 small (1½ pounds) cabbage, trimmed and sliced as for coleslaw

1 cup water

Kosher salt

¼ cup finely chopped toasted walnuts

MAKES 4 SERVINGS

1. Cook the caraway seeds in the oil in a large heavy skillet over medium-high heat, stirring, until the spice gives off fragrance, about 2 minutes. Add the carrots and sugar and cook, turning and tossing, for 5 minutes.

2. Stir in the cabbage and the water. Reduce the heat to low and cook the cabbage, covered, until the liquid is absorbed and the cabbage is soft, about 15 minutes. Uncover and continue to cook, tossing, until excess moisture evaporates. Season to taste with salt. (*The cabbage may be made ahead and set aside for several hours at room temperature or kept, tightly covered, for up to 3 days in the refrigerator.*)

3. Sprinkle with walnuts and serve hot or at room temperature.

Serving Suggestions: Serve this dish with Roasted Chicken Legs with Sage (page 149), Pepper-rubbed Rack of Lamb (page 159), or Fried Clams with Barbecue Spices (page 108).

glazed carrots with cloves

Cloves accentuate the inherent sweetness of carrots. Cut the carrot slices on the diagonal to expose the maximum surface to the cloves and ginger.

1 pound carrots, peeled and sliced ¼ inch thick on the diagonal (3 cups)

½ cup water

½ teaspoon ground cloves

½ teaspoon ground ginger

2 teaspoons unsalted butter or fruity olive oil

1 teaspoon sugar

1. Place the carrots, water, the cloves, ginger, and butter in a heavy skillet and cook, covered, over medium heat until the carrots are tender, about 12 minutes. Uncover and continue to cook until the liquid is absorbed. Add the sugar, and cook, uncovered, stirring, until the sugar melts and glazes the carrots. (*The carrots may be made ahead and set aside for up to 6 hours at room temperature or kept, tightly covered, for up to 3 days in the refrigerator.*)

2. Serve hot, at room temperature, or chilled.

Serving Suggestions: These carrots are incredible served with grilled or sautéed fish, poultry, and meat, such as Flash-grilled Flounder with Ajowan (page 132), Grilled Squab with Fragrant Spice Rub (page 63), and Herb Citrus–rubbed Filet Mignon (page 67). For a composed vegetarian platter, pair the carrots with Smothered Cabbage with Caraway (page 207) and Green Beans with Sichuan Peppercorns (page 205).

turmeric cauliflower

Cauliflower is tinted gold with turmeric, the yellow lemon-flavored powder. Cooked this way, it tastes wonderful without any of the usual butter or cream enrichments. Try to find a small spotless, snow-white cauliflower; it will be more fragrant and fresher tasting than a large old one.

1 small (about 1½ pounds) cauliflower, cut into 1½-inch florets

1 tablespoon canola oil

½ teaspoon turmeric

¼ teaspoon ground red pepper

1 cup chicken stock, low-sodium canned broth, or ½ cup stock and ½ cup water

1½ teaspoons kosher salt

¼ cup finely chopped cilantro

MAKES 4 SERVINGS

1. Heat the oil in a large skillet over medium heat. When the oil is hot, add the turmeric and cook until it gives off aroma. Add the cauliflower, toss until it is coated with oil, and add the pepper, salt, and water, mixing well. Cover the pan, lower the heat, and cook until the cauliflower is tender when pierced with a knife, about 10 minutes. Uncover and continue cooking, turning and tossing, until the excess moisture evaporates and the cauliflower begins to brown, about 5 minutes. Stir in the cilantro. (*The cauliflower may be made ahead and set aside for up to 6 hours at room temperature or kept, tightly covered, for up to 2 days in the refrigerator.*)

2. Serve hot, at room temperature, or chilled.

Serving Suggestions: The cauliflower is good with grilled or sautéed fish such as Grilled Mustard Tuna (page 133) or Shrimp Sauté with Bay (page 141). You can also mince the cooked cauliflower and use it to fill Savory Herb Crêpes (page 253) topped with Fresh Tomato-Ginger Sauce (page 227).

cauliflower with sumac

In this very simple Lebanese recipe, steamed cauliflower is doused with cool minty yogurt and then dusted with sumac, a burgundy powder (see page 47). Sumac gives the cauliflower a tart, cool touch.

1½ cups plain nonfat yogurt

Freshly ground black pepper and kosher salt

1 small (about 1½ pounds) cauliflower, cut into 1½-inch florets

1 teaspoon sumac

1 tablespoon minced mint leaves

MAKES 4 SERVINGS

1. Using a fork, lightly beat the yogurt in a bowl with pepper and salt to taste. Cover and refrigerate until needed.

2. Bring water to a boil in a steamer. Place the cauliflower on the steamer rack and steam until tender but a little crunchy to the bite, about 8 minutes. Drain and place on a platter. Pour the yogurt over the vegetable. Sprinkle with sumac and mint. Serve at room temperature.

Serving Suggestions: Serve the cauliflower with a grilled poultry dish like Grilled Chicken Kabobs with Anise (page 154) or a grilled meat dish like Grilled Leg of Lamb with Smoked Chili Pepper Oil (page 88). You can also make it a light meal accompanied with a bread like Thyme Pita Bread (page 248) or a substantial salad like Bulgur Salad with Allspice (page 173).

cucumber with toasted cumin seeds

An old technique of flavoring vegetables that is popular all the way from the Mediterranean to the extreme east of Asia. Cumin seeds are used whole to retain the lovely pale green color of cucumber.

1 pound cucumbers

1 teaspoon fresh lemon juice

Freshly ground black pepper and kosher salt

1 teaspoon Toasted Cumin Seeds (page 19)

MAKES 4 SERVINGS

1. Peel the cucumbers and cut in half lengthwise. Scrape out the seeds and discard. Slice the cucumber 1/8-inch thick.

2. Place the cucumber slices in a nonstick sauté pan over medium-high heat. When the cucumber begins to steam and sizzle, cover the pan. Lower the heat and steam until the cucumber looks translucent but is still crisp, about 3 minutes.

3. Uncover, sprinkle with lemon juice, pepper, and salt, and toss well. (*The cucumbers may be made ahead and set aside for up to 6 hours at room temperature or kept, tightly covered, for up to 3 days in the refrigerator.*)

4. Just before serving, sprinkle with the cumin seeds. Serve hot, cold, or at room temperature.

Serving Suggestions: Serve with any fish dish such as Bluefish with Tomato-Coriander Sauce (page 130), Steamed Fish with Ginger Essence (page 131), or Grilled Mustard Tuna (page 133).

glazed cucumbers with sesame

Ivory specks of sesame, imbued with their special smoky-nutty aroma, are strewn over pale green cucumber sticks. Sesame seeds are rich in protein but also high in oil content. They turn rancid easily when left in a warm place. Before starting to make this dish, check that the sesame seeds taste fresh.

1 tablespoon sesame seeds

1 pound cucumbers

1 tablespoon unsalted butter

¼ teaspoon kosher salt

¼ teaspoon freshly ground white pepper

MAKES 4 SERVINGS

1. Place the sesame seeds in a small ungreased frying pan over medium-high heat. Toast, stirring and shaking, until the seeds start to smell and turn light gold. Do not let the seeds brown, or they will lose their delicate aroma and turn bitter.

2. Peel the cucumbers and cut in half lengthwise. Scrape out the seeds and discard. Cut the cucumber across into 2-inch pieces. Cut each piece lengthwise into ½-inch-thick sticks.

3. Melt the butter in a sauté pan over medium-high heat. Add the cucumber sticks, salt and pepper. Cook, turning and tossing, for 4 minutes, or until the cucumber begins to turn opaque. Sprinkle 1 tablespoon water over the cucumber and cover the pan. Cook until cucumber is soft, 4 to 5 minutes. Uncover and increase the heat. Cook, shaking and tossing, until the excess moisture evaporates and the cucumber looks glazed. Serve hot, sprinkled with sesame seeds.

Serving Suggestions: This makes a lovely side dish for such subtle fish and poultry preparations as Steamed Sea Bass with Dill (page 138), Shrimp Sauté with Bay (page 141), and Grilled Chicken Kabobs with Anise (page 154).

mushrooms with nutmeg

This method of cooking mushrooms is an effective and foolproof way to bring out their essence. Nutmeg by itself is not a sweet spice, but it draws out the sweetness of anything it is cooked with. Here, mushrooms are first braised in liquid and then pan-roasted with nutmeg. The flavors mellow and the fragrance turns caramel sweet.

1 to 2 tablespoons canola oil

2 large cloves garlic, thinly sliced

1½ pounds fancy mushrooms, such as a combination of cremini and oyster, or white button mushrooms, sliced

¼ cup white wine, chicken stock, or water

¼ teaspoon freshly grated nutmeg

Freshly ground black pepper and kosher salt

2 tablespoons chopped parsley

MAKES 4 SERVINGS

1. Heat 1 tablespoon of the oil in a large sauté pan over medium-high heat. Add the garlic. When the garlic begins to brown, add the mushrooms and cook, stirring, until they begin to steam, about 4 minutes. Add the wine and cook, covered, for 6 minutes, or until the mushrooms are tender.

2. Uncover and increase the heat to high. Cook, turning and tossing, until the moisture evaporates and the mushrooms begin to fry. Reduce the heat to medium-high, sprinkle with nutmeg and, if desired, the remaining 1 tablespoon of oil. Continue pan-roasting the mushrooms for 2 minutes, or until they look glazed. Turn off the heat and season with pepper and salt. Sprinkle with parsley and serve.

Serving Suggestions: These mushrooms are perfect as a luncheon dish or breakfast or brunch dish stuffed in Savory Herb Crêpes (page 253) or Chili Tortilla Bread (page 241) or as an accompaniment to Tarragon Scallops Kedgeree (page 201). The mushrooms make a lovely side dish with Thyme Roasted Chicken (page 151) or Rosemary-crusted Veal Chops (page 160).

chili hash-brown potatoes

Boiled potatoes are slowly pan-roasted until crusty brown, then they are sprinkled with Chili Powder and paprika. The red hue of paprika makes them look hotter than they really are. This dish tastes even better made with day-old potatoes. Keeping that in mind, I always boil a few extra when boiled potatoes are on the dinner menu.

2 tablespoons olive oil

1½ pounds Yukon Gold or white or red new potatoes, scrubbed, boiled, and cut into ½-inch dice

2 teaspoons Chili Powder (page 54)

1 teaspoon Hungarian paprika

Kosher salt

MAKES 4 SERVINGS

Heat the oil in a heavy nonstick sauté pan over medium-high heat until very hot. Add the potatoes and cook, turning and tossing, until they are brown and crusted, about 12 minutes. Sprinkle with Chili Powder, paprika, and salt. Toss for 2 minutes, or until the spices are cooked. Serve immediately.

Serving Suggestions: These potatoes are great at breakfast or brunch or as a side dish with roasted or grilled food like Thyme Roasted Chicken (page 151) or Pan-grilled Flounder with Cajun Spices (page 59). For a vegetarian meal, serve them with Cool Yogurt Dill Sauce with Dried Cranberries and Almonds (page 230) and Parsley Rice (page 192).

cumin potatoes

Cumin and potato are an ideal match; they taste incredibly good together. The cumin also cuts the heavy starchy quality of potatoes. In this dish, they are pan-roasted in a cumin-infused oil, which gives them a light smoky flavor. You can substitute sweet potatoes for some of the potatoes.

1 tablespoon olive oil

1 teaspoon cumin seeds

1 to 1¼ pounds waxy red or white new potatoes, peeled and cut into 1-inch pieces

1 cup water

Freshly ground black pepper and kosher salt

MAKES 4 SERVINGS

1. Heat the oil in a large nonstick sauté pan over medium-high heat. Add the cumin seeds. When they turn several shades darker, add the potatoes, mixing well to coat with the spice oil. Add the water and bring to a boil.

2. Lower the heat and cook, covered, for 18 minutes, or until the potatoes are tender. Uncover and increase the heat. Continue cooking until all the liquid evaporates and the potatoes are lightly browned and glazed. Turn off the heat. Season generously with pepper and add salt to taste. (*The potatoes may be made ahead and set aside for up to 6 hours at room temperature.*)

3. Serve hot or at room temperature.

Serving Suggestions: These potatoes are nice by themselves with cocktails. Serve them with grilled or sautéed main dishes such as Herb Citrus–rubbed Filet Mignon (page 67) or Grilled Mustard Tuna (page 133). For a unique taste experience, serve the potatoes topped with a dip like Cilantro-Walnut Dip (page 229) or Yogurt Dip with Herbs (page 230).

pumpkin with allspice

Pumpkin pieces are coated with a mixture of allspice, black pepper, pineapple juice, and sugar, then baked. Decidedly sweet to the taste, they are crusty on the outside and creamy soft within. Calabaza, or Mexican pumpkin, flattish-round with greenish-yellow spotted skin, is preferred for this recipe.

2 to 2¹/₂ pounds Mexican pumpkin (calabaza) or butternut or acorn squash

1 teaspoon ground allspice

¹/₂ teaspoon freshly ground black pepper

¹/₄ cup pineapple juice

1 tablespoon sugar

Vegetable oil spray

MAKES 6 SERVINGS

1. Preheat the oven to 400°F.

2. Cut open the pumpkin and scrape out and discard the seeds. Cut the pumpkin into 1-inch wedges and peel. Cut each wedge into 1-inch pieces and put them in a bowl. Add the allspice, pepper, and pineapple juice. Toss well and let stand for 10 minutes.

3. Arrange the pumpkin in a baking dish in 1 layer. Pour any remaining marinade over the pumpkin, sprinkle with sugar, and spray lightly with oil. Bake for 30 minutes, or until the pumpkin is tender and lightly crusted. (*The pumpkin may be made ahead and set aside for up to 3 hours at room temperature or kept, tightly covered, for up to 3 days in the refrigerator.*)

4. Serve hot, at room temperature, or cold, straight from the refrigerator.

Serving Suggestions: Serve the pumpkin with dishes of warm spices and winter flavors, such as Rosemary-crusted Veal Chops (page 160), Seared Red Chicken (page 91), Mild Indian Chile with Paprika (page 163), or Lamb Shanks in Black Pepper Sauce (page 157). It can be pureed and used as a stuffing for crêpes or spooned over a cream soup like Kale Soup with Crabmeat and Thyme (page 124).

forever red tomatoes

If we could all get our wish, red vine-ripened tomatoes would be plentiful year round, but that is indeed wishful thinking. Often the tomatoes are yellowish-red, under-ripe, and insipid tasting, particularly in the winter months. In such situations, turmeric is your miracle spice. Simply sprinkle a pinch over a small batch of tomatoes and see the color being drawn out of the tomatoes. For best results, the turmeric must cook with the tomatoes for at least five minutes, to allow the color to blend and smooth out.

1 tablespoon olive oil or canola oil

1 teaspoon minced garlic (optional)

1½ pounds tomatoes, cut into 1-inch wedges

½ teaspoon turmeric

1 teaspoon balsamic vinegar or fresh lemon juice

MAKES 4 SERVINGS

1. Heat the oil in a sauté pan over medium-high heat until hot. Stir in the garlic, if using. Add the tomatoes and sprinkle with turmeric. Cook, turning and tossing occasionally, until the seasoned oil is evenly distributed and the tomatoes are slightly soft, about 5 minutes. Sprinkle with vinegar. (*The tomatoes may be set aside for up to 6 hours at room temperature or kept, tightly covered, for up to 4 days in the refrigerator.*)

2. Serve warm, at room temperature, or cold.

Serving Suggestions: These tomatoes make a spectacular side dish for such grilled poultry or fish dishes as Grilled Chicken Kabobs with Anise (page 154) or Shrimp Sauté with Bay (page 141). The tomatoes can also be folded into pasta or cooked rice or used as a topping for bread.

roasted sweet potatoes with cloves

Deep orange sweet potatoes are extraordinary when flavored with orange juice and clove. In the absence of butter and cream, the caramelized flavor of roasted yam really comes through. I add nuts only when I serve it at Thanksgiving.

2 pounds sweet potatoes, scrubbed

⅓ cup fresh orange juice

½ cup lowfat (2%) milk

¼ teaspoon ground cloves

½ cup pecans, toasted (optional)

MAKES 6 SERVINGS

1. Preheat the oven to 400°F.

2. Place the sweet potatoes in a baking dish. Bake in the middle level of the oven until the sweet potatoes feel very soft to the touch, 45 minutes to 1 hour. When the sweet potatoes are cool enough to handle, peel and place in a bowl. Add the orange juice, milk, and cloves. Mash and beat until thoroughly mixed. If you are using pecans, fold them in. Serve hot.

Serving Suggestions: Serve this with any herb-laced grilled, roasted, or pot-roasted poultry, such as Thyme Roasted Chicken (page 151), Pot Roast of Chicken with Rosemary, Figs, and Pine Nuts (page 146), or Roasted Chicken Legs with Sage (page 149). The sweet potatoes are also good with dishes with Caribbean accents like Jerk Chicken (page 61) and Arroz con Pollo (page 93).

seared pears with cloves

Pan-roasted pears are light and smoky, with caramelized streaks from their own natural sugar. A touch of clove lends color and enhances the sweetness of the pears. For best results, use pears that are ripe but not soft; very ripe ones will turn mushy and fall apart during cooking.

1 tablespoon unsalted butter

4 ripe Anjou pears, peeled, cored, and sliced

1/8 teaspoon ground cloves

1 tablespoon water

MAKES 4 SERVINGS

1. Melt the butter in a large nonstick frying pan over medium-high heat. Add the pear slices and spread them so that most of the slices touch the bottom of the pan. Cook the pears undisturbed for 1 to 2 minutes, or until they are light brown on the underside.

2. Using tongs or a spatula, turn all the pieces and brown the second side. Mix cloves and water and sprinkle over. Continue to sear the pears, turning and tossing, for 1 minute. (*The pears may be made ahead and set aside for up to 6 hours at room temperature or kept, tightly covered, for up to 10 days in the refrigerator.*)

3. Serve hot, at room temperature, or cold, straight from the refrigerator.

Serving Suggestions: Serve with grilled or sautéed dishes like Flash-grilled Flounder with Ajowan (page 132) or Grilled Pork with Epazote (page 162). You can also serve the pears stuffed in Savory Herb Crêpes (page 253) as a side dish or stuffed in Anise-Pistachio Crêpes (page 256) with Saffron Cream (page 261) as a dessert.

stewed apples with white pepper and fennel

These stewed apples are fragrant with clove and complex tasting—spicy, tart, and sweet, all at the same time. The dish combines the season's first apples and the last of the tomatoes, with some prunes thrown in for color and intense sweetness. Although the apples in this dish are flavored with fennel just like the Apple Compote with Fennel, it flavors the dish in a totally different way, because the fennel is cooked in liquid as opposed to being infused in oil.

1 to 1¼ pounds apples, preferably Granny Smiths, peeled and cut into chunks (2 cups)

1 pound yellow or red tomatoes, peeled and chopped (1 cup)

½ cup white wine or apple juice

1 teaspoon minced garlic

½ to 1 teaspoon ground white pepper

1 teaspoon fennel seeds, crushed

4 whole cloves, crushed

½ cup pitted prunes, quartered

MAKES 3 CUPS

1. Combine the apples, tomatoes, wine, garlic, pepper, fennel, and cloves in a small saucepan over medium-high heat and bring to a boil. Reduce the heat and simmer, covered, until the apples are very soft, about 20 minutes. If the moisture evaporates too fast or if the apples are naturally dry to begin with, add a little extra wine or apple juice. Turn off the heat.

2. Stir in the prunes and let stand, covered, for at least 15 minutes to allow the prunes to soak up juices. (*The dish can be made ahead and set aside, covered, for several hours at room temperature or kept, tightly covered, for up to 1 week in the refrigerator.*)

3. Serve warm or at room temperature.

Serving Suggestions: Serve the apples with poultry, game, or pork dishes, such as Roasted Chicken Legs with Sage (page 149), Steamed Duck with Star Anise (page 156), or Grilled Pork with Epazote (page 162).

apple compote with fennel

Apples have a great ability to combine with both sweet and savory flavors. Granny Smith apples, bright green and crisp, are particularly good cooked with onions. What is interesting is that this apple, which is known for its tartness, is rendered sweet without the addition of sugar. The sweetness comes from fennel, which draws out and accentuates the sweetness of onions.

1½ tablespoons olive oil

½ teaspoon fennel seeds

4 large (2¼ to 2½ pounds) Granny Smith apples, peeled, cored, and sliced

1 large (½ pound) onion, peeled, halved, and cut into ⅛-inch-thick slices

¼ teaspoon ground cinnamon

½ teaspoon ground ginger

MAKES 2½ CUPS

1. Heat the oil in a nonstick frying pan over medium-high heat until very hot. Add the fennel seeds and apples. Cook, stirring occasionally, until the apples are cooked but not soft and lightly browned, about 6 minutes. Add the onion, cinnamon, and ginger. Cook for 6 minutes more, or until the onion is soft and translucent. Turn off the heat.

2. Coarsely puree the apple mixture in a food processor or a food mill. Transfer to a bowl. (*The compote can be made ahead and set aside, covered, for several hours at room temperature, refrigerated for up to 5 days, or frozen.*)

3. Serve at room temperature or chilled.

Serving Suggestions: Serve as a relish with grilled or roasted meats like Milk-marinated Grilled Pork Chops with Ajowan (page 161) or Grilled Squab with Fragrant Spice Rub (page 63).

pan-grilled pineapple with young ginger

The natural sugar present in pineapple caramelizes during pan-grilling for a unique accent in the fusion with ginger and lime. This dish excels when you use sweet ripe pineapple. Young ginger, also known as Hawaiian ginger (see page 38), is immature ginger, cream colored and translucent, with bright pink shoots. It arrives at markets, especially those carrying Asian produce, in early summer. It is ambrosial.

¼ cup finely shredded young ginger or very fresh juicy ginger

2 tablespoons rice wine or white wine vinegar

1 teaspoon grated lime zest

¼ to ½ teaspoon freshly ground white pepper

1 medium-size ripe pineapple

Vegetable oil spray

MAKES 4 SERVINGS

1. Combine the ginger, vinegar, lime zest, and pepper in a small bowl. Cover and refrigerate until needed.

2. Peel, core, and cut the pineapple into ¹/₂-inch-thick slices. Heat a griddle large enough to hold all the slices in 1 layer over high heat until very hot. Spray the griddle with oil and place the pineapple on it. Pan-roast until the slices lose excess moisture and look glazed and lightly streaked, turning as often as necessary, about 6 minutes. Remove to a large shallow dish. Leave pineapple whole or cut into 1-inch pieces. Let stand until cool.

3. When completely cool, spread the ginger mixture on top. Cover and refrigerate for at least 30 minutes before serving.

Serving Suggestions: Serve the pineapple as an accompaniment to a main course or as a dessert. It is particularly good with grilled seafood or pork dishes like Chili-stuffed Prawns (page 104), Milk-marinated Grilled Pork Chops with Ajowan (page 162), Black Pepper-rubbed Salmon (page 135), and Curry-grilled Scallops (page 57), or a poultry dish like Steamed Duck with Star Anise (page 156).

pan-grilled plantains with ginger

This is the simplest version of grilled plantain, the Latin American favorite, I have tasted so far, hailing from Guyana. The plantain slices are pan-grilled and basted with a ginger-rum mixture. They are quite extraordinary. If you have never tried plantain, then here is your awakening.

2 very ripe black-skinned plantains

1 teaspoon ground ginger

1 tablespoon rum, fruit juice, or water

Olive oil spray

MAKES 4 SERVINGS

1. Peel the plantains and slice them ¼ inch thick on the diagonal. Stir the ginger into the rum in a small bowl.

2. Spray a large nonstick frying pan with oil and place it over high heat. When it is very hot, place the plantain slices in a single layer on the frying pan. Spray the top with oil. Cook until the underside is streaked brown, about 2 minutes. Turn the slices with a spatula, and pan-grill, basting with ginger-rum until they look brown and caramelized, about 6 minutes. Serve immediately.

Note: The dish can be made with ground cinnamon in place of the ginger.

Serving Suggestions: This dish lends a sweet contrast to spicy dishes, particularly those with Latin American and Caribbean flavors. It is particularly good with Jerk Chicken (page 61) and Island Vegetable Stew with Thyme (page 177). You can also pair it with rich-tasting poultry like Grilled Squab with Fragrant Spice Rub (page 63) or a fish dish like Red Snapper with Anise-Tomato Sauce (page 140).

sauces, salsas, and spicy condiments

parsley sauce

1 cup (8-ounce container) nonfat sour cream or plain nonfat yogurt

2 tablespoons wine vinegar

Kosher salt

1½ teaspoons sugar

1 cup (packed) Italian flat-leaf parsley leaves and tender stems

1 cup (loosely packed) basil leaves

A light and refreshing sauce, this is reminiscent of springtime and summer to come. Make it with Italian flat-leaf parsley, which has more flavor than the curly kind. The sauce goes with all fried foods and grilled and roasted meats. It makes a dip for steamed vegetables, a foil for cooked seafood, such as crab or lobster meat, and a dressing for salad.

MAKES 2 CUPS

Combine all the ingredients in a blender or food processor and process until they turn into a fine puree. Cover and refrigerate. (*The sauce keeps well, covered, for up to 1 week in the refrigerator.*)

lemon saffron sauce

¼ teaspoon saffron threads

2 tablespoons hot water

1 cup (8-ounce container) plain nonfat yogurt

½ teaspoon grated lemon zest

2 teaspoons fresh lemon juice

1 tablespoon sugar

¼ teaspoon freshly ground white pepper

There really is no spice sweeter or more sensuous than saffron. Whether used in a dessert sauce (see page 261) or in a savory one as here, it is magic on the palate. Serve this sauce with subtle steamed and poached dishes. Seafood is particularly enhanced by saffron sauce; try it with Steamed Lobster in Juniper Berry Vapor (page 142).

MAKES 1 CUP

Crush the saffron with your fingertips to a fine powder and place in a 2-cup bowl. Add the hot water and set aside for 10 minutes. Crush the saffron with the back of a spoon to extract the color and flavor. Add all the other ingredients and whisk vigorously until the sugar dissolves. Cover and refrigerate until needed. (*The sauce keeps well, covered, for 10 days in the refrigerator.*)

fresh tomato-ginger sauce

1 pound ripe red tomatoes, peeled, halved, and seeded

¼ pound shallots, peeled

1 tablespoon chopped fresh ginger, preferably Hawaiian ginger (see page 37)

1 teaspoon powdered dry mustard

This lovely salmon-pink sauce can bring forth cheers when made with just-picked homegrown tomatoes and Hawaiian ginger. Its summery flavor is perfect with grilled seafood and chicken, kabobs and fritters. For best flavor, serve the sauce chilled.

MAKES 2 CUPS

Combine the tomatoes and shallots in a food processor and process until pureed as smooth or as coarse as you like. Pour the sauce into a saucepan and bring to a boil. Stir in the ginger and mustard and simmer, uncovered, for 5 minutes. Transfer the sauce to a nice bowl, cover, and refrigerate. (*The sauce keeps well, covered, for up to 3 days in the refrigerator.*) Serve the sauce chilled.

sweet sesame dipping sauce

⅓ cup minced shallots

1 tablespoon sesame seeds

2 teaspoons olive oil

½ cup prune juice

1 tablespoon light (low-sodium) soy sauce

1 tablespoon fresh lemon juice

¼ teaspoon ground red pepper

1 teaspoon creamy peanut butter, without added sugar

¼ teaspoon dark sesame oil or fruity olive oil

½ teaspoon kosher salt

A unique sesame sauce, from the plantation workers of Malaysia, this is without doubt one of the most appealing I have ever encountered in my travels. This is my adaptation of the recipe. Serve the sauce with grilled and fried foods and as a dip for bread.

MAKES ⅔ CUP

Place the shallots, sesame seeds, and oil in a small saucepan over medium-high heat and cook for 3 minutes, or until the shallots are lightly colored. Reduce the heat and add the prune juice, soy sauce, lemon juice, red pepper, peanut butter, sesame oil, and salt. Cook, stirring, for 1 minute, or until the peanut butter is fully dissolved. Transfer the sauce to a bowl, cover, and refrigerate. (*The sauce keeps well, covered, for up to 1 week in the refrigerator or for up to 6 months in the freezer.*) Serve the sauce warm or chilled.

zaatar dip

2 tablespoons sesame seeds

2 tablespoons fresh thyme
leaves or 4 teaspoons dried
thyme

2 teaspoons fresh chopped
marjoram or oregano or
1/2 teaspoon dried marjoram
or oregano

2 teaspoons sumac

Kosher salt

1/4 cup fruity olive oil

Zaatar, used since antiquity in the eastern Mediterranean region, is a blend of toasted sesame seeds, thyme, and sumac, a sour ruby-colored powder (see page 228). Some add a little marjoram or oregano to bolster the sweetness of the sesame as well as to mellow and diffuse the thyme accent. The blend is smoky and very aromatic. Stirred into olive oil, zaatar turns into a marvelous dip for vegetables, breads, and grilled meat or fish. You can also use it to enrich soups and sauces. I like to dribble it over steamed vegetables and greens or use it as an infused oil to cook highly aromatic vegetables like broccoli raab.

MAKES 1/2 CUP

1. Place the sesame seeds in an ungreased frying pan over medium-high heat. Toast, stirring and shaking, until the seeds start to smell and to turn light gold. Do not let the seeds brown or they will lose their delicate aroma and turn bitter. Transfer to a bowl and let cool.

2. Stir in the thyme, marjoram, sumac, 1/4 teaspoon salt, and olive oil. Taste and add more salt, if desired. For best results, let the dip stand for 3 days at cool room temperature for flavors to peak. (*The dip keeps well, covered, for up to 10 days at room temperature or for up to 6 months in the refrigerator.*)

mint sauce

1/4 cup minced mint

1 cup (8-ounce container)
plain nonfat yogurt

1 small cucumber, peeled,
seeded, and grated

2 teaspoons sugar

Kosher salt

Among the best ways to showcase the flavor of mint is this sauce. Mint's spicy lemon scent and cool menthol flavor make it particularly well suited to summertime barbecues and fried foods.

MAKES 1 1/2 CUPS

Combine the mint, yogurt, cucumber, sugar, and salt to taste in a nice 2-cup bowl and whisk until mixed. Cover and refrigerate until needed. *The sauce keeps well, covered, for up to 1 week in the refrigerator.* Serve the sauce chilled.

hot wasabi dipping sauce

1 teaspoon cumin seeds

1/2 cup wine vinegar

2 tablespoons light (low-sodium) soy sauce

2 tablespoons creamy peanut butter, without added sugar

1 teaspoon minced garlic

1 teaspoon grated orange zest

1 tablespoon minced cilantro or parsley

1 tablespoon wasabi paste or 1 1/2 teaspoons wasabi powder

A fusion of Japanese and Southeast Asian flavors, this sauce is enlivened with wasabi (see page 49), which jolts the palate with its characteristic sting. Once exposed to air and light, wasabi loses its punch within an hour, so use the sauce immediately. Serve it with fried foods and grilled or steamed fish and poultry.

MAKES 3/4 CUP

1. Heat a small ungreased frying pan over medium-high heat and add the cumin seeds. Toast, shaking and tossing, until the seeds are several shades darker and give off a nutty aroma. Remove from the pan and let cool completely.

2. Combine the vinegar, soy sauce, peanut butter, garlic, orange zest, and cilantro in a small bowl and whisk until thoroughly blended. Stir in the cumin seeds and let stand for at least 15 minutes or cover and refrigerate for 1 hour. Just before serving, stir in the wasabi. Use within 1 hour.

cilantro-walnut dip

1 cup (packed) cilantro leaves and tender stems

3 fresh chilies, stemmed and seeded

2 cloves garlic

1/4 cup chopped walnuts

2 tablespoons sugar

1/2 cup fresh lemon juice

Kosher salt

This dip of afghan origin is spicy, aromatic, and full of flavor. It is particularly good with steamed seafood, yet its pestolike texture makes it suited to pasta and grains as well.

MAKES 1 CUP

Place the cilantro, chilies, garlic, walnuts, sugar, and lemon juice in the container of blender or food processor. Process, scraping down the sides once or twice, until the mixture is finely pureed. Season with salt to taste. Serve right away or transfer to a bowl, cover, and refrigerate. Serve chilled, straight from the refrigerator. (*The dip keeps well in the refrigerator, covered for up to 1 week or for up to 9 months in the freezer. To prevent discoloration, pour a thin layer of oil on top, to create an airtight seal, before covering with a lid.*)

cool yogurt dill sauce with dried cranberries and almonds

1 cup (8-ounce container) plain nonfat yogurt

1 small cucumber peeled, seeded, and grated

2 teaspoons chopped dill

1 tablespoon chopped dried cranberries or cherries

2 tablespoons sliced almonds, toasted

A holdover from the ancient Persian empire, this dill-scented yogurt sauce is filled with dried fruits and nuts. Traditionally dried sour cherries are used, but dried cranberries work just as well. Serve the sauce with sautéed shellfish, grilled fish or chicken, or roast meat.

MAKES 2 CUPS

Combine the yogurt, cucumber, dill, dried cranberries, and almonds in a nice bowl, cover tightly, and refrigerate until thoroughly chilled, at least 1 hour. (*The sauce keeps well, covered, for up to 2 days in the refrigerator.*) Serve chilled.

yogurt dip with herbs

1 small cucumber

1 cup part skim ricotta

1 cup (8-ounce container) plain nonfat yogurt

1 teaspoon minced garlic

1½ teaspoons fresh lemon juice

1 teaspoon minced mint

2 teaspoons minced basil

Kosher salt (optional)

A refreshing sauce made by combining ricotta and yogurt with herbs, this goes well with grilled meat and kabobs or roasts. You can also serve the dip with steamed vegetables or seafood.

MAKES 2 CUPS

1. Peel and cut the cucumber in half lengthwise. Using a spoon, scrape out the central part with the seeds and discard. Grate the cucumber using the medium hole of a grater and put in a strainer. Press and squeeze, extracting as much cucumber liquid as possible. Put the cucumber shreds in a medium bowl. Set the strainer on top.

2. Place the ricotta in the sieve and press it through, mashing and stirring, directly into the bowl with the cucumber. Add the yogurt and whisk until thoroughly blended. Add the garlic, lemon juice, mint, and basil and continue to whisk until very light and fluffy. Cover and refrigerate until thoroughly chilled, at least 1 hour. (*The sauce keeps well, covered, for up to 4 days in the refrigerator.*) Just before serving, season with salt, if desired.

avocado, onion, and cilantro relish

1 small ripe avocado,
preferably Haas

2 tablespoons balsamic
vinegar

¾ cup finely chopped red
onion

¾ cup chopped tomatoes

¾ cup chopped cilantro

1 tablespoon chopped
jalapeños (optional)

Freshly ground black pepper
and kosher salt (optional)

A familiar combination of ingredients, this avocado relish is tasty enough to be eaten by the spoonful. The only improvement you could possibly make is to add half a cup of cooked black beans, if you happen to have some on hand. Serve the relish with just about any dish, including grilled fish, roast chicken, barbecued meat, and grain salads. The relish should be made fresh and served soon thereafter, as the avocado quickly turns muddy colored.   **MAKES 2 CUPS**

Peel the avocado and remove the pit. Cut the flesh into neat $1/2$-inch dice and put the pieces in a bowl. Add the vinegar and toss to coat. Add the onion, tomatoes, and cilantro. Add the chilies, if using. Mix gently, with a folding motion so as not to crush the avocado too much. Taste and add pepper and salt, if desired. Serve immediately.

mango-mint salsa

2 medium-ripe mangoes, chopped
(2 cups)

¼ cup sliced red radishes

¼ cup chopped black olives,
preferably Mediterranean

2 fresh chilies, stemmed and
chopped with seeds

2 tablespoons fresh lemon juice

2 tablespoons fresh orange juice

2 tablespoons finely chopped mint

Freshly ground black pepper

Sprigs of mint, for garnish

Make the salsa in summer when sweet, aromatic mangoes, free of fiber, are flown in from Mexico. Their sweetness is balanced with hot chilies, sharp red radishes, and saline olives. The flavors come together, grow mellow, and fuse with mint. Serve the salsa to add moisture to grilled food, grain pilafs, or pies. The salsa should be made soon before serving. It keeps for only a couple of hours at room temperature.   **MAKES 3 CUPS**

Place the mango in a nice bowl. Add the radishes, olives, and chilies and toss. Combine the lemon juice and orange juice and pour over the mangoes. Sprinkle with mint and black pepper. Toss lightly. Serve the salsa garnished with mint.

pesto

1 tablespoon olive oil

5 tablespoons white wine

3 cloves garlic

1/3 cup pine nuts, walnuts, or pistachios

2 cups (packed) basil leaves, rinsed and dried

3 tablespoons freshly grated parmesan

Freshly ground black pepper and kosher salt

You'll find pesto is delicious even with just a little oil. This lighter version of the famous basil–pine nut puree can be folded into rice or pasta, especially orzo, the rice-shaped pasta. It also goes with steamed seafood, poultry, and vegetables. **MAKES 1 CUP**

1. Pour the oil and wine into a blender. Add the garlic and process until roughly pureed. Add the nuts and process until finely chopped. Take care not to overprocess, or the nuts will turn into a butter.

2. Add the basil, a little at a time, processing until all is used up. The mixture should be like a slightly grainy puree. Add the cheese and process only until mixed in. Season with pepper and salt to taste. Use right away or transfer to a bowl, cover, and set aside for several hours at room temperature. Or refrigerate and serve chilled. (*The pesto keeps well tightly covered, for up to 1 week, in the refrigerator or up to 6 months in the freezer. To prevent discoloration, pour a thin layer of oil on top, to create an airtight seal, before covering with a lid.*)

cilantro pesto: Substitute cilantro for basil leaves and proceed as directed.

apple-mustard salsa

2 tablespoons canola oil

1 teaspoon mustard seeds, crushed

1 teaspoon crushed red pepper

1 teaspoon minced garlic

1 cup chopped onions

2 cups peeled, cored, and sliced Granny Smith apples (1 pound)

2 cups peeled, seeded, and chopped tomatoes (2 pounds)

4 fresh chilies, stemmed and minced with seeds (optional)

1 teaspoon Hungarian paprika

Kosher salt

In this cooked salsa, apples are sautéed in a mustard-infused oil with tomatoes, chilies, and other flavorings added. The heat is more diffuse than in a fresh salsa, which can be perky, with stings of heat.

MAKES 3 CUPS

1. Heat the oil in a frying pan over medium heat. Add the mustard seeds, red pepper, and garlic. Cook, stirring, for 1 minute, or until the garlic is light gold. Increase the heat to medium-high and add the onions and apples. Cook, stirring occasionally, until the onions begin to soften and look glazed, about 5 minutes.

2. Add the tomatoes, chilies, if using, and paprika and bring the contents to a boil. Lower the heat and simmer, covered, until the tomatoes lose their raw aroma and the mixture looks thick and pulpy, about 10 minutes. Season to taste with salt. When cool, transfer to a bowl, cover, and refrigerate. Serve chilled. (*The salsa keeps well, covered, for up to 3 weeks in the refrigerator or for up to 3 months in the freezer.*)

fresh fig salsa with sesame

2 tablespoons sesame seeds

6 fresh figs, quartered lengthwise

2 small cucumbers, peeled, seeded, and finely diced

¼ cup chopped red onion

Juice of 1 lemon

1 tablespoon minced fresh chilies

1 tablespoon chopped basil

1 tablespoon chopped mint

Kosher salt

The time to make this salsa is when fresh figs are available, usually from June until September. You could use either black Mission or pale green Calimyrna figs. They are combined with cucumber and red onion and the mixture is laced with mint, basil, and chilies. Sesame is essential for texture and to meld the many flavors present in the salsa. Serve the salsa with grilled fish, broiled or barbecued chicken, or rice pilaf. **MAKES 2 CUPS**

1. Place the sesame seeds in an ungreased frying pan over medium-high heat. Toast, stirring and shaking, until the seeds give off an aroma and turn light gold. Do not let the seeds brown, or they will lose their delicate flavor. Transfer to a plate and set aside.

2. Combine the figs, cucumbers, onion, lemon juice, chilies, basil, and mint in a bowl. Toss well. Add salt to taste. Sprinkle with sesame seeds and serve immediately at room temperature. (*The salsa will keep for about 4 hours at room temperature.*)

yellow tomato and green peppercorn salsa

¾ pound yellow tomatoes, washed and chopped

¾ pound red tomatoes, washed and chopped

1 medium cucumber, peeled and finely chopped

1 medium onion, chopped

½ cup (packed) cilantro leaves and tender stems, chopped

1 clove garlic, minced

2 tablespoons dried green peppercorns or green peppercorns in brine, rinsed and drained

Kosher salt

A wonderfully fragrant salsa, studded with tiny pearls of green peppercorn, it takes no time at all to make—all you do is combine the ingredients and serve. Yellow tomatoes can generally be found at farmers' markets in summer; if they are not available, just use all red tomatoes. Serve the salsa with grilled fish, chicken, or meat. It also goes well with rice pilaf and stuffed breads. **MAKES 2½ CUPS**

Combine the yellow tomatoes, red tomatoes, cucumber, onion, cilantro, garlic, green peppercorns, and ½ teaspoon salt in a bowl. Let stand, uncovered, for 15 minutes, for the flavors to blend and for the dried peppercorns to rehydrate. Taste and add more salt, if desired. Serve at room temperature. (*The salsa may be stored for up to 4 days in the refrigerator. It does not freeze well.*)

warm tomato butter with paprika

2 tablespoons vegetable oil

**8 cloves garlic, thickly sliced
(about ¼ cup)**

**1 teaspoon mustard seeds,
crushed**

**1 to 8 fresh chilies, stemmed
and sliced with seeds**

**2 pounds Italian plum
tomatoes, washed and sliced**

**2 teaspoons Curry Powder
(page 56)**

**1 tablespoon Hungarian
paprika**

½ teaspoon kosher salt

Beautifully colored with paprika, this garlicky tomato butter, which is spiced with mustard and curry, is very easy to cook up. You can use as few as one chili or as many as eight, depending on how hot you want the sauce to be. A versatile sauce, it goes well with grains, bread, pasta, and grilled fish or meat. It can be served hot, at room temperature, or chilled. **MAKES 4 CUPS**

1. Place the oil and garlic in a 3-quart saucepan over medium-high heat. Cook the garlic, stirring, until light gold. Stir in the mustard seeds and chilies and cook briefly. Add the tomatoes. When the tomatoes begin to boil, add the Curry Powder, paprika, and salt. Lower the heat and simmer, covered, for 10 minutes, or until fully cooked.

2. Transfer the sauce to a food processor and process until pureed. If the sauce is to be served hot, return to the saucepan and heat until boiling hot. If the sauce is to be served at room temperature, transfer to a bowl. To serve chilled, refrigerate, tightly covered, for at least 2 hours. (*The sauce keeps well, covered, for up to 1 week in the refrigerator and for up to 1 year in the freezer.*)

cranberry relish with apricots, walnuts, and cinnamon

1 package (12 ounces) cranberries, fresh or frozen, picked clean

1 orange, scrubbed, chopped, and seeded

1 cup sugar

1 teaspoon ground cinnamon

$1/2$ teaspoon ground ginger

2 tablespoons fresh lemon juice

1 cup coarsely chopped walnuts

1 cup dried apricots, finely chopped

In this relish, cranberries are combined with dried apricots and walnuts in a cinnamon-scented orange syrup. When just made, the relish has a sharp taste and polarized accents. It needs to be left to ripen to let an exchange and mellowing of flavors take place. Then the nuts and fruits soak up the juice, the spices lend their fragrance, and the cranberries turn sweet. The relish can be served with holiday turkey, goose, or ham. It also goes with roast chicken, grilled fish, and bread.

MAKES 3 CUPS

Combine the cranberries, orange, sugar, cinnamon, ginger, and lemon juice in a nonaluminum saucepan over medium heat. Cook, stirring, just until the sugar dissolves. Increase the heat and boil until the cranberries pop, about 4 minutes. Turn off the heat. Add the walnuts and apricots and let cool completely. Mix again and spoon into jars. Cover with a lid and refrigerate for at least 2 weeks to ripen. Serve at room temperature or chilled. (*The relish keeps well, covered, for up to 1 year in the refrigerator or in the freezer.*)

breads

dill tortilla bread

My tortilla breads are lighter than the traditional kind because they are made with half the amount of fat. In addition, I use a light oil (canola) rather than lard or shortening. The dill cuts the starchy flavor of the bread and lends a nice aroma.

2½ cups unbleached all-purpose flour or whole wheat pastry flour

½ teaspoon baking soda

1 tablespoon thinly sliced garlic

2 tablespoons chopped fresh dill or 2 teaspoons dried dillweed

5 tablespoons canola oil

⅔ cup plain nonfat yogurt

1½ teaspoons kosher salt

MAKES TWELVE 5-INCH BREADS

1. Mix together the flour, baking soda, garlic, and dill in a medium bowl. Add the oil and distribute it evenly in the flour with your fingertips. Blend the yogurt and salt in a measuring cup. Dribble the yogurt over the flour mixture and mix until the dough can be gathered into a mass. Lightly knead until smooth. (*The dough may be set aside for up to 8 hours at room temperature, up to 5 days in the refrigerator, or up to 3 months in the freezer. Bring back to room temperature before rolling out.*)

2. Divide the dough into 12 portions. Working with 1 portion at a time, form the dough into a smooth ball and place it on the work surface. Dust with flour and roll into a 5-inch circle. Keep the rolled-out breads loosely covered with a sheet of plastic wrap. Do not stack.

3. Heat an ungreased griddle or frying pan over high heat until very hot. Reduce the heat and add a bread. Griddle-bake the bread, turning once, until lightly browned and fully cooked. Remove and keep the bread warm, loosely covered in a low oven, while you make all the other breads the same way.

4. To serve, briefly place the breads in a single layer under the broiler or on top of the grill, until heated through.

5. Serve warm or at room temperature. (*The tortillas keep well for up to 2 days, in plastic bags or wrapped in aluminum foil, at room temperature or, tightly wrapped in aluminum foil, for up to 3 months in the freezer. To reheat, place the thawed tortillas, loosely wrapped in foil, in a preheated 400°F. oven for 5 minutes.*)

Serving Suggestions: Serve the bread with a hearty soup like Black Bean Soup with Epazote (page 115) or use it to wrap a sandwich like the Rolled Vegetable-Cheese Sandwiches with Green Peppercorns (page 176).

chili tortilla bread

I like to make these tortillas in summer when the farmers' market has many colorful chilies in varying degrees of heat. I combine them two to one—two of the mild to one of the hot—but you can use all mild or all hot. Just remember to be careful when you pair the bread with milder dishes, as very hot tortillas together with a spicy-hot entree may be too much for some to enjoy.

2 1/2 cups unbleached all-purpose or whole wheat pastry flour

1/2 teaspoon baking soda

6 fresh chilies and/or bell peppers, stemmed, seeded, and thinly sliced

1 teaspoon cumin seeds, crushed

5 tablespoons canola oil

1 tablespoon fresh lemon juice

2/3 cup plain nonfat yogurt

1 1/2 teaspoons kosher salt

MAKES TWELVE 5-INCH BREADS

1. Mix together the flour, baking soda, chilies, and cumin in a medium-sized bowl. Add the oil and distribute it evenly in the flour with your fingertips. Blend the lemon juice, yogurt, and salt in a measuring cup. Dribble the yogurt over the flour mixture and mix until the dough can be gathered into a mass. Lightly knead until smooth. (*The dough may be set aside for up to 8 hours at room temperature, up to 5 days in the refrigerator, or up to 3 months or in the freezer. Bring back to room temperature before rolling out.*)

2. Divide the dough into 12 portions. Working with 1 portion at a time, form the dough into a smooth ball and place it on the work surface. Dust with flour and roll into a 5-inch circle. Keep the rolled-out breads loosely covered with a sheet of plastic wrap. Do not stack.

3. Heat an ungreased griddle or frying pan over high heat until very hot. Reduce the heat and add 1 bread. Griddle-bake the bread, turning once, until lightly browned and fully cooked. Remove and keep the bread warm, loosely covered in a low oven, while you make all the other breads the same way.

4. To serve, briefly place the tortillas in a single layer under the broiler or on top of the grill, until heated through. Serve warm or at room temperature. (*The tortillas keep well for up to 2 days, in plastic bags or wrapped in aluminum foil, at room temperature or, tightly wrapped in aluminum foil, for up to 3 months in the freezer. To reheat, place the thawed tortillas, loosely wrapped in foil, in a preheated 400°F. oven for 5 minutes.*)

Serving Suggestions: Serve the bread with Island Vegetable Stew with Thyme (page 177) or use it to make a rolled sandwich with grilled food, such as Grilled Chicken Kabobs with Anise (page 154) or Grilled Pork with Epazote (page 162).

currant and mace puffs

Currant-studded puffs have a delicate buttery-sweet taste. A hint of mace makes them taste sweeter than they really are. If you like, fold a quarter of a cup of finely chopped walnuts into the dough with the currants.

¹⁄₄ cup chopped dried currants or dark raisins

¹⁄₂ teaspoon ground mace

2 tablespoons light rum, milk, or fruit juice

4 tablespoons (¹⁄₂ stick) unsalted butter

¹⁄₄ cup sugar

1 cup water

1 cup unbleached all-purpose flour

4 large eggs

Vegetable oil spray (optional)

MAKES 16 PUFFS

1. Combine the currants, mace, and rum in a small bowl. Set aside.

2. Combine the butter, sugar, and water in heavy saucepan over medium-high heat and bring to a boil. Add the flour all at once, stirring constantly. Cook for 1 minute, or until the dough thickens and begins to pull away from the sides of the pan. Transfer the dough to a food processor while still warm. With the machine running, add the eggs one at a time, blending well after each addition. Transfer the dough to a bowl. Fold in the currant mixture. (*The dough can be kept, tightly covered, for up to 2 days in the refrigerator.*)

3. Preheat the oven to 375°F. Choose 2 large nonstick baking sheets or lightly spray 2 large baking sheets.

4. Drop the dough by the heaping tablespoonful onto the baking sheets, spacing the puffs 2 inches apart.

5. Bake for 40 minutes, or until puffed and light brown. Pierce the puffs with a toothpick to allow the steam to escape. Bake for 5 minutes more.

6. Serve hot or at room temperature. (*The puffs keep well for up to 2 days, in plastic bags or wrapped in aluminum foil, at room temperature or, in plastic bags or tightly wrapped in aluminum foil, for up to 3 months in the freezer. To reheat, place the thawed puffs, loosely wrapped in foil, in a preheated 400°F. oven for 6 minutes.*)

Serving Suggestions: These puffs are particularly good with veal, pork, and poultry, including such dishes as Rosemary-crusted Veal Chops (page 160), Milk-marinated Grilled Pork Chops with Ajowan (page 161), and Roast Duck with Hot Pepper and Plums (page 155).

parmesan-chive puffs

Parmesan cheese makes these velvety herbal puffs crusty on the outside. You can prepare several batches at a time by simply multiplying the ingredients in the recipe.

2 tablespoons unsalted butter

2 tablespoons olive oil

½ teaspoon kosher salt

¼ teaspoon ground red pepper

1 cup water

1 cup unbleached all-purpose flour

4 large eggs

1 cup freshly grated parmesan

2 tablespoons snipped fresh chives or 1 tablespoon dried chives

Vegetable oil spray (optional)

MAKES 16 PUFFS

1. Combine the butter, oil, salt, red pepper, and water in a heavy saucepan over medium-high heat and bring to a boil. Add the flour all at once, stirring constantly. Cook for 1 minute, or until the dough thickens and begins to pull away from the sides of the pan. Transfer the dough to a food processor while still warm. With the machine running, add the eggs one at a time, blending well after each addition. Add the cheese and chives and process only until just mixed. Do not overprocess, crushing the chives excessively. Transfer the dough to a bowl. (*The dough can be kept, tightly covered, for up to 2 days in the refrigerator.*)

2. Preheat the oven to 375°F. Choose 2 large nonstick baking sheets or lightly spray 2 large baking sheets.

3. Drop dough by the heaping tablespoonful onto the baking sheets, spacing the puffs 2 inches apart. Bake for 40 minutes, or until puffed and light brown. Pierce the puffs with a toothpick to allow the steam to escape. Bake for 5 minutes more.

4. Serve hot or at room temperature. (*The puffs keep well for up to 2 days, in plastic bags or wrapped in aluminum foil, at room temperature or, in plastic bags or tightly wrapped in aluminum foil, for up to 3 months in the freezer. To reheat, place the thawed puffs, loosely wrapped in foil, in a preheated 400°F. oven for 6 minutes.*)

Serving Suggestions: Serve the puffs with Lentil Soup with Smoked Turkey and Tarragon (page 118) or Split Pea and Winter Vegetable Stew with Warm Spices (page 178).

ham puffs with black pepper

Ham has a special affinity with two spices—cloves and black pepper. In this bread, pepper lends itself harmoniously to the sweet ham. Use only one half to one teaspoon black pepper if you want the rolls to be just mildly peppery.

2 tablespoons unsalted butter

2 tablespoons olive oil

½ teaspoon powdered dry mustard

1 cup water

1 cup unbleached all-purpose flour

4 large eggs

1 cup swiss cheese or extra sharp cheddar

¼ cup finely diced ham, preferably smoked

1 to 2 teaspoons black peppercorns, cracked

Vegetable oil spray (optional)

MAKES 16 PUFFS

1. Combine the butter, oil, mustard, and water in a heavy saucepan over medium-high heat and bring to a boil. Add the flour all at once, stirring constantly. Cook for 1 minute, or until the dough thickens and begins to pull away from the sides of the pan. Transfer the dough to a food processor while still warm. With the machine running, add the eggs one at a time, blending well after each addition. Add the cheese and process until mixed. Transfer the dough to a bowl. Fold in the ham and black pepper. (*The dough can be kept, tightly covered, for up to 2 days in the refrigerator.*)

2. Preheat the oven to 375°F. Choose 2 large nonstick baking sheets or lightly spray 2 large baking sheets.

3. Drop the dough by the heaping tablespoonful onto the baking sheets, spacing the puffs 2 inches apart.

4. Bake for 40 minutes, or until puffed and light brown. Pierce the puffs with a toothpick to allow the steam to escape. Bake for 5 minutes more.

5. Serve hot or at room temperature. (*The puffs keep well for up to 2 days, in plastic bags or wrapped in aluminum foil, at room temperature or, in plastic bags or tightly wrapped in aluminum foil, for up to 3 months in the freezer. To reheat, place the thawed puffs, loosely wrapped in foil, in a preheated 400°F. oven for 6 minutes.*)

Serving Suggestions: Serve the puffs with any soup or sautéed dish with a sauce, such as Bluefish with Tomato-Coriander Sauce (page 130). The puffs are also good to nibble with cocktails, to take on picnics, or to pair with Tarragon Scallops Kedgeree (page 201) at brunch.

raisin and caraway rolls

These dinner rolls with raisins and caraway, which enhance rising, are based on a standard dinner roll dough that I have been making for decades. They are feathery light inside and slightly crusty outside. You can replace one cup of the all-purpose flour with an equal amount of millet, barley, rye, whole wheat, or potato flour.

3 cups unbleached all-purpose flour

1½ teaspoons caraway seeds, crushed

1 package active dry yeast

1¼ cups warm water

3 tablespoons sugar

2 teaspoons kosher salt

½ cup dark raisins

2 ½ tablespoons melted unsalted butter

1 large egg, beaten with 1 tablespoon water

MAKES 16 ROLLS

1. Combine the flour and 1 teaspoon of the caraway seeds in a large mixing bowl.

2. Dissolve the yeast in ¼ cup of the warm water in a small bowl. Set aside in a warm place to proof for about 10 minutes, or until bubbly. Stir in the remaining water, the sugar, salt, raisins, and 2 tablespoons of the butter.

3. Pour the liquid over the flour and mix well to form a dough. Turn out onto a floured work surface and wash out and dry the bowl. Knead the dough for 10 minutes, or until smooth and satiny. Shape the dough into a ball, place in the bowl, and brush the top with the remaining ½ tablespoon butter. Cover the bowl and set aside in a warm place to rise until doubled in bulk, about 2 hours.

4. Preheat the oven to 400°F. Grease a large baking sheet.

5. Punch down the dough, knead briefly, and divide into 16 portions. Shape each portion into a smooth ball. Place the balls on the baking sheet, about 2 inches apart. Cover loosely with plastic wrap or a towel and let rise until doubled in size, about 30 minutes.

6. Brush the tops of the rolls with the egg wash and sprinkle with the remaining caraway seeds. Bake in the upper level of the oven for 15 minutes, or until light gold. Cool the rolls on racks.

7. Serve warm or at room temperature. (*When completely cool, transfer the rolls to plastic bags and freeze. The rolls may be frozen for up to 3 months. To reheat, place the thawed rolls, loosely wrapped in foil, in a preheated 375°F. oven for 5 minutes.*)

Serving Suggestions: These rolls are good with peppery dishes like Spicy Tomato Spread (page 99). Or serve them with cocktails or as a snack.

cumin rolls

Cumin rolls can be made with raw or toasted cumin seeds. Raw cumin seeds lend spicy flavor to the rolls; toasted seeds give them a smoky scent. Either way, the cumin acts as a preservative, keeping the rolls fresh longer.

3 cups unbleached all-purpose flour

1½ teaspoons cumin seeds, raw or toasted (see page 18)

1 package active dry yeast

1¼ cups warm water

3 tablespoons sugar

2 teaspoons kosher salt

2½ tablespoons melted unsalted butter

1 large egg, beaten with 1 tablespoon water

MAKES 16 ROLLS

1. Combine the flour and 1 teaspoon of the cumin seeds in a large mixing bowl.

2. Dissolve the yeast in ¼ cup of the water in a small bowl. Set aside in a warm place to proof for about 10 minutes, or until bubbly. Stir in the remaining water, the sugar, salt, and 2 tablespoons of the butter.

3. Pour the liquid over the flour and mix well to form a dough. Turn out onto a floured work surface and wash out and dry the bowl. Knead the dough for 10 minutes, or until smooth and satiny. Shape the dough into a ball, place in the bowl, and brush the top with the remaining ½ tablespoon butter. Cover the bowl and set aside in a warm place to rise until doubled in bulk, about 2 hours.

4. Preheat the oven to 400°F. Grease a large baking sheet.

5. Punch down the dough, knead briefly, and divide into 16 portions. Shape each portion into a smooth ball. Place the balls on the baking sheet, about 2 inches apart. Cover loosely with plastic wrap or a towel and let rise until doubled in size, about 30 minutes.

6. Brush the tops of the rolls with the egg wash and sprinkle with the remaining cumin seeds. Bake in the upper level of the oven for 15 minutes, or until light gold. Cool the rolls on racks. Serve warm or at room temperature. (*When completely cool, transfer the rolls to plastic bags and freeze. The rolls may be frozen for up to 3 months. To reheat, place the thawed rolls, loosely wrapped in foil, in a preheated 375°F. oven for 5 minutes.*)

Serving Suggestions: Cumin rolls are very versatile. They can be served with anything from dips and soups to main course dishes. Plain cumin rolls pair more naturally with soups, vegetable spreads, and fish, like Fragrant Fish Chowder with Celery Seed (page 123), while those made with toasted seeds go better with rich meats and hearty stews, like Lamb Shanks in Black Pepper Sauce (page 157).

five pepper rolls

From time to time I get a sudden urge to soak my palate in some peppery hot concoction. It's at that moment that I make these rolls, which are laced with peppers and chilies in all forms and flavors. Sumac adds a delicate trace of piquancy and gives the rolls an earth-tone color. They are hot, and they are delicious.

3 cups unbleached all-purpose flour

2 tablespoons Five Pepper Mix (page 68)

1 package active dry yeast

¼ cup warm milk

3 tablespoons maple syrup

2 teaspoons kosher salt

1 teaspoon sumac (see page 47) or 1 tablespoon fresh lemon juice

2 tablespoons chopped cilantro

1 cup water

2½ tablespoons olive oil

MAKES 16 ROLLS

1. Combine the flour and Five Pepper Mix in a large bowl.

2. Dissolve the yeast in the milk in a small bowl. Set aside in a warm place to proof for about 10 minutes, or until bubbly. Stir in the maple syrup, salt, cilantro, water, and 2 tablespoons of the olive oil.

3. Pour the liquid over the flour and mix well to form a dough. Turn out onto a floured work surface and wash out and dry the bowl. Knead the dough for 10 minutes, or until smooth and satiny. Shape the dough into a ball, place in the bowl, and brush the top with the remaining ½ tablespoon olive oil. Cover the bowl and set aside in a warm place to rise until doubled in bulk, about 2 hours.

4. Preheat the oven to 400°F. Grease a large baking sheet.

5. Punch down the dough, knead briefly, and divide into 16 portions. Shape each portion into a smooth ball. Place the balls on the baking sheet, about 2 inches apart. Cover loosely with plastic wrap or a towel and let rise until doubled in size, about 30 minutes.

6. Brush the tops of the rolls with the egg wash. Cut a cross on top with scissors. Bake in the upper level of the oven for about 15 minutes, or until light gold. Cool the rolls on racks.

7. Serve warm or at room temperature. (*When completely cool, transfer the rolls to plastic bags and freeze. The rolls may be frozen for up to 3 months. To reheat, place the thawed rolls, loosely wrapped in foil, in a preheated 375°F. oven for 5 minutes.*)

Serving Suggestions: These rolls are good with a chilled beverage like Raspberry Tea with Sage (page 283) or Basil-Ginger Tea (page 285). They are good with salads like Mozzarella and Fennel with Cumin Vinaigrette (page 169) and cold soups like Iced Pear Soup with Mint (page 126).

thyme pita bread

With the popularity of souvlaki and shish kabob sandwiches, pita bread has become a household word in America. Homemade pitas are easy to make and can be dressed up in countless ways, with dried tomatoes and basil, or garlic and bay, or dates and walnuts. The simplest and most versatile version is this one, scented with thyme. I often use lemon thyme and place long sprigs on top of the rolled dough; they look very attractive when baked.

3 cups unbleached all-purpose flour

1 teaspoon kosher salt

1/2 package (1 teaspoon) active dry yeast

2 teaspoons sugar

1/2 cup warm water

3/4 cup skim milk

3 tablespoons olive oil

2 tablespoons fresh thyme leaves or 2 teaspoons dried thyme

1 1/2 teaspoons fresh lemon juice

MAKES SIX 5-INCH BREADS

1. Combine the flour and salt in a large bowl.

2. Dissolve the yeast and sugar in the water in a small bowl. Set aside in a warm place to proof for 10 minutes, or until bubbly. Stir in the milk and pour the mixture over the flour. Mix to make a soft and sticky dough. Turn the dough out onto a floured work surface and wash out and dry the bowl. Knead for 10 minutes, or until smooth and satiny. Shape the dough into a ball, place it in the bowl, and brush the top with some of the oil. Cover the bowl and set aside in a warm place to rise until doubled in bulk, 2 to 4 hours.

3. Preheat the oven to 500° to 550°F. Set aside 2 large baking sheets.

4. Punch down the dough, knead briefly, and divide into 6 portions. Form each into a smooth ball. Cover with plastic wrap or a towel and let rise until doubled in bulk, about 30 minutes.

5. Working three at a time, roll out each ball into a circle about 5-inches in diameter, dusting often with flour. Place the breads on a baking sheet. Combine the oil, thyme, and lemon juice and brush over the top. Bake on the lowest rack of the oven for 10 minutes, or until firm to the touch. Take out the loaves and place briefly under the broiler to give them a browned look and mildly charred taste, if desired. Cool the loaves in a cloth-lined basket.

6. Serve warm or at room temperature. (*When completely cool, transfer the pitas to plastic bags and freeze. The pitas may be frozen for up to 3 months. To reheat, place the thawed pitas, loosely wrapped in foil, in a preheated 375°F. oven for 5 minutes.*)

Serving Suggestions: Thyme pita is delicious with spreads and dips, including Lima Bean Spread with Cumin Vinaigrette (page 83) and Yogurt Dip with Herbs (page 230). It is also great sopping up gravies and sauces in braised dishes like Mild Indian Chile with Paprika (page 163) and Ginger Ragout of Lamb (page 158).

sesame pita bread

In this pita bread, the rolled-out dough is sprinkled with sesame seeds before going in the oven. As the bread bakes, the seeds get toasted and release a lovely caramel aroma. The bread is rich tasting and a good source of vegetable protein.

3 cups unbleached all-purpose flour

1 teaspoon kosher salt

½ package (1 teaspoon)
 active dry yeast

2 teaspoons sugar

½ cup warm water

¾ cup skim milk

Olive oil spray

1 large egg, mixed with
 3 tablespoons water

3 tablespoons sesame seeds

MAKES SIX 5- TO 6-INCH BREADS

1. Combine the flour and salt in a large bowl.

2. Dissolve the yeast and sugar in the water in a small bowl. Set aside in a warm place to proof for 10 minutes, or until bubbly. Stir in the milk and pour the mixture over the flour. Mix to make a soft and sticky dough. Turn the dough out onto a floured work surface and wash out and dry the bowl. Knead for 10 minutes, or until smooth and satiny. Shape the dough into a ball, place in the bowl, and spray with oil. Cover the bowl and set aside in a warm place to rise until doubled in bulk, 2 to 4 hours.

3. Preheat the oven to 500° to 550°F. Set aside 2 large baking sheets.

4. Punch down the dough, knead briefly, and divide into 6 portions. Form each into a smooth ball. Cover with plastic wrap or a towel and let rise until doubled in bulk, about 30 minutes.

5. Roll each ball into a 5- to 6-inch circle, dusting often with flour. Place the flat breads on the baking sheets. Brush the tops with egg wash and sprinkle with sesame seeds. Bake on the lowest rack of the oven for 10 minutes, or until puffed and firm to the touch. Remove and place the pita under the broiler for a few seconds to lightly brown the top. Cool the loaves in a cloth-lined basket. Repeat with the remaining 3 balls.

6. Serve warm or at room temperature. (*When completely cool, transfer the pitas to plastic bags and freeze. The pitas may be frozen for up to 3 months. To reheat, place the thawed pitas, loosely wrapped in foil, in a preheated 375°F. oven for 5 minutes.*)

Serving Suggestions: These nutty pita breads are good to eat with grilled foods like Grilled Chicken Kabobs with Anise (page 154), accompanied with a salsa like Mango-Mint Salsa (page 231), or with an elaborate salad like Chick Pea Salad with Cumin (page 172) or Lentil and Endive Salad with Juniper Berries (page 171).

mini pita with basil and dried tomatoes

Little rounds of pita, flavored with fragrant basil leaves and tart dried tomatoes, are great with cocktails. They can be made ahead in large batches and frozen until ready to serve.

½ package (1 teaspoon) active dry yeast

1 tablespoon sugar

1 ¼ cups warm water

2 tablespoons olive oil

3 cups unbleached all-purpose flour

1 teaspoon kosher salt

⅓ cup julienned dried tomatoes (see page 98)

⅔ cup shredded large basil leaves or whole small leaves

Olive oil spray

1 egg, beaten with 3 tablespoons water

MAKES TWELVE 3-INCH BREADS

1. Dissolve the yeast and sugar in ½ cup of the water in a small bowl. Set aside in a warm place to proof for 10 minutes, or until bubbly. Stir in the remaining ¾ cup water and the oil.

2. Combine the flour and salt in a large bowl. Add the yeast mixture and mix to make a soft and sticky dough. Add half the tomatoes and half the basil to the dough. Turn the dough out onto a floured work surface and wash out and dry the bowl. Knead for 10 minutes, or until smooth and satiny. Shape the dough into a ball, place it in the bowl, and spray with oil. Cover the bowl and set aside in a warm place to rise until doubled in bulk, 2 to 4 hours.

3. Preheat the oven to 500° to 550°F. Set aside 2 large baking sheets.

4. Punch down the dough, knead briefly, and divide into 12 portions. Form each into a smooth ball. Cover with plastic wrap or a towel and let rise until doubled in bulk, about 20 minutes.

5. Working with six at a time, roll out each ball into a 3-inch circle, dusting often with flour. Brush the tops lightly with egg wash and press a few shreds of the remaining tomatoes and basil on top of each. Place the rolled-out breads on a baking sheet. Bake on the lowest rack of the oven for 7 minutes, or until firm to the touch. The breads may not puff fully because of the indentations. Remove and place under the broiler for a few seconds to lightly brown the top. Cool loaves in a cloth-lined basket. Repeat with the remaining 6 balls.

6. Serve warm or at room temperature. (*When completely cool, transfer the pitas to plastic bags and freeze. The pitas may be frozen for up to 3 months. To reheat, place the thawed pitas, loosely wrapped in foil, in a preheated 375°F. oven for 5 minutes.*)

Serving Suggestions: These flavorful pita breads can be served with such hearty dishes as Vegetarian Pumpkin, Eggplant, and Lima Bean Chile (page 180) and Green Mussels Curry (page 95).

stuffed sage roti bread with olives

Roti breads are similar to tortillas except they are stuffed; the dough is rich and flaky. This one, studded with olive bits and imbued with the warm scent of sage, is an eagerly awaited treat on cold winter days.

2½ cups unbleached all-purpose or whole wheat pastry flour

1 teaspoon minced fresh sage or ½ teaspoon ground dried sage

½ teaspoon baking soda

1½ teaspoons kosher salt

3 tablespoons olive oil

¾ cup plain nonfat yogurt, or more as needed

½ cup chopped black olives, preferably Mediterranean

8 sprigs of sage or large sage leaves

MAKES EIGHT 5-INCH BREADS

1. Mix together the flour, sage, baking soda, and salt in a medium bowl. Add the oil and distribute it evenly in the flour with your fingertips. Dribble the yogurt over the flour mixture and mix until the flour can be gathered into a mass. Turn it out onto a floured work surface. Lightly knead the dough until smooth. Wrap the dough in plastic wrap. (*The dough may be set aside for up to 8 hours at room temperature, up to 5 days in the refrigerator, or up to 6 months in the freezer. Defrost the dough before rolling out.*)

2. Divide the dough into 8 portions. Roll a portion into a 6-inch circle. (The circle does not have to be perfect, as it will be folded.) Scatter about 1 tablespoon of the chopped olives on the dough, as for pizza. Bring the edges of the circle together to the center to enclose the filling completely. Pinch the dough to seal. Dust with flour and roll the bread into a 5-inch circle. Place a sage sprig or leaf on top and roll over to make it adhere to the bread. Continue until all the breads are ready. Keep the breads loosely covered with a sheet of plastic wrap.

3. Heat a large ungreased griddle or 2 frying pans over high heat until hot. Reduce the heat to medium and add as many breads as fit without overcrowding. Griddle-bake the breads, turning once, until lightly browned and fully cooked, about 4 minutes. Remove and keep the bread warm, loosely covered in a low oven. Continue until all the breads are done. Briefly place the breads in a single layer under the broiler or on top of the grill until heated through.

4. Serve warm or at room temperature. (*Roti breads keep well, wrapped in foil, for up to 2 days at room temperature or up to 5 days in the refrigerator. Or, when they are completely cool, transfer the rotis to plastic bags and freeze for up to 3 months. To reheat, place the thawed rotis, loosely wrapped in foil, in a preheated 400°F. oven for 5 minutes.*)

Serving Suggestions: Serve with Lentil Soup with Smoked Turkey and Tarragon (page 118) or braised and stewed dishes like Pot Roast of Chicken with Rosemary, Figs, and Pine Nuts (page 146).

stuffed tarragon roti bread with ham and mushrooms

These roti breads are packed with smoky chunks of ham and glazed mushrooms. Tarragon adds a delicate licorice perfume. It also draws out the sweetness of the mushrooms, counterbalancing the saltiness of the ham.

2½ cups all-purpose or whole wheat pastry flour

¾ teaspoon baking soda

3 tablespoons unsalted butter

¾ cup plain nonfat yogurt, or more as needed

1 to 2 tablespoons olive oil

1½ pounds white button mushrooms, sliced

2 tablespoons minced shallots or onions

1 cup chopped cooked ham, preferably smoked

2 tablespoons chopped fresh tarragon or 2 teaspoons dried tarragon

Freshly ground black pepper

MAKES EIGHT 5-INCH BREADS

1. Mix the flour and baking soda in a medium bowl. Add the butter and distribute it evenly in the flour with your fingertips. Dribble the yogurt over the flour mixture and mix until the flour can be gathered into a mass. Turn it out onto a floured work surface. Lightly knead the dough until smooth. Wrap the dough in plastic. (*The dough may be set aside for up to 8 hours at room temperature, up to 5 days in the refrigerator, or up to 6 months in the freezer. Defrost the dough before rolling out.*)

2. Combine the oil, mushrooms, and shallots in a large frying pan over medium-high heat. Cook, stirring, until the mushrooms are soft and glazed, about 10 minutes. The mushrooms will render liquid, which will evaporate during cooking. Add the ham and tarragon and cook for 2 minutes more. Turn off the heat. Sprinkle generously with pepper.

3. Divide the mushroom filling and the dough into 8 portions each. Working with 1 portion at a time, roll the dough into a 6-inch circle. (The circle does not have to be perfect as it will be folded.) Scatter 1 portion of the filling on the dough, as for pizza. Bring the edges of the circle together to the center to enclose the filling completely. Pinch the dough to seal. Dust with flour and roll the bread into a 5-inch circle. Continue until all the breads are ready. Keep the breads loosely covered with a sheet of plastic wrap.

4. Heat a large ungreased griddle or 2 frying pans over high heat until hot. Reduce the heat to medium and add as many breads as fit without overcrowding. Griddle-bake the breads, turning once, until lightly browned and fully cooked, about 4 minutes. Remove and keep the bread warm, loosely covered, in a low oven. Continue until all the breads are done. Briefly place the breads in a single layer under the broiler or on top of the grill until heated through. Serve warm or at room temperature. (*Roti breads keep well, wrapped in foil,* *for up to 2 days at room temperature or up to 5 days in the refrigerator. Or, when they are completely cool, transfer the rotis to plastic bags and freeze for up to 3 months. To reheat, place the thawed rotis, loosely wrapped in foil, in a preheated 400°F. oven for 5 minutes.)*

Serving Suggestions: Serve the bread with stewed and braised vegetables like Sofrito Green Beans and Potatoes (page 179) or a bean soup like Winter Bean Soup with Bay Leaf (page 117).

savory herb crêpes

I don't know why anyone would think crêpes are difficult. In my opinion, they are easier than fried eggs. To make good crêpes easily, you need the right pan; six to ten inches in diameter, lightweight, and nonstick. Second, you need a good wrist movement to tilt the pan, spreading and swirling the batter quickly and evenly to coat the bottom of the pan. The rest of the magic happens naturally. For best results with these crêpes, use only fresh herbs, even if all you have is parsley; dried herbs give them a gritty texture.

1 cup plus 2 tablespoons skim milk

2 large eggs

1 teaspoon sugar

1/2 teaspoon baking powder

1 tablespoon freshly grated parmesan

1 cup bleached all-purpose flour

2 tablespoons minced mixed herbs, such as a combination of basil, thyme, cilantro, and oregano, or parsley

Kosher salt (optional)

Olive oil spray

MAKES TWELVE 6-INCH CRÊPES

1. Combine the milk, eggs, sugar, baking powder, cheese, and flour in a blender or food processor and process until the batter is smooth. Transfer the batter to a bowl and stir in the herbs. Add salt to taste, if desired.

2. Spray a 6- to 7-inch nonstick frying pan and place over high heat. When the pan is hot, reduce the heat to medium-high. Using a small ladle or 1/4-cup measure, pour about 3 tablespoons batter into the pan. Tilt immediately to spread the batter and coat the bottom of the pan evenly. Cook for 2 minutes, or until the underside of the crêpe is lightly browned. Turn it over and cook the other side for 15 to 30 seconds. Remove the crêpe and keep warm, loosely covered, in a low oven. Continue with the remaining batter the same way. Serve warm or at room temperature. (*The crêpes keep well, wrapped in foil, for up to 2 days in the refrigerator or for up to 3 months in the freezer. Defrost, and reheat in a frying pan.*)

Serving Suggestions: These crêpes are great for wrapping delicate salads and spreads such as Lobster Sandwich in Curry Mayonnaise (page 85) or Avocado Spread with Tahini (page 81). They are also a nice accompaniment to fish and poultry dishes like Red Snapper with Anise-Tomato Sauce (page 140), Steamed Sea Bass with Dill (page 138), Grilled Chicken Kabobs with Anise (page 154), and Steamed Duck with Star Anise (page 156).

desserts

anise-pistachio crêpes

These slightly sweet crêpes with specks of anise seed and bits of buttery pistachio are very simple to make. Just remember to agitate the batter every time you spoon it up since nuts have an annoying habit of sinking to the bottom.

You can serve the crêpes warm with cool sliced fruits, such as mangos and strawberries, and garnished with a mint sprig. They are also good served with a dessert sauce, such as Mango Sauce with Nutmeg (page 259).

1¼ cups whole milk

3 large eggs

3 tablespoons sugar

¼ teaspoon kosher salt

½ teaspoon baking powder

1 cup bleached all-purpose flour

1 teaspoon anise seeds, crushed

¼ cup finely chopped unsalted roasted pistachio nuts

3 tablespoons unsalted butter

MAKES TWELVE 6-INCH CRÊPES

1. Combine the milk, eggs, sugar, salt, baking powder, and flour in a blender or food processor and process until the batter is smooth. Transfer to a bowl and stir in the anise and pistachio. (*The batter keeps well, covered, for up to 3 days in the refrigerator or for up to 6 months in the freezer. Defrost and whisk before using.*)

2. Melt ½ teaspoon of the butter in a 6- to 7-inch nonstick frying pan over medium-high heat until very hot. Using a small ladle or ¼-cup measure, pour about 3 tablespoons batter into the pan. Tilt immediately to spread the batter and coat the bottom of the pan evenly. Cook for 2 minutes, or until the underside of the crêpe is lightly browned. Turn it over and cook the other side for 15 to 30 seconds. Remove the crêpe and keep warm. Continue with the remaining batter the same way. Serve warm or at room temperature. (*The crêpes keep well, tightly covered in foil, for up to 2 days in the refrigerator or for up to 3 months in the freezer. Defrost, and reheat in a frying pan before serving.*)

blueberry-cinnamon sauce

Blueberries have a very subtle sweetness that often gets overpowered by other ingredients. A little cinnamon usually does the trick of bringing it out. This sauce is full of natural flavor and loaded with blueberries. It is good warm, at room temperature, or chilled.

Spoon the sauce over ice cream or waffles or pancakes or use it to make blueberry shortcake. Packed in an attractive jar, the sauce makes a lovely homemade gift. Remember, though, to note on the label that the sauce is perishable and must be kept refrigerated.

2 pints fresh blueberries, picked over

1/2 teaspoon ground cinnamon

1/2 cup apple cider or apple juice

6 tablespoons sugar

Zest of 1 medium lemon

Juice of 1 medium lemon

2 teaspoons cornstarch, mixed with 2 tablespoons apple cider

2 tablespoons blackberry or orange liqueur (optional)

MAKES 1 1/2 CUPS

1. Combine the blueberries, cinnamon, cider, sugar, lemon zest, and lemon juice in a large heavy saucepan over medium-high heat. When the contents come to a boil, add the cornstarch mixture and cook, stirring, until the sauce thickens. Remove from the heat.

2. When the sauce is cool, mix in the liqueur, if using. Lightly crush some of the berries with the back of a spoon. Serve the sauce immediately or spoon it into jars, cover with lids, and refrigerate. (*The sauce keeps well, covered, for up to 3 weeks in the refrigerator.*)

banana-ginger cream

A snowy mound of banana and yogurt is laced with ginger. A little nutmeg and vanilla are added to cut the acid tang of the yogurt. The trick in this recipe is to use frozen banana; freezing not only makes it possible to whip the banana to a light airy mass but mellows its flavor from a tropical bolt to a teasing scent. For best results, use a fully ripe banana with spotless ivory flesh.

The cream is great served with Ginger Crisps (page 274).

1 very ripe banana

1 cup (8-ounce container) plain nonfat yogurt

1/4 teaspoon ground ginger

1/4 teaspoon freshly grated nutmeg

1 teaspoon pure vanilla extract

2 tablespoons honey

1 tablespoon ginger liqueur (optional)

MAKES 2 SERVINGS

Peel and roughly chop the banana, seal it in a plastic bag, and freeze for at least 4 hours or up to 3 months. When ready to serve, combine the banana pieces, yogurt, ginger, nutmeg, vanilla, and honey in a blender or food processor and process until whipped to a light foam. Spoon the banana cream into tall dessert glasses. Sprinkle with ginger liqueur, if desired, and serve.

mango sauce with nutmeg

If ever there was a sauce to bring back memories of the balmy air and turquoise waters of the Caribbean, it's this mango sauce. In this elegant interpretation, the mangos are pureed in nutmeg-laced pineapple juice to retain and heighten their delicate perfume. A little lemon juice, though not essential, helps tone down the sweetness of mango. Use highly aromatic, nonfibrous mangos imported from Mexico. They are round and range in color from deep-green to reddish-yellow. Judging a mango from the outside is a gamble. In the event your mango turns out to be fibrous, pass the sauce through a fine-mesh sieve.

Serve the sauce with crêpes, such as Anise-Pistachio Crêpes (page 256), Rice Pudding with Cardamom (page 264), Old-fashioned Vanilla Ice Cream (page 266), or sliced fruits.

2¹/₂ cups chopped ripe mango

¹/₂ cup pineapple, peach, or pear juice

¹/₄ cup sugar

2 teaspoons fresh lemon juice

¹/₂ teaspoon freshly grated nutmeg

¹/₂ cup light rum

MAKES 3 CUPS

Combine all the ingredients in a food processor. Process until smoothly pureed. If the mango is fibrous, pass the sauce through a fine mesh sieve. Cover and refrigerate the sauce for at least 2 hours. (*The sauce keeps well, covered, for up to 3 days in the refrigerator.*) Serve chilled.

dried fruit compote with allspice

A lovely bowl of stewed fruit can grace a holiday dessert table as well as an everyday breakfast table. The success of the dish depends very much on the quality of the dried fruits. The fresher and more fragrant, the more likely the compote will be ambrosial. Allspice diffuses the sweetness of the fruits while it lends a spicy undertone.

Serve the fruit compote with its juices, chilled, in attractive dessert bowls, topped, if desired, with Saffron Cream (page 261) or vanilla yogurt and accompanied with Ginger Crisps (page 274). The compote is also delicious spooned over Old-fashioned Vanilla Ice Cream (page 266), pancakes, waffles, or warm cereal.

3 cups mixed dried fruits, such as pitted prunes, apricots, pineapple, apples, cranberries, strawberries, red currants, and raisins

2 cups water

¹/₂ cup sugar

1 teaspoon finely slivered lemon zest

¹/₂ teaspoon ground allspice

2 tablespoons orange liqueur or ¹/₄ teaspoon grated orange zest (optional)

MAKES 6 SERVINGS

Combine all the ingredients except the liqueur in a saucepan and bring to a boil. Lower the heat and simmer, covered, for 10 minutes. Uncover and continue cooking until the fruits are soft and the syrup is thick. Stir in the liqueur, if using. Cover and refrigerate for at least 12 hours or overnight. (*The compote keeps well, covered, for up to 1 week in the refrigerator.*) Serve chilled.

saffron cream

This is a creamy cloud, tinged with the hue and scent of saffron. A little mace and sugar are added to heighten the sweetness of saffron. Saffron Cream reminds me of the Italian frozen dessert called *tortoni*. The cream too can be frozen in three-ounce ramekins.

Serve the chilled cream in parfait glasses, garnished with crushed Ginger Crisps (page 274). Or spoon over sliced fruits like pineapple, peaches, or kiwis, or fold into berries.

¼ teaspoon (lightly packed) saffron threads

2 tablespoons warm skim milk

1 cup (8-ounce container) nonfat sour cream

⅛ teaspoon ground mace or freshly grated nutmeg

3 tablespoons confectioners' sugar

MAKES ABOUT 1 CUP

Crush the saffron with your fingertips to a fine powder and place it in a medium bowl. Add the milk and set aside for 10 minutes. Crush the saffron with the back of a spoon to release more flavor and color. Add the sour cream, mace, and sugar and whisk until smooth and fluffy. Or combine the soaked saffron and milk with the other ingredients in a blender or food processor and process until smoothly blended. Cover and refrigerate until needed. (*The sauce keeps well, covered, for up to 4 days in the refrigerator.*) Serve chilled.

blueberry tart with saffron cream

As the forsythia fades in my garden and robins appear eagerly picking at the soft earth, I start dreaming of long summer days and berry tarts—juicy succulent berries in flavored cream, nestled in a crunchy crust. In this rendition of my dream, the cream base, made with nonfat yogurt, is delicately perfumed with saffron, its flavor heightened by nutmeg and orange. For best results, assemble the tart just before serving. You can make it with blackberries, red raspberries, or tiny champagne grapes.

Saffron Cream Filling

1 cup (8-ounce container) drained plain nonfat yogurt or part skim ricotta

3 tablespoons sugar

¼ teaspoon powdered saffron

½ teaspoon freshly grated nutmeg

2 teaspoons grated orange zest

Nut Crust

1 cup bleached all-purpose flour

½ cup coarsely ground walnuts

2 tablespoons sugar

½ teaspoon kosher salt

1 teaspoon grated lemon zest

¼ cup walnut or canola oil

¼ cup drained plain nonfat yogurt or part skim ricotta

Fresh orange juice

2 tablespoons blueberry or red currant jelly, heated

1 pint fresh blueberries

Confectioners' sugar

MAKES 8 SERVINGS

1. Preheat the oven to 375°F.

2. Combine all the ingredients for the filling in a mixing bowl and whisk thoroughly until smoothly blended. Set aside.

3. Combine all the crust ingredients except the orange juice in another bowl. Mix thoroughly, adding just enough orange juice to form a soft dough. Place the dough on the work surface and, dusting often with flour, roll it out into a 12-inch circle. Lift the dough, wrapped around the rolling pin, and unroll it on top of a 9-inch tart pan. Press the dough into the pan. Or press the kneaded dough straight into a 9-inch tart pan. Prick the dough evenly.

4. Bake in the upper level of the oven for 25 minutes. Remove from the oven and brush with 4 teaspoons of the jam. Bake for 5 minutes more. Remove from the oven and brush with the remaining 2 teaspoons jam. Cool completely.

5. Pour the filling into the crust. Smooth the top with a spatula. Pick over the blueberries and distribute them evenly over the filling. Just before serving, dust the blueberries lightly with sugar. Serve right away.

baked saffron custard

Soft, moist, and permeated with the floral scent of saffron, this baked custard is perfect for entertaining and for the holiday table, especially since it can be prepared ahead. It is made with milk, which heightens the sweetness of saffron and sugar.

4¼ cups whole or lowfat (2%) milk

½ teaspoon kosher salt

½ teaspoon (loosely packed) saffron threads

7 tablespoons sugar

¾ teaspoon pure vanilla extract

5 large eggs, lightly beaten

MAKES 8 SERVINGS

1. Preheat the oven to 325°F. Lightly butter eight 5-ounce ramekins.

2. Combine the milk and salt in a 3-quart saucepan and bring to a simmer over high heat. Crush ¼ teaspoon of the saffron threads with your fingertips to a fine powder and add to the milk. Add the sugar. Lower the heat to medium and simmer, stirring occasionally, for 5 minutes, or until the saffron's golden color is infused into the milk. Turn off the heat and stir in the vanilla. Add the eggs in a slow stream while stirring the milk rapidly.

3. Pour the custard into the ramekins. Place them in a baking pan and pour boiling water into the pan to a depth of 1 inch. Bake in the middle level of the oven for 30 minutes. Carefully sprinkle the remaining ¼ teaspoon of saffron on top of the custards. Continue to bake for 20 minutes more, or until a toothpick inserted in the center comes out clean. Cool the custard, then refrigerate for at least 4 hours. (*The custard keeps well, covered, for up to 3 days in the refrigerator.*) Serve chilled.

rice pudding with cardamom

Soul-soothing and comforting, rice pudding is everyone's favorite dessert. In the following East Indian version, no cream or eggs are used. Instead milk is cooked down until very thick. Cardamom gives natural sweetness to the pudding.

2 cups whole milk

2 cans (10 ounces each) evaporated milk

¼ cup uncooked rice

⅓ cup sugar

½ teaspoon ground cardamom

¼ cup golden raisins, for garnish

¼ cup sliced almonds, for garnish

MAKES 4 SERVINGS

Combine the milk and evaporated milk in a deep pot and bring to a boil. Add the rice and simmer over very low heat for 1 hour, or until the rice is cooked and the milk has reduced and thickened. During the last 5 minutes, stir in the sugar and cardamom. Serve warm or chilled, garnished with raisins and almonds. (*The pudding keeps well, covered, for up to 5 days in the refrigerator.*)

raspberry yogurt bavarian with mace and pistachio

A cool springtime dessert to make when fresh raspberries begin to appear in the market. The mildly sweet bavarian cream is flavored with mace, vanilla, and orange zest. The crunch of the pistachios is a delightful surprise. You can substitute roasted cashew nuts or almonds for the pistachio nuts.

³/₄ cup plain nonfat or lowfat yogurt

³/₄ cup part skim ricotta

¹/₄ teaspoon powdered mace

¹/₄ teaspoon pure vanilla extract

1 teaspoon grated orange zest

¹/₄ cup sugar

¹/₄ cup finely chopped unsalted roasted pistachio nuts

2 pints raspberries or a combination of raspberries and blueberries

2 tablespoons crystallized ginger slivers

MAKES 8 SERVINGS

1. Combine the yogurt, ricotta, mace, vanilla, orange zest, and sugar in a mixing bowl. Whip until smooth and creamy. Cover and refrigerate for at least 4 hours or overnight. (*Bavarian cream keeps well, tightly covered, for up to 1 week in the refrigerator.*)

2. When ready to serve, fold in the pistachios. Divide the berries among 8 dessert dishes and spoon the bavarian cream evenly over the fruit. Garnish with crystallized ginger and serve.

old-fashioned vanilla ice cream

No dessert is more satisfying to me than a simple scoop of perfectly made vanilla ice cream. Needless to say, the quality of the vanilla bean is of utmost importance here, not only for flavor but for texture as well.

A British Raj heirloom, this recipe is almost a century old; I enjoyed it as a child at parties at the Officers' Mess where my father was a member.

In the Raj tradition, serve the ice cream topped with either Tomato-Ginger Jam (page 271) or Sweet Tomato Conserve with Cloves (page 272).

2 cups light cream or half-and-half

1 vanilla bean

¼ cup sugar

1 can (14 ounces) condensed milk

1 extra large egg

2 cups heavy cream

MAKES ABOUT 2½ PINTS

1. Pour the light cream into a medium saucepan. Score the vanilla bean along its length and add to the cream. Bring to a boil, stirring, over medium-high heat. Turn off the heat, cover the pan, and set aside. Let steep for 15 minutes. Remove the bean, carefully scrape out the seeds, and add them to the cream. Stir in the sugar and condensed milk.

2. Transfer 1 cup of the vanilla cream to the top of a double boiler or a bowl set over a large pan of simmering water. Whisk in the egg and cook, stirring, until the mixture thickens. Return the custard to the cream mixture. Stir in the heavy cream. Cover, cool, and refrigerate until thoroughly chilled, about 4 hours.

3. Pour the cream into an ice-cream maker and process according to the manufacturer's directions. For best results, let the ice cream rest in the freezer to ripen for at least 4 hours before serving.

peach ice cream with marjoram

Make this ice cream only if you have garden- or farm-fresh ripe peaches. Supermarket peaches are so completely devoid of flavor that in the end your ice cream will taste like marjoram-sweetened cream. When peaches are in their glory, on the other hand, the balmy marjoram will come through as only a teasing suggestion.

1 cup whole milk

¼ cup minced marjoram leaves

1 pound very ripe peaches, peeled, pitted, and finely diced (about 2 cups)

¼ cup peach brandy

4 large eggs, separated

2 cups half-and-half or light cream

¾ cup sugar

MAKES 2½ PINTS

1. Bring the milk to a boil in a small saucepan. Add the marjoram, cover the pan, and remove from the heat. Set aside to cool completely.

2. Toss together the peaches and brandy in a ceramic or glass bowl. Cover and refrigerate until needed.

3. Beat the egg whites in a large bowl until soft peaks form. Set aside until needed.

4. Combine the egg yolks, half-and-half, and sugar in a medium bowl and lightly beat until blended and smooth. Transfer the mixture to a saucepan over medium-low heat, cook, stirring constantly, until the custard thickens enough to coat the back of a spoon, 10 to 15 minutes. Immediately remove from the heat. Beat the hot custard into the egg whites. Let the mixture cool.

5. Strain the marjoram-scented milk into the custard, discarding the marjoram leaves. Add the peaches with the brandy.

6. Pour the mixture into an ice-cream maker and process according to the manufacturer's directions. For best results, let the ice cream rest in the freezer to ripen for at least 4 hours before serving.

cardamom ice cream

Relatively simple but very delicious, this ice cream is still uncommon, perhaps because cardamom, like saffron, is associated with the mysterious East. It is quite similar in appearance to vanilla ice cream, with tiny specks of seed scattered throughout.

1 teaspoon cardamom seeds, crushed

3 cups light cream

¾ cup sugar

4 large eggs, separated

1 teaspoon pure vanilla extract

MAKES ABOUT 2½ PINTS

1. Combine the cardamom, cream, and sugar in a large heavy skillet over medium-high heat and bring to a boil, stirring often. Remove from the heat.

2. Lightly beat the egg yolks in a medium bowl. Gradually whisk in 1 cup of the hot cream, whisking until blended and smooth. Stir into the remaining cream in the skillet. Cook over medium-low heat, stirring constantly, for 12 minutes, or until the custard thickens enough to coat the back of a spoon.

3. Beat the egg whites in a large bowl until soft peaks form. Beat in the hot custard until well blended. Stir in the vanilla. Let cool completely.

4. Strain the custard into an ice-cream maker and process according to the manufacturer's directions. For best results, let the ice cream rest in the freezer to ripen for at least 4 hours before serving.

basil-pineapple ice

Palate-tingling and alive with tropical flavor, this pineapple ice is a refreshing ice you can enjoy all summer long. White pineapple with its very sweet and juicy flesh is preferred, but it is expensive and not that easily available outside Hawaii. Holy basil (see page 8), which has a sharp anise-peppery aroma, is available at markets selling Asian produce. Still, any perfectly ripe pineapple and fresh local basil will yield excellent results. Underripe or inferior pineapple will not work in this recipe.

1 large ripe pineapple, preferably white

2 to 4 tablespoons fresh lemon juice, or as needed

1¼ cups water

½ cup sugar

½ cup finely chopped basil, preferably holy basil

¼ teaspoon freshly ground white pepper

¼ cup light rum (optional)

Sprigs of basil, for garnish

MAKES 1 ½ PINTS

1. Peel, core, and chop the pineapple into chunks and put in a blender. Add 2 tablespoons of the lemon juice and process until the pineapple is completely liquefied. It may be necessary do this in 2 batches. Transfer the juice to a bowl. Taste and add more lemon juice if needed. Set aside until needed.

2. Combine the water and sugar in a small saucepan and cook over medium heat, stirring, until the sugar dissolves completely. Boil the syrup for 3 minutes, then turn off the heat. Add the basil, stir vigorously, and cover the pot. Set aside to cool. When completely cool, strain the syrup into the pineapple juice. Add pepper and rum, if using.

3. Transfer the liquid to an ice-cream maker and process according to the manufacturer's directions. Transfer to a covered container and put in the freezer for at least 2 hours, or until the ice is firm.

chocolate-cinnamon ice

A deep chocolate taste comes through this ice, thanks to the addition of cinnamon. The ice is just as lovely served by the fireside on a cold winter night as it is scooped up from an ice box at the beach, to counter the heat of summer.

$3/4$ cup sugar

$1/2$ cup unsweetened cocoa powder

$1/2$ teaspoons pure vanilla extract

1 teaspoon instant coffee powder

1 egg white

$1/2$ teaspoon ground cinnamon

1 cup Marsala or similar wine

$2^1/2$ cups 1% or skim milk

MAKES 1 QUART

Combine all the ingredients in a bowl and beat until they are thoroughly blended and the sugar is dissolved. Pour the liquid into an ice-cream maker and process according to the manufacturer's directions. Transfer to a covered container and put in the freezer for at least 2 hours, or until the ice is firm.

tomato-ginger jam

Sweet and gingery, with chunks of tomatoes and thick shreds of ginger, this is as much an English jam as orange marmalade, popular throughout the old British colonies. Although making the jam takes place over two days, the process itself is simple and straightforward. Make the jam in summer, when tomatoes are at their peak and young Hawaiian ginger (see page 38) is available at produce markets. The jam is delicious spread on toasted muffins or spooned over ice cream or crêpes.

MAKES 2 CUPS

2 pounds ripe tomatoes, peeled, seeded, and cut into ¼-inch wedges

½ cup peeled and julienned fresh ginger

¼ teaspoon kosher salt

1½ cups sugar

¼ cup fresh lemon juice

1. Toss together the tomatoes, ginger, and salt in a ceramic or glass bowl. Cover and let stand in a cool place for 8 hours or refrigerate overnight.

2. Strain all the accumulated juices into a nonaluminum saucepan. Stir in the sugar. Bring to a boil over high heat. Cook, uncovered, until thick and syrupy, about 8 minutes.

3. Add the tomatoes and ginger and the lemon juice. Continue to cook, stirring, until the mixture reaches the consistency of jam, about 10 minutes. Turn off the heat. When cool, transfer the jam to a covered container and refrigerate. (*The jam keeps well, covered, for up to 3 months in the refrigerator.*)

sweet tomato conserve with cloves

This vibrant tomato conserve, sweet and peppery, flavored with cloves and ginger, is delicious served with dessert crêpes, over ice cream, or on toast. Packed in attractive jars, it makes a nice homemade gift. Remember to mention on the label, though, that the conserve is perishable and must be refrigerated.

$^3/_4$ pound ripe tomatoes

$^1/_4$ cup peeled and julienned fresh ginger

$^2/_3$ cup sugar

8 whole cloves

6 tablespoons white vinegar

$^1/_2$ teaspoon kosher salt

1 teaspoon black peppercorns, cracked

$^1/_3$ cup chopped walnuts, toasted

MAKES 1 PINT

1. Peel and seed the tomatoes and cut them into $^1/_2$-inch wedges. Combine the tomatoes, ginger, and sugar in a glass or ceramic bowl and mix well. Set aside for 8 hours or refrigerate overnight.

2. Strain the accumulated juices into a nonaluminum saucepan, add the cloves, and bring to a boil. Boil the syrup over medium-low heat for 25 minutes, or until reduced to half. Add the reserved tomato-ginger mixture and continue to cook for 10 minutes more.

3. Add the vinegar and salt and cook for 15 minutes more, or until the mixture is thick and reaches jam consistency. Turn off the heat. When completely cool, mix in the peppercorns and walnuts. Spoon into jars, cover with lids, and refrigerate. (*The conserve keeps well, tightly covered, for up to 1 year in the refrigerator.*)

cookies and beverages

ginger crisps

Gingery cookies with the crisp crunch of sesame are an all-time favorite. They are wonderful with creamy desserts, puddings, ice creams, and ices. Serve Banana-Ginger Cream (page 258) with these crisps.

$^1/_4$ cup sesame seeds

1 cup unbleached all-purpose flour

$^1/_4$ cup sugar

1 teaspoon ground ginger

3 tablespoons unsalted butter

1 large egg yolk

Chilled water

MAKES SIXTEEN 2-INCH COOKIES

1. Toast the sesame seeds in an ungreased skillet over low heat, stirring and shaking, until lightly colored, about 5 minutes. Transfer to a plate and let cool.

2. Preheat the oven to 350°F.

3. Combine the flour, sugar, and ginger in a bowl. Add the butter and distribute it evenly in the flour with your fingertips. The mixture will resemble coarse meal. Add the sesame seeds, egg yolk, and just enough chilled water to make a dough. Lightly knead dough until smooth. (*The dough may be made ahead and frozen for up to 6 months. Freeze in small portions. Defrost dough thoroughly before rolling out.*)

4. Roll out the dough on a floured work surface and cut into 2-inch rounds. Place on an ungreased baking sheet about 2 inches apart and bake in the middle level of the oven for 15 minutes, or until light gold. Cool the crisps on racks. Store in an airtight container. (*Crisps may be stored at room temperature for up to 3 weeks in an airtight container or frozen for up to 3 months.*)

saffron scones

Saffron masks the taste of baking powder in these slightly sweet, golden tea biscuits. Serve the scones with tea, coffee, or a chilled beverage such as Raspberry Tea with Sage (page 283). They are great with Tomato-Ginger Jam (page 271).

½ teaspoon (lightly packed) saffron threads

½ cup buttermilk

2 large eggs

12 tablespoons (1½ sticks) unsalted butter

2 cups bleached all-purpose flour

½ cup sugar

2 teaspoons baking powder

1 teaspoon baking soda

¼ teaspoon kosher salt

⅓ cup dried currants

MAKES 8 SCONES

1. Preheat the oven to 425°F.

2. Crush the saffron to a fine powder in a small bowl. Add the buttermilk and eggs and whisk until well blended. Set aside. Melt 4 tablespoons of the butter in a saucepan. Set aside to cool.

3. Combine the flour, sugar, baking powder, baking soda, and salt in a large bowl. Cut the remaining butter into small dice and scatter over the flour mixture. Cut in the butter until the mixture resembles coarse meal. Stir in the currants. Pour the saffron-milk mixture over the flour, tossing to moisten the dough. Quickly stir into a mass and pat the dough into a ball. The dough will be very moist and sticky. (*The dough may be set aside for up to 1 week in the refrigerator or for up to 3 months in the freezer. Bring back to room temperature before rolling out.*)

4. Roll out the dough on a well-floured work surface into an 8-inch square about ½ inch thick. Using a floured knife, cut the square into four 4-inch squares. Cut each square into 4 triangles. Place the 16 triangles on a heavy baking sheet, about 1 inch apart. Brush lightly with the melted butter. Bake in the upper level of the oven for 12 to 15 minutes, or until lightly browned and firm to the touch.

5. Serve warm or at room temperature or let cool and store. (*Scones may be stored at room temperature for up to 2 weeks in an airtight container or frozen for up to 3 months.*)

anise biscotti

Traditional Italian biscotti display the elegance of sweet and aromatic anise seeds. Serve the biscotti with cardamom or cinnamon coffee (page 288) or with espresso. The tea-drinking world would serve biscotti with Cardamom-Citrus Tea (page 286) or Mint Tea (page 284).

5 large eggs

1³/₄ cups superfine sugar

2 tablespoons anise-flavored liqueur

2 teaspoons grated lemon zest

2 teaspoons pure vanilla extract

2 teaspoons anise seeds, crushed

3³/₄ cups unbleached all-purpose flour

2 teaspoons baking powder

1 cup finely chopped walnuts, toasted

MAKES 5 DOZEN 2-INCH COOKIES

1. Preheat the oven to 350°F.

2. Place the eggs and sugar in a bowl and beat until the mixture is pale and thick and forms a ribbon. Stir in the liqueur, lemon zest, vanilla, and anise seeds. Combine the flour and baking powder and gradually fold into the egg mixture. The dough will be stiff, as for bread. Fold in the nuts and form the dough into 2 loaves about 3 inches thick and 24 inches long. Place on an ungreased baking sheet. Press the loaves along the length to slightly flatten them. Bake in the middle level of the oven for 20 to 25 minutes, or until light gold. Cool briefly on a rack.

3. Using a serrated knife, slice the loaves on the diagonal into ³/₄-inch-thick slices. Lay the slices on the baking sheet and return them to the middle level of the oven. Bake for 15 minutes, or until the biscotti are nicely browned. Cool the biscotti on racks.

4. When completely cool, store in airtight containers for 1 day before serving. (*Biscotti may be stored at room temperature for up to 6 weeks in an airtight container.*)

anise cookies

These sweet and crisp German cookies, rich with anise seeds, are delicious with a beverage or just to nibble at any time. Packed in attractive tins, the cookies are a much-appreciated homemade gift.

3 extra large eggs

1 cup superfine sugar

1 teaspoon pure vanilla extract

1 teaspoon almond extract

1 tablespoon anise seeds, crushed

2 cups bleached all-purpose flour

1/2 teaspoon baking powder

MAKES 5 DOZEN 2-INCH COOKIES

1. Preheat the oven to 350°F. Grease 2 large baking sheets.

2. Place the eggs and sugar in a bowl and beat until the mixture is pale and thick and forms a ribbon. Stir in the vanilla extract, almond extract, and 1^1/2 teaspoons of the anise seeds. Combine the flour and baking powder and gradually fold into the egg mixture. Beat just enough to mix ingredients. Cover and let the dough rest for 1 hour. It will be very soft, even runny after resting.

3. Place the dough by the tablespoonful on the baking sheets, 2 inches apart. Sprinkle the cookies lightly with the remaining anise seeds. Press lightly over the top with the back of a spoon to make the seeds stick. Set aside for 2 hours in a cool dry place, to let a crust form on the cookies. Bake for 10 minutes, or until lightly colored. Cool the cookies on racks.

4. Serve or store in airtight containers. (*The cookies may be stored at room temperature for up to 3 months in an airtight container.*)

caraway cookies

Caraway is one of those spices that adapts itself to both savory and sweet preparations. These slightly flaky caraway cookies of Scandinavian origin should be served for dessert along with ice cream, such as Peach Ice Cream with Marjoram (page 267), or a fruit compote like the Dried Fruit Compote with Allspice (page 260).

1 tablespoon caraway seeds

2 cups unbleached all-purpose flour

2 teaspoons baking powder

2 teaspoons ground fennel seeds

1 teaspoon kosher salt

4 tablespoons (½ stick) unsalted butter or margarine, softened

½ cup sugar

1 large egg

⅔ cup whole milk

1 teaspoon pure vanilla extract

1 teaspoon grated orange zest

MAKES 4 DOZEN 2-INCH COOKIES

1. Toast the caraway seeds in a heavy skillet over medium-high heat until they give off an aroma, about 3 minutes. Remove to a plate and let cool thoroughly.

2. Combine the flour, baking powder, ground fennel, and salt in a bowl. Beat the butter in a large bowl until pale. Add the sugar and continue beating until light and fluffy. Stir in the egg, milk, vanilla, orange zest, and caraway seeds. Pour the milk mixture over the flour and mix into a dough. Divide the dough into 2 pieces. (*The dough may be set aside for up to 1 week in the refrigerator or for up to 3 months in the freezer. Bring back to room temperature before rolling out.*)

3. Preheat the oven to 375°F.

4. Roll out 1 piece of the dough, dusting often with flour, until it is ⅛ inch thick. Using a 2-inch cookie cutter, cut out cookies and arrange them on an ungreased baking sheet. Continue with the remaining dough the same way. Finally, gather up the scraps, reroll, and cut into cookies. Bake in the middle level of the oven for 12 minutes, or until light gold. Cool on racks. (*The cookies may be stored at room temperature for up to 3 weeks in an airtight container.*)

cardamom cookies

Imbued with the sweet scent of cardamom, these miniature cookies, made with ground cashews, are fairly dry, hence ideal to go with such beverages as Mogul Spice Tea (page 284) and Peach Cooler with Sage (page 282).

8 tablespoons (1 stick) unsalted butter, softened

1/2 cup (packed) light brown sugar

1 large egg

1 teaspoon pure vanilla extract

1 teaspoon fresh lemon juice

2 cups sifted unbleached all-purpose flour

1/2 cup cashew nuts, ground

3/4 teaspoon baking powder

1/2 teaspoon kosher salt

1 1/2 teaspoons ground cardamom

MAKES 4 DOZEN 1-INCH COOKIES

1. Preheat the oven to 350°F.

2. Cream the butter and brown sugar. Add the egg, vanilla, and lemon juice and beat until light and fluffy. Combine the flour, ground cashews, baking powder, salt, and cardamom. Add to the butter-sugar mixture and mix thoroughly. (*The dough may be set aside for up to 1 week in the refrigerator or for up to 3 months in the freezer. Bring back to room temperature before rolling out.*)

3. Using a 1/2-teaspoon measuring spoon, scoop heaping spoonfuls of dough, roll into neat balls, and place on ungreased baking sheets 1 to 1 1/2 inches apart. Bake for 12 to 15 minutes, or until cooked but not brown. Cool on racks. Serve or store in tightly covered containers. (*The cookies may be stored at room temperature for up to 3 months in an airtight container.*)

holiday spice cookies

Every holiday season a friend of mine used to share with me a batch of cookies that his mother would bake and send from Germany. They were buttery, chewy, and laced with spices. I always meant to ask him for the recipe, but he died suddenly. The following recipe, reconstructed from memory, is a sweet remembrance.

6 tablespoons (³/₄ stick) unsalted butter, softened

¹/₃ cup sugar

1 large egg

1 teaspoon pure vanilla extract

¹/₄ cup maple syrup

1 cup bleached all-purpose flour

¹/₂ teaspoon baking powder

¹/₂ teaspoon kosher salt

1¹/₂ teaspoons Warm Spice Blend (page 64)

¹/₂ cup dried currants

MAKES 2 DOZEN 2-INCH COOKIES

1. Preheat the oven to 350°F.

2. Cream the butter and sugar. Add the egg, vanilla, and maple syrup and beat until light and fluffy. Combine the flour, baking powder, salt, and spice blend. Add to the butter-sugar mixture and mix thoroughly. Stir in the currants. (*The dough may be set aside for up to 1 week in the refrigerator or for up to 3 months in the freezer. Bring back to room temperature before rolling out.*)

3. Using a ¹/₂ teaspoon measuring spoon, scoop dough, roll into neat balls, and place on ungreased baking sheets 1 to 1¹/₂ inches apart. Bake for 12 to 15 minutes, or until lightly browned on edges. Cool on racks. Serve or store in tightly covered containers. (*The cookies may be stored at room temperature for up to 3 months in an airtight container.*)

candied fennel seeds

Candied spices are common throughout Asia and the Middle East, where they are enjoyed as cookies are in Europe and America. At the same time, the spices refresh the breath. Candied fennel can be added to salads for crunch or to a beverage to perfume it. A few seeds in a cup of coffee or tea or a glass of wine are magical.

1½ cups fennel seeds

¼ cup sugar

2 tablespoons water

⅛ teaspoon baking soda

MAKES 1½ CUPS

1. Toast the fennel seeds in a heavy skillet over medium heat until light gold. Transfer to a plate and set aside to cool.

2. Place the sugar and water in a heavy saucepan over low heat and cook until the sugar dissolves. Increase the heat and boil for 1 minute, or until the liquid is thick and syrupy. Remove from the heat and add the baking soda and toasted fennel seeds.

3. Mix rapidly to coat the seeds with syrup. Immediately pour the mixture onto a baking sheet, pressing and separating the mixture to break up clumps. Let cool. When completely cool, transfer to a tightly covered container. (*The candied seeds may be stored, tightly covered, for up to 3 months in a cool dry place.*)

peach cooler with sage

12 sage leaves

1 pound ripe peaches

¼ cup fresh lime juice

¼ cup sugar

Plain ice cubes

1 cup chilled water

¼ teaspoon Angostura bitters

4 lime slices, for garnish

A sweet fruity drink of fresh peaches with a hint of sage, this is a lovely nonalcoholic beverage to offer at parties. If fresh ripe peaches are not available, use nectarines, apricots, or even pears, but do not reach for canned peaches or canned peach nectar—they totally lack the delicate fragrance of the fruit.

MAKES 4 SERVINGS

1. Place 1 sage leaf in each compartment of an ice-cube tray. Fill the tray with water and freeze for at least 8 hours or overnight.

2. Cut 4 small peach wedges and set aside for garnish. Peel the remaining peaches, remove and discard the pits, and roughly chop the flesh. Save the peel to hang on the glasses as garnish. Puree the chopped peaches, lime juice, and sugar in a blender. Add 8 plain ice cubes and process until the ice is crushed.

3. Pour the puree into a tall pitcher. Stir in the water and bitters. Divide the sage ice cubes among 4 tall glasses. Add more plain ice cubes to fill the glasses. Pour the punch over. Garnish each glass with a peach slice, a lime slice, and some of the peel. Serve right away.

raspberry tea with sage

1 cup raspberries

5 cups water

3 sage leaves, bruised

5 heaping teaspoons orange pekoe tea leaves or 4 orange pekoe tea bags

4 large sage leaves, for garnish

4 large raspberries, for garnish

This crimson tea could pass for red wine—if it weren't so perfumed with raspberry and sage. The flavors of the raspberries and the tea are fused with the floral accents of sage. Serve this refreshing drink at brunch, lunch, afternoon tea, or the cocktail hour.

MAKES 6 SERVINGS

1. Combine the raspberries and 1 cup of the water in a blender or food processor. Process until the raspberries are liquefied. The liquid will have some texture because of the raspberry seeds. Add the remaining 4 cups of water. Strain the raspberry liquid through a double layer of cheesecloth into a pitcher.

2. Add the bruised sage leaves and tea, cover, and let steep in the refrigerator for at least 8 hours or overnight. Pour the tea into tall glasses filled with ice cubes, straining it if loose tea was used. Push the stem of a sage leaf through each raspberry and add to the glasses. Serve immediately.

mint tea

3 heaping teaspoons green tea leaves

2 heaping tablespoons dried mint leaves, preferably spearmint

3 cups boiling water

A brew of green tea and mint can be incredibly refreshing. The trick to getting great flavor lies in using the right mint. Surprisingly, dried, not fresh, mint produces better results. The best kind to use is home-dried spearmint. You can also find good mint at Indian and Middle Eastern groceries that carry a wide range of spices and herbs. The North Africans, who excel in the art of mint teas, prefer hot mint tea, but you can serve it chilled too. It tastes just as good.

MAKES 4 SERVINGS

Rinse out a teapot with hot water. Add the tea, mint leaves, and the boiling water. Cover the pot and let the tea steep for 3 minutes. To serve hot, strain the tea into teacups. To serve chilled, strain the tea, cool it, then refrigerate for at least 2 hours. Pour the tea into 4 tall glasses filled with ice cubes.

mogul spice tea

4 heaping teaspoons orange pekoe tea leaves or 4 orange pekoe tea bags

2 teaspoons Mogul Potpourri (page 73), crushed

6 cups boiling water

Honey (optional)

Milk (optional)

This tea is really a spice blend that was favored by the great Mogul emperor, Shah Jahan, who built the Taj Mahal. You can serve the tea hot or cold, plain or sweetened with a little milk and honey or sugar, as the English drink it. In all its forms, the brew is highly aromatic with sweet scents of cinnamon, cardamom, cloves, other spices, and roses.

MAKES 6 SERVINGS

Rinse out a teapot with hot water. Add the tea, potpourri, and boiling water. Stir well for 10 seconds to release the spice fragrance. Cover the pot and let the tea steep for 3 minutes. To serve hot, stir the tea and strain it into teacups. To serve chilled, strain the tea, cool it, then refrigerate for at least 2 hours. Pour the tea into 4 tall glasses filled with ice cubes. Serve accompanied with honey and milk, if desired.

chilled anise tea

½ teaspoon anise seeds, lightly bruised

2 cups bottled water

2 heaping teaspoons orange pekoe tea leaves or 2 orange pekoe tea bags or 2 teaspoons green tea leaves

1 piece (2 inches) fresh or dried orange zest

3 tablespoons honey

Light and refreshing with sweet undertones, anise tea is one of the best thirst quenchers I know. You can make this tea with either black or green tea. With black tea it will be strong, dark, and pungent, with green, delicate, almost colorless, and sweetly herbal.

MAKES 2 SERVINGS

Combine the anise seeds and water in a saucepan and bring to a boil. Simmer for 2 minutes. Turn off the heat. Add the tea and orange zest and cover the pan. Let the tea steep for 3 minutes. Stir in the honey, strain the tea, cool it, then refrigerate for at least 2 hours. Pour the tea into 2 tall glasses filled with ice cubes.

basil-ginger tea

1½ cups bottled water

½ cup (loosely packed) basil leaves

1 quarter-size slice fresh ginger, preferably young ginger

2 heaping teaspoons green tea leaves

1 tablespoon honey

Tender basil leaves, young Hawaiian ginger (see page 38), and green tea leaves are an impeccable combination. It is not only a delight to the palate but soothing to the psyche and body. Sip this to ward off a cold, or at day's end as a picker-upper after work, or after a workout on the treadmill. For a more concentrated tea, chill the strained tea and serve it without adding ice cubes.

MAKES 2 SERVINGS

Bring the water to a boil in a small saucepan. Add the basil and ginger and continue to boil for 1 minute. Add the tea and honey. Turn off the heat. Let the tea brew for 2 minutes. Strain the tea, cool it, then refrigerate for at least 2 hours. Pour the tea into 2 tall glasses filled with ice cubes. Stir and serve.

cardamom-citrus tea

1 lemon, scrubbed

1 orange, scrubbed

1 grapefruit, scrubbed

7 cups water

10 cardamom pods

1 quarter-size slice fresh
   ginger

3 heaping teaspoons green
   tea leaves

A fragrant infusion of citrus essence, cardamom, and green tea that is refreshing either hot or chilled. It is a great thirst quencher, ideal to take along to the beach or a picnic or to serve at an outdoor cookout. For a stronger brew, increase the amount of tea to five teaspoons.

MAKES 8 SERVINGS

1. Using a swivel-bladed vegetable peeler, cut a strip of zest, about 3 inches long and $1/2$ inch wide, from the lemon, the orange, and the grapefruit.

2. Bring the water to a boil in a medium nonaluminum saucepan. Add the citrus zest and cardamom. Remove from the heat, cover the pan, and let steep for 30 minutes. Discard citrus zest.

3. Bring the citrus brew to a second boil. Remove from the heat and add the tea. Cover and steep for 2 to 4 minutes, depending on how strong you like your tea.

4. To serve hot, rinse out a teapot with hot water, strain the prepared tea into the teapot, and pour into teacups. To serve chilled, cool the tea, then refrigerate for at least 2 hours. Pour the tea into tall glasses filled with ice cubes.

great chocolate milk with cinnamon

1 cup water

¹/₂ cup unsweetened cocoa
powder

³/₄ cup sugar

1 teaspoon instant coffee
powder

1¹/₂ tablespoons pure vanilla
extract

¹/₄ teaspoon ground cinnamon

2³/₄ cups milk or water,
hot or cold

This intense and elegant chocolate milk starts with a syrup. When you're ready to serve, stir the syrup into hot or cold water or milk. The flavors are more pronounced with water.

MAKES 4 SERVINGS

Combine the water, cocoa, sugar, coffee, vanilla, and cinnamon in a small saucepan and cook over low heat until the sugar is dissolved and thoroughly blended. (*The syrup keeps, tightly covered, for up to 3 months in the refrigerator without change of flavor although it becomes thick*.) To serve hot, stir in hot milk or water. To serve chilled, mix cold syrup into cold milk or water using a blender or a whisk. Transfer to a pitcher and refrigerate for at least 2 hours before serving.

chocolate milk for one: Combine 1 cup hot or cold milk or water, 2 tablespoons unsweetened cocoa powder, 3 tablespoons sugar, ¹/₄ teaspoon instant coffee powder, ¹/₄ teaspoon pure vanilla extract, and a pinch of ground cinnamon and mix until thoroughly blended, using a blender or whisk if cold. Serve hot or cold over ice.

cardamom coffee

3 cardamom pods

2 cups water

1 to 2 heaping tablespoons coarsely ground coffee

1 tablespoon honey (optional)

Cooking coffee in water to release its fragrance is a common technique used in the Middle East. Usually the process of boiling and cooling is repeated several times, resulting in an intensely flavored brew. Often a spice is added to enhance the coffee flavor and to act as an aphrodisiac. Cardamom is one of the most frequently used spices. In the following toned-down Egyptian version, ground coffee is boiled in cardamom water just once to produce a coffee of medium strength but full flavor. Although traditionally served hot, the infusion is also refreshing chilled.

MAKES 2 SERVINGS

Place the cardamom pods in a small plastic bag and lightly crush them, just enough to bruise them, using a rolling pin or wooden mallet. Combine the cardamom and water in a small saucepan and bring to a boil. Simmer for 3 minutes. Add the coffee and bring back to a rolling boil. Remove from the heat. Cover and let steep for 2 minutes. The grounds and cardamom will settle at the bottom of the pan. Strain the coffee into cups and serve. Pass honey, if desired.

cinnamon coffee

1 stick (3 inches) cinnamon, crushed into bits

2 cups water

1 to 2 heaping tablespoons finely ground coffee

I enjoyed this infusion of coffee with cinnamon at a stall in the market in Zanzibar. It's uncomplicated and soothing, and it has a unique feature: In the sultry heat of Zanzibar, the cinnamon-scented coffee has a gentle coolness, while in the chill of winter in the United States, it gives a glowing warmth all over.

MAKES 2 SERVINGS

Combine the cinnamon with the water in a small saucepan and bring to a boil. Simmer for 1 minute. Add the coffee and let the water come back to a rolling boil. Remove from the heat. Cover and let steep for 2 minutes. Strain the coffee into cups and serve.

mail order sources

Adriana's Caravan
409 Vanderbilt Street
Brooklyn, NY 11218
(800) 316-0820

Balducci's
Shop from Home Service
42-26 13th Street
Long Island City, NY 11101
(800) 225-3822

Big River Nurseries
P.O. Box 487
Mendocino, CA 95460
(707) 937-5026

Dean & Deluca
Retail and mail order
560 Broadway
New York, NY 10012
(800) 221-7714

Elderflower Farm
501 Callahan Road
Roseburg, OR 97470
(503) 672-9803

Foods of India
120 Lexington Avenue
New York, NY 10016
(212) 683-4419

International Grocery Store
529 Ninth Avenue
New York, NY 10036
(212) 279-5514

La Cuisine
323 Cameron Street
Alexandria, VA 22314-3219
(800) 521-1176

McFadden Farm
Powerhouse Road
Potter Valley, CA 95469
(800) 544-8230

**Meadowbrook Herb
Garden Catalog**
93 Kingstown Road
Wyoming, RI 02898
(401) 539-0209

Mountain Butterfly Herbs
P.O. Box 1365
Hamilton, MT 59840
(406) 363-6683

Penzey's Spice House Ltd.
P.O. Box 1448
Waukesha, WI 53187
(414) 579-0277

Richters
Box 26
Goodwood, Ontario
Canada, LOC 1AO
(416) 640-6677

Shahrazad
351 Hempstead Avenue
W. Hempstead, NY 11552
(516) 483-1256

Shallah Middle Eastern Foods
290 White Street
Danbury, CT
(203) 743-4181

Sultan's Delight
59 88th Street
Brooklyn, NY 11209
(800) 852-5046

Williams-Sonoma
100 North Point Street
San Francisco, CA 94133
(800) 541-2233

**Windy River Farm: Cottage
Garden Herbs**
P.O. Box 312
Merlin, OR 97532
(503) 476-8979

references

American Spice Trade Association. *A History of Spices*. New York: American Spice Trade Association, 1966.

Bayley, S. *Taste*. New York: Pantheon Books, 1991.

Bensky, D. and Gamble A., with Kaptchuk, T. *Materia Medica: Chinese Herbal Medicine*. Seattle: Eastland Press, 1986.

Burland, C. A. *The Travels of Marco Polo*. New York: McGraw Hill, 1970.

Chishti, Shaykh H. M. *The Book of Sufi Healing*. Vermont: Inner Traditions International, 1991.

Claiborne, Craig. *An Herb and Spice Cook Book*. New York: Harper & Row, 1963.

David, Elizabeth. *Spices, Salt and Aromatics in the English Kitchen*. London: Penguin Books, 1970.

Davidson, Basil. *Africa in History*. New York: Collier Books, Macmillan, 1968.

Densmore, F. *How Indians Use Wild Plants for Food, Medicine and Crafts* (former title: *Uses of Plants by the Chippewa Indians*). New York: Dover Publications, 1974.

Edwards, J. *The Roman Cookery of Apicius*. Rider Books, 1984.

Farrell, K. T. *Spices, Condiments and Seasonings*. Westport: AVI Publishing, 1985.

Freeman, M. B. *Herbs for the Mediaeval Household: For Cooking, Healing and Divers Uses*. New York: The Metropolitan Museum of Art, 1943.

Grieve, M. A. *A Modern Herbal*. London: Penguin Books, 1976.

Heath, Henry. *Flavour Technology*. Westport: AVI Publishing, 1978.

Hippocrates. *4 Volumes*. Translated by Jones, W.H.S. Cambridge: Harvard University Press, 1923.

Hitti, P. K. *History of the Arabs*. New York: St. Martin Press, 1968.

The Holy Bible, Authorized King James Version. Cambridge: Cambridge University Press, England.

Leung, A. Y. *Chinese Herbal Remedies*. New York: Phaidon Universe, 1984.

Levi-Strauss, Claude. *The Raw and the Cooked* (translated from the French *Le Cru et le Cuit* by John and Doreen Weightman). New York: Harper & Row, 1969.

Meyer, Joseph E. *The Herbalist.* New York: Rand McNally–Conkey Division, 1918.

Miller, J. I. *The Spice Trade of the Roman Empire: 29 B.C. to 641 A.D.* Oxford: Clarendon Press, 1898.

Ortiz de Montellano, B. R. *Aztec Medicine, Health and Nutrition.* New Brunswick and London: Rutgers University Press, 1990.

Parry, J. W. *The Story of Spices: Spices Described.* New York: Chemical Publishing, 1953.

Parry, J. W. *The Story of Spices: Their Morphology, Histology and Chemistry.* New York: Chemical Publishing, 1962.

Pliny the Elder. *Natural History.* Translated by Rackham, H. T. et al. London: William Heinemann, 1960.

Pruthi, J. S. *Spices and Condiments.* India: National Book Trust, 1976.

Purseglove, J. W., Brown, E. G., Green, C. L., and Robbins, S.R.J. *Spices.* Harlow: Longman Group, 1981.

Rosengarten, F., Jr. *The Book of Spices.* London: Livingston Publishing, 1969.

Sheriff, A. *Slaves, Spices and Ivory in Zanzibar.* Dar Es Salaam: Tanzania Publishing House, 1987.

Sigerist, H. C. *A History of Primitive and Archaic Medicine.* New York: Oxford University Press, 1967.

Skinner, Charles M. *Myths and Legends of Flowers, Trees, Fruits and Plants—In All Ages and in all Climes.* Philadelphia: Lippincott, 1911.

Stuart, M. *The Encyclopedia of Herbs and Herbalism.* London: Orbis Publishing, 1968.

Theophrastus. *Enquiry into Plants.* Translated by A. F. Hort. London: William Heinemann, 1916.

Von Reis, A. *Drugs and Food from Little-Known Plants.* Cambridge: Harvard University Press, 1973.

index

basil *(continued)*
  storing, 9
  sweet, 8
  with tomatoes, 8
  in yogurt dip with herbs, 230
bay leaf (*Laurus nobilis*), 9
  in chili powder blend, 54
  ground, 9
  in Mediterranean cooking, 9
  in Mogul potpourri, 73
  red lentil soup with pepper
    cream and, 120–121
  shrimp sauté with, 141
  storing, 9
  summer peach pilaf with, 197
  vapor, salmon steamed in, 136
  winter bean soup with, 117
bean and pasta soup with oregano,
  116
beef:
  herb citrus–rubbed filet mignon,
    67
  mild Indian chile with paprika,
    163
benne, *see* sesame
biscotti, anise, 276
bishop's weed, *see* ajowan
black bean:
  and mango salad with herb citrus
    dressing, 170
  soup with epazote, 115
black pepper (*Piper nigrum*), 10–11
  adding to water-based dishes, 10
  Allepey, 10
  in Cajun spice blend, 58
  in curry powder, 56
  in five pepper mix, 68
  in fragrant spice rub, 62
  ham puffs with, 244
  in jerk spice blend, 60
  medicinal properties of, 10
  in pepper sticks, 110
  –rubbed salmon, 135
  sauce, lamb shanks in, 157
  Tellicherry, 10
blends, spice and herb, *see* spice and
  herb blends
blueberry:
  –cinnamon sauce, 257
  tart with saffron cream, 262
bluefish with tomato-coriander
  sauce, 130
borscht with caraway, chilled, 121
braised:
  chicken in cardamom sauce, 147
  fish fillet in vanilla sauce, 139
  pomegranate chicken, 150
bread:
  chili tortilla, 241
  cumin rolls, 246
  currant and mace puffs, 242
  dill tortilla, 240
  five pepper rolls, 247
  ham puffs with black pepper, 244

mini pita, with basil and dried
  tomatoes, 250
  Parmesan-chive puffs, 243
  raisin and caraway rolls, 245
  sesame pita, 249
  stuffed sage roti with olives, 251
  stuffed tarragon roti, with ham
    and mushrooms, 252–253
  thyme pita, 248
broccoli, penne with turmeric and,
  187
broiled vegetables with oregano,
  103
brown rice salad with basil dressing,
  174
brussels sprouts with fennel, 206
bulgur salad with allspice, 173
butternut squash allspice in, 6

Cabbage with caraway,
  smothered, 207
Cajun:
  shrimp boil, 143
  spice blend, 58
  spices, pan-grilled flounder with,
    59
cakes, steamed spice, 65
candied fennel seeds, 281
capsaicin, 13
Capsicum annuum (pimiento), 6, 10
caraway (*Carum carvi*), 11
  bruising whole seeds, 11
  chilled borscht with, 121
  cookies, 278
  dressing, warm potato salad with,
    168
  and raisin rolls, 245
  smothered cabbage with, 207
cardamom (*Elettaria cardamomum*),
  33–34
  –citrus tea, 286
  coffee, 288
  cookies, 279
  green vs. white pods, 34
  hulling, 34
  ice cream, 268
  in Mogul potpourri, 73
  purchasing pods and seeds, 34
  rice pudding with, 264
  sauce, chicken braised in, 147
carminative herbs, 18
  basil, 8
  black pepper, 10
  caraway, 11
  dill, 19
  fennel, 20
  juniper, 39
  mint, 21–22
  nutmeg, 23
  oregano, 23
  paprika, 14–15
  parsley, 24
  star anise, 47
  turmeric, 48

carrot(s):
  allspice in, 6
  with cloves, glazed, 208
  and mozzarella in harissa sauce,
    marinated, 79
  salad with coriander vinegar,
    166
  soup with mace, chilled, 119
cashew nuts, white pepper, 109
cassia cinnamon (*Cinnamomum
  cassia*), 16
cauliflower:
  fennel, and green bean soup
    with celery seed, 122
  risotto of, with oregano, 198–
    199
  soup, five pepper–laced creamy,
    69
  with sumac, 210
  turmeric, 209
cayenne, *see* ground red pepper
celery root salad with celery seeds,
  167
celery seed (*Apium graveolens*), 11–
  12
  bruising whole seeds, 12
  in Cajun spice blend, 58
  celery root salad with, 167
  in chili powder blend, 54
  crushing, 12
  –curry dressing, tuna and grape
    salad in, 134
  fennel, green bean, and
    cauliflower soup with, 122
  fragrant fish chowder with, 123
  medicinal properties of, 12
chavicine, 10, 41
cheese:
  and potato croquettes with
    nutmeg, 175
  -vegetable sandwich with green
    peppercorns, rolled, 176
cherry coulis, quick, for barbecued
  tarragon game hens, 153
chicken:
  arroz con pollo, 93
  with basil, 148–149
  braised in cardamom sauce, 147
  escabeche of, in allspice sauce,
    105
  jerk, 61
  kabobs with anise, grilled, 154
  legs with sage, roasted, 149
  pan-grilled, with sweet-and-hot
    wasabi sauce, 87
  and papaya salad with
    pomegranate dressing, 153
  pomegranate braised, 150
  pot roast of, with rosemary, figs,
    and pine nuts, 146–147
  seared red, 91
  thyme-roasted, 151
  wings, barbecued, 71–72
chick pea salad with cumin, 172

chile:
  con carne, 55
  with paprika, mild Indian, 163
  vegetarian pumpkin, eggplant,
    and lima bean, 180
chili pepper (*Capsicum annuum*),
  12–13
  angel hair with olives, basil, and,
    188
  in apple-mustard salsa, 233
  capsaicin in, 13
  in chicken with basil, 148–149
  in fresh fig salsa with sesame, 234
  green, in green curry paste, 94
  handling, 13
  hash-brown potatoes, 214
  oil, smoked, 88
  oil, smoked, grilled leg of lamb
    with, 88–89
  storing, 13
  -stuffed prawns, 104
  tortilla bread, 241
  vinegar, green, 76
  vinegar shrimp fritters, green, 77
  vitamin C in, 13
  see also specific types of chili peppers
chili powder blend, 54
chilled:
  borscht with caraway, 121
  carrot soup with mace, 119
Chinese parsley, *see* cilantro
chive-Parmesan puffs, 243
chocolate:
  -cinnamon ice, 270
  milk with cinnamon, great, 287
chowder, fragrant fish, with celery
    seed, 123
cilantro (*Coriandrum sativum*), 15–
  16
  avocado, and onion relish, 231
  in bulgur salad with allspice, 173
  in carrot salad with coriander
    vinegar, 166
  in celery root salad with celery
    seeds, 167
  in green curry paste, 94
  handling, 15–16
  in lamb shanks in black pepper
    sauce, 157
  in lentil and endive salad with
    juniper berries, 171
  in mild Indian chile with
    paprika, 163
  sauce, linguine with, 186
  storing, 15–16
  in sweet-and-hot wasabi sauce,
    86
  in turmeric cauliflower, 209
  -walnut dip, 229
  see also coriander
cinnamon (*Cinnamomum
    zeylanicum*), 16–17
  in apple compote with fennel,
    221

  in barbecue spice blend, 70
  -blueberry sauce, 257
  cassia (*Cinnamomum cassia*), 16
  -chocolate ice, 270
  coffee, 288
  cranberry relish with apricots,
    walnuts, and, 237
  in curry powder, 56
  great chocolate milk with, 287
  in jerk spice blend, 60
  in Mogul potpourri, 73
  -orange pilaf, 196
  in roast duck with hot pepper
    and plums, 155
  in warm spice blend, 64
cinnamon basil (*Ocimum basilicum
    cinnamon*), 8
citrus:
  herb blend, 66
  herb–rubbed filet mignon, 67
clams, fried, with barbecue spices,
    108
clear mushroom and shrimp soup
    with wasabi, 125
clove (*Eugenia aromatica*), 17
  antibacterial properties of, 17
  in barbecue spice blend, 70
  in curry powder, 56
  in fragrant spice rub, 62
  glazed carrots with, 208
  grinding, 17
  in Mogul potpourri, 73
  in orange-cinnamon pilaf, 196
  purchasing, 17
  roasted sweet potatoes with,
    218
  seared pears with, 219
  in stewed apples with white
    pepper and fennel, 220
  sweet tomato conserve with,
    272
  in warm spice blend, 64
coffee:
  cardamom, 288
  cinnamon, 288
compote:
  apple, with fennel, 221
  dried fruit with allspice, 260
conserve, sweet tomato, with
    cloves, 272
cookies:
  anise, 277
  anise biscotti, 276
  caraway, 278
  cardamom, 279
  ginger crisps, 274
  holiday spice, 280
  saffron scones, 275
cooler, peach, with sage, 282
cool yogurt:
  dill sauce with dried cranberries
    and almonds, 230
  soup with toasted cumin seeds,
    128

coriander (*Coriandrum sativum*),
    34–35
  in chicken braised in cardamom
    sauce, 147
  in chicken with basil, 148–149
  in curry powder, 56
  fresh, *see* cilantro
  in Mogul potpourri, 73
  substitutes for, 35
  toasting, 35
  -tomato sauce, bluefish with, 130
  using whole vs. ground, 35
  vinegar, carrot salad with, 166
coulis, quick cherry, for barbecued
    tarragon game hens, 153
crabmeat, kale soup with thyme
    and, 124
crackers:
  ajowan, 112
  cumin, 111
cranberry relish with apricots,
    walnuts, and cinnamon, 237
cream:
  banana-ginger, 258
  saffron, 261
crêpes:
  anise-pistachio, 256
  savory herb, 253
crisps, ginger, 274
croquettes, potato and cheese, with
    nutmeg, 175
crushed red pepper (*Capsicum
    annuum*), 13–14
  in brussels sprouts with fennel,
    206
  in harissa, 78
  penne with mushrooms and, 189
cucumber:
  with sesame, glazed, 212
  with toasted cumin seeds, 211
cumin (*Cuminum cyminum*), 18
  in barbecue spice blend, 70
  in Cajun spice blend, 58
  chick pea salad with, 172
  in chili powder blend, 54
  crackers, 111
  cucumber with toasted, 211
  in curry powder, 56
  in fragrant spice rub, 62
  grinding, 18
  in harissa, 78
  in mild Indian chile with
    paprika, 163
  potatoes, 215
  purchasing, 18
  rolls, 246
  toasted, cool yogurt soup with,
    128
  toasting, 18–19
  -tomato rice, 193
cumin vinaigrette, 82
  lima bean spread with, 83
  mozzarella and fennel with, 169
currant and mace puffs, 242

I have been cooking and exploring cuisines for over thirty-five years. International travels have taken me from bustling spice bazaars in leading spice ports of the world to spice plantations and herb fields on remote islands. I have searched for the finest spices and herbs and collaborated with a spice source to bring you my great blends. Custom blended and packed by hand in small batches, these seasoning mixes—all ready-made—will be really handy!

Of course, they are free of preservatives, salt, and sugar.

Herb Citrus Blend	**Chili Powder**
Cajun Spice Blend	**Curry Powder**
Barbecue Spice Blend	**Fragrant Spice Rub**
Jerk Spice Blend	**Five Pepper Mix**
Warm Spice Blend	**Mogul Potpourri**

For information on spice blends, call 1-718-625-4865, or write to Savory Spices & Herbs, P.O. Box 023792, Brooklyn, NY 11202-3792.

—Julie Sahni